HAWAII'S STORY

BY
HAWAII'S QUEEN

Dec 11, 1980

To Cindy

aloha

Dol (Ollie)

HAWAII'S STORY

BY
HAWAII'S QUEEN

by LILIUOKALANI

CHARLES E. TUTTLE COMPANY
Rutland, Vermont & Tokyo, Japan

Representatives
Continental Europe: BOXERBOOKS, INC., *Zurich*
British Isles: PRENTICE-HALL INTERNATIONAL, INC., *London*
Australasia: BOOK WISE (AUSTRALIA) PTY. LTD.
104-108 Sussex Street, Sydney 2000

Published by the Charles E. Tuttle Company, Inc.
of Rutland, Vermont & Tokyo, Japan
with editorial offices at
Suido 1-chome, 2-6, Bunkyo-ku, Tokyo, Japan

Copyright in Japan, 1964 by Charles E. Tuttle Co., Inc.

Library of Congress Catalog Card No. 63-23301

International Standard Book No. 0-8048-1066-4

First edition, 1898 by
Lothrop, Lee & Shepard Co., Boston

First Tuttle edition, 1964
Eighteenth printing, 1979

0222-000309-4615
PRINTED IN JAPAN

CONTENTS

Contents

Contents

xi   Contents

LIST OF ILLUSTRATIONS

The throne room of the palace. The widowed queen is standing, and
the Princess Poomaikelani, her sister, is sitting by the king's casket. The
plume standards are Kahilis, which are emblems of royalty and nobility.

The car obstructs the view of Arion Hall, where the American troops
were stationed — less than two hundred feet from the palace. When Mr.
Poepoe and Mr. Walker protested against their occupancy, Mr. Stevens
replied, " We are here, and we mean to stay."

This view is near the place where the men from the Boston drew into
line Jan. 16, 1893. The face of Admiral Skerrett is blurred. The man in
white with his hand to his hat is President Dole. Next to him is Captain
Wiltze, and in front facing Admiral Brown is Lieutenant Washburne. To
the right of the admiral, and wearing a light colored derby, stands H. W.
Severance, United States Consul during the time of Minister Stevens.

Here all receptions of State were held, here King Kalakaua's body lay
in state, and here the Provisional Government held the trial of her majesty
Liliuokalani, and compelled her to sign her abdication.

Mr. Soper, representing the Provisional Government, reads their dismissal, with Captain Nowlein in command of the guard by his side.

PUBLISHER'S FOREWORD

In accordance with our policy of making available significant out-of-print books pertaining to the Pacific area, we are reprinting this story of 19th-century Hawaii. Originally published in 1898, it has long been unobtainable. *Hawaii's Story by Hawaii's Queen* could as aptly be called *The Queen's Story of Hawaii,* for here is a compelling and personal account of the last years of a monarchy that was inevitably and inexorably swept along toward democracy. Told with pride in, and love for, her royal predecessors as well as her people, the facts of Queen Liliuokalani's account do not differ from those of other writers and historians of the era, but her presentation, naturally enough, is colored by her deep affection and loyalty.

Liliuokalani would have been an outstanding woman in any age, any country. What is most amazing is that a woman of Victorian times, born and educated in a tiny Pacific island kingdom at the time when its written language was less than twenty years old, could attain such a level of knowledge, understanding, and accomplishment. The answer is undoubtedly the combination of her natural intelligence, her eagerness to learn, her deeply religious zeal, and her sympathy and love for her subjects.

A paradoxical personality—imperious, warmhearted,

stubborn, modest, poised, devout—Liliuokalani believed firmly in the divine right of absolute monarchy, yet she personally organized and supported efforts to improve the native Hawaiians' health, welfare, and education in an age when more "advanced" rulers did relatively less. She traveled, observed, and learned in both the United States and Europe, where she met in regal style the royalty and leaders of all the countries she visited. An honored guest at Queen Victoria's Jubilee in 1887, she continued her friendship with the queen until Victoria's death. President and Mrs. McKinley entertained Liliuokalani both publicly and privately. A lavish and generous hostess, even by Hawaii's fabulous standards, she entertained many world-famous figures at her various homes. The Duke of Edinburgh, Victoria's son, was a memorable visitor, and it is said that the *luau* she gave in his honor at her Waikiki villa has never been surpassed.

If Liliuokalani had never done more than follow her avocation as a musical composer, she would be forever famed as the writer of the once-heard-never-forgotten "Aloha Oe." And this is only one of her many musical works.

The great qualities of her character are most clearly revealed in the final chapter of the book. Deposed, retired, widowed, she begs for understanding, not of herself but of her cause: Hawaiian autonomy. Without rancor or passion and in simple and eloquent manner, she states her case and pleads that the American conscience judge. It is an especially moving document despite the fact that a Hawaiian kingdom was a political and practical impossibility in a world where smaller entities could no longer prevail against or compete with the ever-growing great powers.

Now that Hawaii is the fiftieth American state, Liliuo-kalani's story is part of the American heritage, and, to place it in its frame, a brief background setting is necessary.

Uncounted centuries ago the Hawaiian archipelago burst through the then unnamed Pacific Ocean from a submerged volcano, and during many more hundreds of years the resultant rock mass gradually became verdant land, unknown and uninhabited for possibly an equally long period. One theory is that the first settlers were migrant seafarers from Polynesia around the 5th century A.D. Evidence of their existence is found in temple remains, fish ponds, and irrigation canals. These first settlers vanished mysteriously at some later date, and it was not until about A.D. 1000 that a second migratory group arrived—this time, it is believed, from Tahiti. The newcomers were a very different type—rulers, warriors, priests—and they settled on the various islands, bringing with them their amazing collection of awe-inspiring gods, superstitions, and taboos. Since they did not read or write, only their chants remain to tell of their fierce and constant warfare through the next several centuries. Corroboration is found in the accounts of the first white men to visit the islands. Captain Cook is credited with their discovery in 1778, although it is likely that unrecorded white men had landed there a hundred or two hundred years before. Cook, who was killed on the big island, Hawaii, named the archipelago after his patron, the Earl of Sandwich, and for many years and on old maps and charts they were known as the Sandwich Islands. After a lapse of some years, other white explorers began to arrive at these islands, and two of them —an American and an Englishman—were captured by the Hawaiians and eventually made chiefs. These men later became influential advisers to Kamehameha I, the warrior who during this period succeeded in conquering and uniting all the islands under his rule and that of his successors.

The influence of the white man led to an interest in the Christian faith on the part of the native rulers, and after the conversion of some of the chiefs the old idols and taboos were overthrown. The moment was appropriate for the arrival of the first missionary group in 1820—a band of about twenty sturdy Congregationalist New Englanders. Their efforts and successes in teaching and converting were crowned by their establishment of the first Hawaiian alphabet. The Hawaiians' ardent desire to read and write accounts for their achieving widespread literacy in an incredibly brief space of time. Gratitude toward the missionaries led the rulers to seek their guidance in other fields —government, agriculture, public health, commerce—and their advice became a dominating factor in the life of the islands.

Naturally not all was idyllic in the development of this island kingdom to a modern American state. Opposing the missionary viewpoint were business and shipping interests, adventurers from many nations. Disease and disaster struck in these beguiling islands as elsewhere in the world. Political differences arose, were settled, and arose again. External influences, however, gradually weakened the monarchist hold, and during the next sixty to seventy years various constitutions were promulgated, lessening the kings' power. Good and bad rulers came and went, and eventually the greater strength of the white man, along with other pressures, brought about the situation and the events of the story so movingly told in the following pages by Liliuokalani, Hawaii's last monarch.

HAWAII'S STORY

CHAPTER I

A SKETCH OF MY CHILDHOOD

THE extinct crater or mountain which forms the background to the city of Honolulu is known as the Punch-Bowl; at its base is situated the Queen's Hospital, so named because of the great interest taken in its erection by Emma, the queen of Kamehameha IV. Funds for the cause were solicited by the reigning sovereigns in person, and the hospital building was completed in 1860. Very near to its site, on Sept. 2, 1838, I was born. My father's name was Kapaakea, and my mother was Keohokalole; the latter was one of the fifteen counsellors of the king, Kamehameha III., who in 1840 gave the first written constitution to the Hawaiian people. My great-grandfather, Keawe-a-Heulu, the founder of the dynasty of the Kamehamehas, and Keoua, father of Kamehameha I., were own cousins (he was also brother of Mrs. Bishop's ancestress, Hakau), and my great-grandaunt was the celebrated Queen Kapiolani, one of the first converts to Christianity. She plucked the sacred berries from the borders of the volcano, descended to the boiling lava, and there, while singing Christian hymns, threw them into the lake of fire. This was the act which broke forever the power of Pele, the fire-goddess, over the hearts of her people. Those interested in genealogies are referred to the tables at the close of this volume, which show the descent of our family from the highest chiefs of ancient days. It has often happened in the history of nations that the most eminent men have won the crown, and then, instead of ascending the throne, have placed the executive office in the hands of another. Kamehameha I. was, indeed, the founder of Hawaiian unity, and worthy of the surname of the Great; but it is truthfully recorded in the early histories of the Islands, — those written by such men as Mr. Pogue, Mr. Dibble, and others, — that he owed his selection for the monarchy to the chiefs from whom the latest reigning family, my own, is descended. This indebtedness was fully recognized during the life of that monarch.

Naihe, the husband of Kapiolani, was the great orator of the king's reign; his father, Keawe-a-Heulu, was chief counsellor to Kamehameha I.; while had it not been for the aid of the two chiefs, Keeaumoku and Kameeiamoku, cousins of the chief counsellor, the Hawaiian Islands must have remained for a long time, if not until this day, in a state of anarchy. My grandfather, Aikanaka, had charge of the guns of the fort on Punch-Bowl Hill, which had been brought from the larger island of Hawaii; as the chiefs, their families, and followers had settled here from the time of the final battle, when all the forces contending against Kamehameha I. were driven over the Pali.

For the purpose of enhancing the value of their own

mission, it has been at times asserted by foreigners that the abundance of the chief was procured by the poverty of his followers. To any person at all familiar, either by experience or from trustworthy tradition, with the daily life of the Hawaiian people fifty years ago, nothing could be more incorrect than such assumption. The chief whose retainers were in any poverty or want would have felt, not only their sufferings, but, further, his own disgrace. As was then customary with the Hawaiian chiefs, my father was surrounded by hundreds of his own people, all of whom looked to him, and never in vain, for sustenance. He lived in a large grass house surrounded by smaller ones, which were the homes of those the most closely connected with his service. There was food enough and to spare for every one. And this was equally true of all his people, however distant from his personal care. For the chief always appointed some man of ability as his agent or overseer. This officer apportioned the lands to each Hawaiian, and on these allotments were raised the taro, the potatoes, the pigs, and the chickens which constituted the living of the family; even the forests, which furnished the material from which was made the tapa cloth, were apportioned to the women in like manner. It is true that no one of the common people could mortgage or sell his land, but the wisdom of this limitation is abundantly proved by the homeless condition of the Hawaiians at the present day. Rent, eviction of tenants, as understood in other lands, were unknown; but each retainer of any chief contributed in the productions of his holding to the support of the chief's table.

But I was destined to grow up away from the house of my parents. Immediately after my birth I was wrapped in the finest soft tapa cloth, and taken to the house of another chief, by whom I was adopted. Konia, my foster-mother, was a granddaughter of Kamehameha I., and was married to Paki, also a high chief; their only daughter, Bernice Pauahi, afterwards Mrs. Charles R. Bishop, was therefore my foster-sister. In speaking of our relationship, I have adopted the term customarily used in the English language, but there was no such modification recognized in my native land. I knew no other father or mother than my foster-parents, no other sister than Bernice. I used to climb up on the knees of Paki, put my arms around his neck, kiss him, and he caressed me as a father would his child; while on the contrary, when I met my own parents, it was with perhaps more of interest, yet always with the demeanor I would have shown to any strangers who noticed me. My own father and mother had other children, ten in all, the most of them being adopted into other chiefs' families; and although I knew that these were my own brothers and sisters, yet we met throughout my younger life as though we had not known our common parentage. This was, and indeed is, in accordance with Hawaiian customs. It is not easy to explain its origin to those alien to our national life, but it seems perfectly natural to us. As intelligible a reason as can be given is that this alliance by adoption cemented the ties of friendship between the chiefs. It spread to the common people, and it has doubtless fostered a community of interest and harmony.

At the age of four years I was sent to what was then known as the Royal School, because its pupils were exclusively persons whose claims to the throne were acknowledged. It was founded and conducted by Mr. Amos S. Cooke, who was assisted by his wife. It was a boarding-school, the pupils being allowed to return to their homes during vacation time, as well as for an occasional Sunday during the term. The family life was made agreeable to us, and our instructors were especially particular to teach us the proper use of the English language; but when I recall the instances in which we were sent hungry to bed, it seems to me that they failed to remember that we were growing children. A thick slice of bread covered with molasses was usually the sole article of our supper, and we were sometimes ingenious, if not over honest, in our search for food: if we could beg something of the cook it was the easier way; but if not, anything eatable left within our reach was surely confiscated. As a last resort, we were not above searching the gardens for any esculent root or leaf, which (having inherited the art of igniting a fire from the friction of sticks), we could cook and consume without the knowledge of our preceptors.

I can remember now my emotions on entering this the first school I ever attended. I can recall that I was carried there on the shoulders of a tall, stout, very large woman, whose name was Kaikai (she was the sister of Governor Kanoa, and they were of a family of chiefs of inferior rank, living under the control and direction of the higher chiefs). As she put me down at the entrance to the schoolhouse, I shrank from its

doors, with that immediate and strange dread of the
unknown so common to childhood.   Crying bitterly, I
turned to my faithful attendant, clasping her with my
arms and clinging closely to her neck.   She tenderly
expostulated with me; and as the children, moved by
curiosity to meet the new-comer, crowded about me, I
was soon attracted by their friendly faces, and was induced to go into the old courtyard with them.   Then
my fears began to vanish, and comforted and consoled,
I soon found myself at home amongst my playmates.

Several of the pupils who were at school with me
have subsequently become known in Hawaiian history.
There were four children of Kinau, daughter of Kame-
hameha I., the highest in rank of any of the women
chiefs of her day; these were Moses, Lot (afterwards
Kamehameha V.), Liholiho (afterwards Kamehameha
IV.), and Victoria, of whom I shall soon speak.   Next
came Lunalilo, who followed Kamehameha V. as king.
Then came Bernice Pauahi, who married Hon. Charles
R. Bishop.   Our family was represented by Kaliokalani,
Kalakaua, and myself, two of the three destined to as-
cend the throne.   Besides these I must mention Emma
Rooke, who married one of the Kamehamehas, Peter
Kaeo, Jane Loeau, Elizabeth Kaaniau, Abigail Maheha,
Mary Paaina, and John Kinau Pitt; although these were
all not there at the same time.   Queen Emma, I remem-
ber, did not come in until after I had been at school
some years.

We never failed to go to church in a procession
every Sunday in charge of our teachers, Mr. and Mrs.
Cooke, and occupied seats in the immediate vicinity of

the pew where the king was seated. The custom was for a boy and girl to march side by side, the lead being taken by the eldest scholars. Moses and Jane had this distinction, next Lot and Bernice, then Liholiho with Abigail, followed by Lunalilo and Emma (after the latter had joined the school), James and Elizabeth, David and Victoria, and so on, John Kinau and I being the last.

With the Princess Victoria, who died on the 29th of May, 1866, my younger life was connected in the following manner. When I was taken from my own parents and adopted by Paki and Konia, or about two months thereafter, a child was born to Kinau. That little babe was the Princess Victoria, two of whose brothers became sovereigns of the Hawaiian people. While the infant was at its mother's breast, Kinau always preferred to take me into her arms to nurse, and would hand her own child to the woman attendant who was there for that purpose. So she frequently declared in the presence of my adopted mother, Konia, that a bond of the closest friendship must always exist between her own baby girl and myself as *aikane* or foster-children of the same mother, and that all she had would also appertain to me just as if I had been her own child; and that although in the future I might be her child's rival, yet whatever would belong to Victoria should be mine. This insistence on the part of the mother was never forgotten; it remained in the history of Victoria's girlhood and mine until her death, although Kinau herself never lived to see her prophetic predictions fulfilled. Kinau died on the 4th of April, 1839, not long after the birth of her youngest child, Victoria.

On any occasion where the Princess Victoria was
expected to be present I was always included in the
invitation, so that whenever Kekauluohi, the sister of
Kinau, invited her niece to be with her, I was also summoned to her residence. This aunt lived in a large
stone house called Pohukaina, which stood not more
than two hundred feet from the Royal School; and for
our enjoyment she used to prepare all sorts of sweet-
meats and delicacies peculiar to the Hawaiians, such as
(to call them by our native names) *kulolo, paipaiee*,
and *koele-palau*, with which our childish tastes were
delighted.

In 1847 Moses left school, and went to reside with
his father. In 1848 Jane Loeau married a Mr. Jasper.
Abigail Maheha also left about the same time to reside
with her aunt, the Princess Kekauonohi, and it was at
this date that the epidemic of measles spread through
the land; of those who fell victims to it were Moses
Kekuaiwa, William Pitt Leleiohoku, who was a cousin
of the Princess Kekauonohi and first husband of the
Princess Ruth (when later my younger brother was
born, and adopted by Ruth, he took the name of her
deceased husband); the third of these deaths in the
families of the royal children was that of my little sister
Kaiminaauao, who had been adopted by Kamehameha
III. and his queen, Kalama.

This sad event made a great impression upon my
younger days; for these relatives and companions of my
youth died and were buried on the same day, the coffin
of the last-named resting on that of the others. They
were all buried in the royal mausoleum, which then was

located where is now the yard of Iolani Palace. Since the erection of another building up the Nuuanu Valley, their remains have been removed with those of their ancestors.

From the year 1848 the Royal School began to decline in influence ; and within two or three years from that time it was discontinued, the Cooke family entering business with the Castles, forming a mercantile establishment still in existence.

Mr. Cooke and Mr. S. N. Castle were both sent to Honolulu by the American Board of Commissioners for Foreign Missions. As soon as they had become accustomed to life in the Hawaiian Islands, they severed all connection with the board, entered secular and mercantile pursuits, founding the firm of Castle & Cooke. This has now become a very wealthy concern ; and although the senior partners are dead, it is still conducted under their name by their descendants or associates. The sons of Mr. Castle have also been actively interested in the present (1893–1897) government of the Hawaiian Islands.

From the school of Mr. and Mrs. Cooke I was sent to that of Rev. Mr. Beckwith, also one of the American missionaries. This was a day-school, and with it I was better satisfied than with a boarding-school.

CHAPTER II

SOME INCIDENTS OF MY YOUTH

I WAS a studious girl; and the acquisition of knowledge has been a passion with me during my whole life, one which has not lost its charm to the present day. In this respect I was quite different from my sister Bernice. She was one of the most beautiful girls I ever saw; the vision of her loveliness at that time can never be effaced from remembrance; like a striking picture once seen, it is stamped upon memory's page forever. She married in her eighteenth year. She was betrothed to Prince Lot, a grandchild of Kamehameha the Great; but when Mr. Charles R. Bishop pressed his suit, my sister smiled on him, and they were married. It was a happy marriage. When Mr. and Mrs. Bishop were first married they established their modest home at the termination of the beautiful Nuuanu Valley, directly opposite the tombs of the Hawaiian monarchs. They then began housekeeping in a small house on Alakea Street, near the site of the present Masonic Temple. At this time I was still living with Paki and Konia, and the house now standing and known as the Arlington Hotel was being erected by the chief for his residence. It was completed in 1851, and occupied by Paki until 1855, when he died. Then my sister and her husband moved to that residence, which still remained my home.   It was there that the years of my girlhood were passed, after school-days were over, and the pleasant company we often had in that house will never cease to give interest to the spot.

Mr. Bishop was a popular and hospitable man, and his wife was as good as she was beautiful.   The king, Kamehameha IV., Alexander Liholiho, would often appear informally at our doors with some of his friends ; the evening would be passed in improvised dances, and the company always grew larger when it became known that we were thus enjoying ourselves ; sometimes we would all adjourn to the house of some friend or neighbor from whom we had reason to expect like hospitality, and the night would be half gone ere we noticed the flight of time.

It was now that the young man who subsequently became my husband first became specially interested in me, and I in him, although we had been very near neighbors during our school-days, and we had seen each other more than once.   A Mr. and Mrs. Johnston, a married couple of rather advanced age, established a day-school for children of both sexes in the house next to that of Mr. Cooke ; their lot was separated from ours by a high fence of adobe, or sun-baked brick.   The boys used to climb the fence on their side for the purpose of looking at the royal children, and amongst these curious urchins was John O. Dominis.   His father was a sea-captain, who had originally come to Honolulu on Cape Horn voyages, and had been interested in trade both in China and in California.   The ancestors of

Captain Dominis were from Italy; but Mrs. Dominis
was an American, born at Boston, and was a descendant
of one of the early English settlers.   The house known
as Washington Place was built by Captain Dominis for
a family residence.   As will appear shortly, Mr. Dominis was not my first or only suitor.   My social and
political importance would, quite apart from any personal qualities, render my alliance a matter of much
solicitude to many.   This is not, however, a subject on
which I shall care to say more than is necessary.

On June 13, 1855, Paki, my adopted father, died.
Soon after this the betrothal was announced of Alexander Liholiho and Emma Rooke.   Some of those interested in the genealogies of the historic families of the
Hawaiian chiefs, on hearing of this intended marriage,
went to the king, and begged him to change his mind.
"And why should I?" asked Liholiho.   "Because, Your
Majesty, there is no other chief equal to you in birth
and rank but the adopted daughter of Paki."   The king
took offence at this counsel, and dismissed the objec-
tors from his presence.   Emma was descended from a
half-brother of Kalaniopuu, the latter being first cousin
to Kamehameha the Great.   The royal wedding took
place on June 19, 1856.   The bridesmaids were Princess Victoria, myself, and Mary Pitman; the groomsmen
were Prince Lot (afterwards Kamehameha V.), Prince
William, and my brother, David Kalakaua.   Honolulu
was for the time the scene of great festivity.   The
ceremony filled the great Kawaiahao church; and thereafter there were picnics, parties, *luaus*, and balls without number.   Each of the nations represented on the

island, even to the Chinese, gave its own special ball
in honor of the wedding.

The king was returning from Moanalua with a large
escort, a cavalcade of perhaps two hundred riders of
both sexes.   Amongst these was General J. O. Dominis, then a young man on the staff of Prince Lot.   He
was riding by my side when an awkward horseman
forced his horse between us, and in the confusion Mr.
Dominis was thrown from his horse and his leg broken.
He gained the saddle, however, and insisted on accompanying me to my home, where he dismounted, and
helped me from my horse.   He then rode home ; but by
the time he had reached his own house his leg had
become so swollen and painful that he could not dis-
mount without assistance, and for some time, until the
bone had become united, was confined to his house.

In the following November I accompanied Konia,
my mother, to Hawaii, where she went for her health.
We visited Kona, Kaei, and Kaleakekua Bay, the latter
celebrated as the scene of the death of Captain Cook,
the discoverer.   The Princess Miriam Likelike (my own
sister) was there brought up, and was well contented ;
but to one accustomed as I was to the bustle of the city
and the life of the court, it seemed to be an excessively
quiet and dismal place.   After some months spent on
Hawaii we went to Lahaina ; there I received a letter
from my brother Kalakaua, telling me that he was engaged to the Princess Victoria, and asking me to come
to Honolulu.   So, attended by five women, all from the
families of high chiefs, I started for that city ; but upon
my arrival I found that the engagement was broken,

for the Princess Victoria had gone to Wailua, and my
brother had heard nothing from her for a fortnight : so
I made preparations to return to Maui, but receiving an
invitation to remain for a ball to be given by Prince Lot,
I deferred my journey.   At the ball the Princess Victoria
appeared with her suite, and it was said was engaged to
Prince William.   Be that as it may, we all had a very
gay time at the ball, which continued until daybreak.

   At two o'clock the day following Prince Lot and
Mr. Dominis, with the five ladies of noble birth, attended me to the old schooner Kekauluohi, by which I
was to make the passage across the channel.   My retinue was very large, and nearly filled the cabin.   Prince
William, who ascended the throne in 1874 under the
title of Lunalilo, was the owner of the vessel, and was
also at this time on board.   He came to me, and insisted
on my taking his cabin; and when the berth had been
emptied of oranges with which I found it filled, his wearing apparel, boots, and other belongings also cleared out,
I complied.   He then asked me in the presence of my
attendants why we shouldn't get married.   There was
an aged native preacher on board, Pikanele by name, who
at once offered to perform the ceremony.   But having
heard the prince was engaged to his cousin Victoria,
I did not consider it right to marry him on the impulse
of the moment.   When we arrived at Lahaina he escorted me to my home, there repeating his offer ; and I
took the matter into serious consideration, agreeing to
write to him.   He joined his father at Kona ; and to that
place I directed my letter, sending it by the schooner
Kamamalu, which also was the Hawaiian name of the

princess. It seemed that she declined to be the bearer of messages to her fickle swain, for the schooner was lost at sea. In the mean time Victoria Kamamalu had written to Prince William, reminding him of his obligations to her, and asking him to return to Honolulu, which he did, stopping at Lahaina on the way to tell me that, having received no answer from me, he supposed that I had rejected his proposal; but on my explanation of the matter, he again renewed his offer, and we became engaged. In May of that year my mother returned with me to Honolulu; but her health was not permanently improved, and on July 2, 1857, she died.

The death of Paki and Konia placed me more yet under the charge of Mr. and Mrs. Bishop, but Prince William claimed that our engagement was in full force. Mr. Bishop asked the king if he considered it a good match, to which Alexander replied that if I were his daughter he should not approve of it, but that if each of us were pleased, he should not oppose it, but advise us to marry. But there were certain other incidents which came to the surface ere long which led me to break the engagement. Neither Prince William Lunalilo nor the Princess Victoria was ever married.

CHAPTER III

KAMEHAMEHA IV

ALEXANDER LIHOLIHO, known to history as Kamehameha IV., had all the characteristics of his race ; and
the strong, passionate nature of the Kamehamehas is
shown in his benevolent as in his less commendable
acts.   To him was due the introduction of the Anglican
Mission.   He personally translated the English Prayer-
Book into our language.   He also founded the Queen's
Hospital, as has already been noticed ; and both the foreign and domestic affairs of his government were ably
administered.   Hon. R. C. Wylie continued as his Minister of Foreign Affairs throughout his reign.

In 1859, or just prior to my engagement to Mr.
Dominis, a pleasant party was made up in Honolulu for
an excursion to the other islands, on which I went,
being, as indeed I always was at this time, under the
special charge of Mrs. Bishop.   We visited the volcano
on Hawaii, and descended to the city of Hilo, on whose
beautiful bay was then lying the United States ship
Levant.   At this place we were joined by the king with
his party ; and having many most agreeable acquaintances amongst the naval officers, the time sped quickly
in social pleasures.   We lived in a large grass house,
one side of which was occupied by the ladies and the

other by the gentlemen, while the centre was a room used for banquet-hall or ballroom, besides answering the purpose of separating the two lateral apartments so widely that no conversation could be heard from one to the other. When any of the royal party had occasion to go from one place to another, we were drawn in carriages of native construction, the people themselves furnishing the power usually supplied by horses. Sometimes we were stuck in some mud-hole or water-course, from which the most determined efforts of our devoted followers could not extricate us ; and it was then necessary to have a horse led to the side of the vehicle to take us off on horseback. But we were light-hearted, merry, and happy ; the naval officers were perfect gentlemen, and gallant in their attentions. The king enjoyed the pleasures to which his presence and that of others of the royal line gave a great charm. He even mischievously prevented us from taking an affectionate adieu of our friends aboard the Levant by suddenly signalling that we were to be at once on board of the Kilauea ; and that steamer started without as much as a " By your leave, sir," to the naval commander. At Lahaina the whole party left the ship, and at that port was further increased by the accession of the king's friends and retainers.

The next trip (1860) proposed by His Majesty was to the extinct volcano of Healeala, and orders were given that we should all go in boats from Lahaina to Wailuku. It was a beautiful sight ; the waters were calm, each boat was ornamented with the Hawaiian flag, the royal standard fluttered from that of the king, and as we coasted along the shores, we could see the people on the land following our course and interested in our progress; there were, I think, twelve boats in all. We arrived without accident, ascended the mountain, and passed a night on the border of the crater. We had our tents, and there was shelter in the caves and crevices for the remainder of the party. All passed off gayly. There was little sleep, however, some of us being afflicted with asthmatic attacks which the excessive rarity of the air at that altitude made very severe. Such was my portion; but as I sat up, not daring to lie down lest I might lose my breath, I could hear the merry sounds of the singing and dancing which from one tent or another was going on around me.

The first halt in our enjoyment was when word was received that the little Prince of Hawaii, then but a little more than a year old, was ill.

The king was deaf to the entreaties of the queen to be allowed to go directly to her child, because he thought it would delay his own departure and arrival at the bedside of his boy. Fortunately the illness passed away without serious consequences; yet it seemed the first break in our festivities, and was followed by an event of a most tragical nature.

We descended the mountain and returned to Lahaina, where I, accompanied by Mrs. Bishop, left them, and went back to Honolulu. The first news we received was that the king in a fit of passion had shot and mortally wounded one of the party, his own secretary, Mr. H. A. Neilson. After the occurrence all that the tenderest of brothers could have done was proffered by the

king to the wounded man; but after lingering for some
months, Mr. Neilson died. No legal notice of the event
was in any way taken; no person would have been fool-
hardy enough to propose it. It is not my purpose to
defend the right of the king to this execution of sum-
mary vengeance, especially as it was done in a moment
of anger; yet beyond the sadness of the act, it has a
certain bearing on this sketch of my life as one of the
descendants from the ruling families of Hawaii.

There were causes which were apparent to any of our
people for something very like righteous anger on the
part of the king. His Majesty was trying to make us
each and all happy; yet even during moments of relaxation, undue familiarity, absence of etiquette, rudeness,
or any other form which implied or suggested disrespect
to royalty in any manner whatsoever, would never be
tolerated by any one of the native chiefs of the Hawaiian people. To allow any such breach of good
manners to pass unnoticed would be looked upon by his
own retainers as belittling to him, and they would be
the first to demand the punishment of the offender. It
was in this case far too severe. No one realized that
more than the king himself, who suffered much distress
for his victim, and was with difficulty dissuaded from
the abdication of his throne. The temper of the Kamehamehas had descended to the young prince, and was
also the cause of his death. For when the child was
about four years old, he became dissatisfied with a pair
of boots, and burst into an ungovernable fit of passion.
His father sought to cool him off by putting the boy
under an open faucet of cold, running water. The lit-

tle one appeared to be unharmed, but later in the day
broke down with nervous weeping, and could not be
comforted.   Then it was discovered that the cold
douche and shock had brought on an attack of brain
fever.   From this he did not recover, but died on the
27th of August, 1862.   The king and queen had the
sympathy of all parties in their bereavement ; but Kamehameha IV. completely lost his interest in public life,
living in the utmost possible retirement until his death.

It may be in place here to notice the opening of the
reign of Kamehameha IV.'s successor.   It has already
been seen that the right of life and death was unchal-
lenged ; that whatever it may be in other countries, as
late as an epoch thirty years in the past it belonged
to the highest chief of the Hawaiian people.   In like
manner it may be said that the whole people owed its
national life to the throne.   The first constitution was
given to the realm in 1840, and was a voluntary act on
the part of the king, Kamehameha III.   The second succeeded it in 1852.   Both of these were doubtless drafted
under the supervision and advice of the missionaries, of
whom, even at the latter date, the Hawaiian nation was
beginning to feel a little justifiable jealousy.   So when
Prince Lot came to the throne in 1863, under the title
of Kamehameha V., his first official act was to refuse
to take the oath to maintain the existing constitution.
His success as Minister of the Interior under his brother
had been remarkable, and his character was said to re-
semble that of Kamehameha the Great ; it is presumable,
therefore, that he understood the needs of his people better than those of foreign birth and alien affinities.   In

the month of May, 1864, the king issued a call for a
constitutional convention, subsequently making a tour of
the islands to explain his plans to the electors.   In July
of that year the convention assembled in Honolulu ; but
its time being given to what Kamehameha considered
useless deliberations instead of business, on Aug. 13 he
declared the convention dissolved, dismissed the delegates, publicly abrogated the constitution of 1852, and
one week after that date he proclaimed a new constitution of his own devising, under which Hawaii was happily
ruled for twenty-three years.   There will be no disput-
ing the fact that this was a period of increasing prosperity ; yet until the late King Kalakaua was constrained
by the foreign element to abrogate this constitution
(which my brother did much against his own will and
better judgment in 1887), all parties had lived together
in harmony throughout the kingdom of the Hawaiian
Islands, under a constitution devised and promulgated
by one man, and he of the race of the Hawaiian chiefs.
I hope this fact will be recalled when I come to speak
of the history of the reign of my brother Kalakaua, and
my own administration of public affairs.   Let it be repeated : the promulgation of a new constitution, adapted
to the needs of the times and the demands of the people,
has been an indisputable prerogative of the Hawaiian
monarchy.

CHAPTER IV

MY MARRIED LIFE

I WAS engaged to Mr. Dominis for about two years; and it was our intention to be married on the second day of September, 1862. But by reason of the fact that the court was in affliction and mourning, our wedding was delayed at the request of the king, Kamehameha IV., to the sixteenth of that month; Rev. Dr. Damon, father of Mr. S. M. Damon, at present the leading banker of the Islands, being the officiating clergyman. It was celebrated at the residence of Mr. and Mrs. Bishop, in the house which had been erected by my father, Paki, and which, known as the Arlington Hotel, is still one of the most beautiful and central of the mansions in Honolulu. To it came all the high chiefs then living there, also the foreign residents; in fact, all the best society of the city.

My husband took me at once to the estate known as Washington Place, which had been built by his father, and which is still my private residence. It is a large, square, white house, with pillars and porticos on all sides, really a palatial dwelling, as comfortable in its appointments as it is inviting in its aspect; its front is distant from the street far enough to avoid the dust and noise. Trees shade its walls from the heat of noonday;

WASHINGTON PLACE

The Private Residence of the Queen, formerly the Home of General John Owen Dominis, the Prince Consort

its ample gardens are filled with the choicest flowers and shrubs; it is, in fact, just what it appears, a choice tropical retreat in the midst of the chief city of the Hawaiian Islands. Opposite its doors is the edifice, recently erected, known as the Central Union Church, which is attended by the missionary families, and indeed most of the foreign residents of American birth or sympathies.

Captain Dominis, father of my husband, had but little enjoyment from the homestead he had planned. He last sailed from the port in 1846, just as the house was on the point of completion, and the ship he commanded was never heard of more. His widow expected, hoped, and prayed, but no tidings of his fate were ever received; slowly she was compelled to recognize the truth so many sailors' wives are constantly learning, and to hope long deferred succeeded grief for irreparable loss. For this reason she clung with tenacity to the affection and constant attentions of her son, and no man could be more devoted than was General Dominis to his mother. He was really an only child, although there had been two daughters older; but while he was an infant they both died in the United States, where they had been left to gain their education. Mrs. Dominis was a native of Boston.

As she felt that no one should step between her and her child, naturally I, as her son's wife, was considered an intruder; and I was forced to realize this from the beginning. My husband was extremely kind and considerate to me, yet he would not swerve to the one side or to the other in any matter where there was danger

of hurting his mother's feelings. I respected the close-
ness of the tie between mother and son, and conformed
my own ideas, so far as I could, to encourage and assist
my husband in his devotion to his mother. Later in
life Mrs. Dominis seemed to fully realize that there
had been some self-sacrifice, and she became more and
more a tender and affectionate mother to me as her
days were drawing to a close.

Soon after our marriage, Prince Lot invited my husband and myself, with Mr. and Mrs. Robert Davis, who
were married about the same time, to accompany him
on a trip to Hawaii, the largest island of the group,
from which its name is taken. We accepted, and it
became really my bridal tour. Prince Lot's accession
to the throne as Kamehameha V. was then very near.
Invitations were also extended to Mr. and Mrs. John
Sumner, Mr. Haalelea, another member, like my husband, of the staff of His Royal Highness, and a few
other friends of the royal party. It was a most enjoy-
able trip; we were gone many weeks, but the time
passed away most delightfully.

As there are no hotels in our islands, a few words as
to the entertainment of the chiefs, with such guests as
they might have with them, may not be out of place
here. I have always said that under our own system in
former days there was always plenty for prince or for
people. The latter were not paid in money, nor were
they taxed in purse. The chief, by the overseer he appointed, took proper care of their needs, and they in turn
contributed to the support of his table. It was a repetition of the principle of family life by extending the same

over a large number of retainers. So on the estates of
the high chiefs who generally resided at Honolulu were
built houses which were sacred to their residence, exclusively devoted to such occasions as the present, when
they might choose to visit their people.

Prince Lot had his houses and lands in Hawaii and
elsewhere. It was to these we went. His people welcomed our presence ; and no matter how protracted our
stay, Hawaiian hospitality, or love and loyalty, which-
ever it may please the reader to call it, was never exhausted. It was the same with all the chiefs of the
ancient families, with Mrs. Bishop, for example, who
would have found a home on any part of her landed
estate ; nor has the custom altogether passed away by
the many changes which have been wrought through
the hands of the foreigner in the Hawaiian Islands.
Were any person of the blood of the chiefs, myself for
example, to visit Hawaii to-day, scarcely would the
knowledge that we had reached the port of Hilo get to
the ears of our people when a house would be provided
for our occupancy, food would be brought to our doors,
and we would be made welcome amongst our people for
weeks, months, indeed years, if we chose to continue
our residence.

On this visit to Hilo (1862) occurred the first chapter of an interesting history of which the sequel was the
nomination of a younger brother of mine to the throne,
although he did not live to enter upon his reign. One
of the retainers of the Princess Ruth was in our company, and it was near the time of that lady's confine-
ment. As Kalaikuaiwa, one of her people, was about to

return to the neighboring island of Oahu, she inquired
of Prince Lot what message she could carry back to
Honolulu, to be delivered to Princess Ruth in regard to
the little stranger about to enter this world. The prince,
in reply, told the attendant to charge his sister from him
on no account to give the coming child away, to which
that messenger responded that it had been already promised to Mrs. Pauahi Bishop, her cousin. The prince repeated his injunction with still more emphasis, saying,
"You must go back and tell my sister that on no account
is she to give that child to another. I am an adopted
child myself, deprived of the love of my mother, and yet
I was a stranger in the house of my adoption." He referred to his own and Lunalilo's grandfather, Hoapili-
kane. The prince made no further explanations, save
to impress it upon the messenger that such must be
the message delivered ; and as we started for our trip
around the great island of Hawaii, the attendant left
for her mistress's houses and home in Honolulu.

I may anticipate a little in order to continue the
thread of this story. When our tour was over, and we
returned to Honolulu, the first day of our arrival was a
day of rest ; but on the succeeding day, possibly a little
later, Prince Lot, Queen Emma, Mrs. Bishop, and perhaps some others, were summoned to be present at the
birth of the child of the Princess Ruth. The babe was
born that afternoon at about three o'clock, in the house
called Halaniani, on the veranda of which the prince
waited for tidings of the mother and child for hours.
Finally, at half-past five, Queen Emma appeared, and addressing the prince, asked him if he had heard from his

sister, to which he replied that he had not. She expressed much surprise, and told him that the newly born infant had been taken away as her own by Mrs. Bishop over an hour ago. This intelligence was extremely unpleasant to the prince, and he at once declared that he would never have anything to do with that child. He carried his purpose into immediate execution by insisting within a week from that time that his sister Ruth should legally adopt as her own my brother Leleiohoku, whom she had taken from his parents at birth. He then made out two instruments of adoption for his sister to sign. By one she gave her child to Mrs. Bishop irrevocably, cutting it off from all interest in her property, and by the other she adopted as her child and heir, William Pitt Leleiohoku, the second of that name. All the papers were carefully drawn up by the prince, and everything connected with the adoption was made complete, so that in no event could the legality of my brother's position be doubted. The innocent cause of this disturbance, the child thus adopted by Mrs. Bishop and named Keolaokalani, died in about six months; my brother lived to be named heir apparent, and indeed to fill the office of regent during the absence of Kalakaua.

After making the tour of Hawaii, Prince Lot, accompanied by his guests, returned as far as the island of Maui, where it is possible we might have remained longer had it not been for the illness of his brother, the reigning king. Having been notified that this was approaching a fatal termination, and that his presence was required at the capital, His Royal Highness returned at once to Honolulu, where Alexander, Kamehameha IV.,

died on Nov. 30, 1863, after a reign of nine years, and
being at the time of his death still a young man of
twenty-nine.   His widow, Queen Emma, although once
a candidate for the throne, was never again in public
life.   She went abroad, however, in 1865, being received
in England in a manner becoming her rank.   She
returned to Honolulu in 1866 on the United States
ship Vanderbilt, commanded by Admiral Henry Knox
Thatcher, only to learn at once of a new affliction in the
death of her adopted mother, Mrs. T. C. B. Rooke.

On the accession to the throne of Prince Lot as
Kamehameha V., the last of the Hawaiian monarchs to
bear that name, my husband was at once appointed his
private secretary and confidential adviser, which position he occupied during the entire reign.   The king was
surrounded by his own people, with whom he was in
perfect accord, but showed this mark of royal favor to
my husband simply because he preferred to advise with
him on matters of public importance.   My husband was
further made governor of the island on which Honolulu
is situated ; and although the appointment was nomi-
nally for four years, yet it was always renewed, without
the least discussion or hesitation, as long as he lived.
It was a part of his official duty to make a tour of the
whole island at least once a year ; this was always
rendered a most agreeable excursion, and I invariably
accompanied him in the journey.   Besides this position
he held other offices of importance under the Hawaiian
government, being at one time governor of the island
of Maui ; commissioner of the administration of the
crown lands ; attached to the suite of my brother, the

late King Kalakaua, on his visit to this country in 1874 in the interest of reciprocity; and finally being a member of the Hawaiian embassy which visited this country and Great Britain in 1887, representing our nation at the Queen's Jubilee. But in the fall of 1891, Governor Dominis, who was then lieutenant-general of the kingdom with the rank of His Royal Highness Prince Consort, was in rapidly failing health; and on the 27th of August of that year, seven months after my accession to the throne, he died. His remains were laid in state in the palace; and on Sunday, Sept. 6, he was buried with royal honors.

His death occurred at a time when his long experience in public life, his amiable qualities, and his universal popularity, would have made him an adviser to me for whom no substitute could possibly be found. I have often said that it pleased the Almighty Ruler of nations to take him away from me at precisely the time when I felt that I most needed his counsel and companionship.

CHAPTER V

HAWAIIAN MUSIC, AND A DUCAL GUEST

THE Hawaiian people have been from time immemorial lovers of poetry and music, and have been apt in improvising historic poems, songs of love, and chants of worship, so that praises of the living or wails over the dead were with them but the natural expression of their feelings. My ancestors were peculiarly gifted in this respect, and yet it is remarkable that there are few if any written compositions of the music of Hawaii excepting those published by me.

In my school-days my facility in reading music at sight was always recognized by my instructors. At the schools I attended, and of which mention has already been made, there was one boy by my side who could read the airs of new tunes which the teachers were anxious to introduce to the pupils. His name, I remember, was Willie Andrews. The untried music was handed to us ; and we sang it by note, the rest of the pupils following by ear until the whole assembly were acquainted with the new music. After leaving school, my musical education was continued from time to time as opportunity offered, but I scarcely remember the days when it would not have been possible for me to write either the words or the music for any occasion on which poetry or song was needed. To compose was as natural to me as to breathe ; and this gift of nature, never having been suffered to fall into disuse, remains a source of the greatest consolation to this day. I have never yet numbered my compositions, but am sure that they must run well up to the hundreds. Of these not more than a quarter have been printed, but the most popular have been in such demand that several editions have been exhausted. Hours of which it is not yet in place to speak, which I might have found long and lonely, passed quickly and cheerfully by, occupied and soothed by the expression of my thoughts in music ; and even when I was denied the aid of any instrument I could transcribe to paper the tones of my voice.

In the early years of the reign of Kamehameha V. he brought to my notice the fact that the Hawaiian people had no national air. Each nation, he said, but ours had its expression of patriotism and love of country in its own music ; but we were using for that purpose on state occasions the time-honored British anthem, " God save the Queen." This he desired me to supplant by one of my own composition. In one week's time I notified the king that I had completed my task. The Princess Victoria had been the leader of the choir of the Kawaiahao church ; but upon her death, May 29, 1866, I assumed the leadership. It was in this building and by that choir that I first introduced the " Hawaiian National Anthem." The king was present for the purpose of criticising my new composition of both words and music, and was liberal in his commendations to me on my success. He admired not only the beauty of the music, but spoke enthusiastically of the appropriate words, so well adapted to the air and to the purpose for which they were written.

This remained in use as our national anthem for some twenty years or more, when my brother composed the words of the Hawaii Ponoi. He was at the time the reigning king, and gave directions to the master of the band to set these to music. He, being a German, found some composition from his own country which he deemed appropriate; and this has been considered of late years our national air.

In the changes of the past few years, the words written by His Majesty Kalakaua have been found no longer adapted to public occasions; so while the music is still played, such sentiments as " Look to the people " have been substituted for the ancient injunction to " Look to the king."

In the year 1869 the Duke of Edinburgh, Prince Alfred of England, arrived in the harbor of Honolulu, being in command of Her Britannic Majesty's ship-of-war Galatea. As soon as the king learned of the duke's presence he made special preparations for his reception; and for his better accommodation on shore he assigned for his use the residence of the late Kekuanaoa, who died in November of the preceding year. My own mother having died about three months prior to the arrival of the Galatea, I was not taking part in any festivities, being in retirement from society. But this was considered an exceptional occasion, and the king signified his wish to me that I would not fail to do it honor. So at his specific request I gave a grand *luau* at my

Waikiki residence, to which were invited all those connected with the government, indeed, all the first families
of the city, whether of native or foreign birth.   Major
J. H. Wodehouse, so long the ambassador of Great Britain at Honolulu, had just arrived with Mrs. Wodehouse;
and they were of the invited guests, the prince specially
inviting them to drive out to my house with him.   I
suppose the feast would be styled a breakfast in other
lands, for it was to begin at eleven o'clock in the forenoon.   The sailor-prince mounted the driver's box of
the carriage, and taking the reins from that official,
showed himself an expert in the management of horses.
All the members of the royal family of England are, I
understand, excellent horsemen; and in doing this the
Duke of Edinburgh was only following customs to which
he had been trained in his own land.   The Queen Dowager Kalama, widow of Kamehameha III., drove out to
Waikiki in her own carriage of state, accompanied by
her adopted son, Kunuiakea, and my sister, Miriam
Likelike; these two being at that time betrothed in
marriage, although the latter married Hon. A. S. Cleghorn, and became the mother of the Princess Kaiulani.
The drivers of these carriages wore the royal feather
shoulder-capes, and the footmen were also clad in like
royal fashion.   It was considered one of the grandest
occasions in the history of those days, and all passed off
as becoming the high birth and commanding position of
our visitor.   The guests were received with every mark
of courtesy by my husband and myself, as well as by His
Majesty Kamehameha V., who was one of the first arrivals.   When the prince entered he was met by two very

pretty Hawaiian ladies, who advanced, and, according
to the custom of our country, decorated him with *leis*, or
long, pliable wreaths of flowers suspended from the neck.

As Mrs. Bush, considered one of the most beautiful
women in the Hawaiian Islands, advanced, and proceeded
to tie the flowery garland about the neck of the prince,
he seemed perhaps a bit confused at the novel custom ;
but, submitting with the easy grace of a gentleman, he
appeared to be excessively pleased with the flowers and
with the expression of friendly welcome conveyed to
him by the act. Balls, picnics, and parties followed
this day of enjoyment ; and the prince gave an entertainment in return at his own house, which was attended
by my husband and myself, and by most of the distinguished persons in the city. The day of departure for
the Galatea arrived ; and the prince called on me to express the pleasure he had taken during his visit, and
the regrets he felt at leaving us. On this occasion he
presented me with an armlet emblematic of his profes-
sion ; it was of solid gold, a massively wrought chain
made after the pattern of a ship's cable, with anchor
as a pendant. He also gave me copies of two of his
own musical compositions ; and to this day I keep and
cherish these three souvenirs of the son of England's
good queen, and at the same time one of England's
noblest sailors. We have met once since those days,
at the Queen's Jubilee, during my visit to London in
1887. Our past acquaintance was cordially recognized
by the prince, who was then my escort on a state occasion, my nearest neighbor on the other hand being the
present Emperor of Germany.

CHAPTER VI

KAMEHAMEHA V

EARLY in December, 1872, occurred the death of Prince Lot, as he was often called, even after his accession to the throne under the title of Kamehameha V. On the 10th of that month my husband and I were summoned to the palace to attend the dying monarch; one by one other chiefs of the Hawaiian people, with a few of their trusted retainers, also arrived to be present at the final scene; we spent that night watching in silence near the king's bedside. The disease was pronounced by the medical men to be dropsy on the chest.

At nine o'clock on the day following we were drawn up in a little circle about his bed. Among other considerations forced upon us at this solemn moment was that of a successor to the throne, which, respecting the right of nomination, rested with the king. Those present were his half-sister, the Princess Ruth, Mrs. Pauahi Bishop, Mrs. Fanny Young, the mother of Queen Emma, and myself, all eligible candidates in the female line. At the doors of the apartment were Prince William Lunalilo and my brother, David Kalakaua, also heirs presumptive to the throne, while watching at a respectful distance were retainers of these chiefs.

The attorney-general, Hon. Stephen H. Phillips, Hon. P. Nahaolelua, afterwards a member of my brother's cabinet, my husband, General Dominis, Kamakou, and two women in attendance occupied the space between us and the doors. Although nearing the end, the mind of the king was still clear; and his thoughts, like our own, were evidently on the selection of a future ruler for the island kingdom, for, turning to Mrs. Bishop, he asked her to assume the reins of government and become queen at his death. She hesitated a moment, and then quietly inquired why His Majesty did not appoint as his successor his sister, the Princess Ruth Keelikolani, to which question the king replied that the princess would not be capable of undertaking with success the responsibilities of government, to which Mrs. Bishop rejoined, " Oh, but we will all help her to the best of our ability." Having obtained her opinion, he next turned to Nahaolelua, and demanded of him who would be the proper person to be named for the succession. To this the counsellor gave a very truthful, yet scarcely fortunate response, saying, " Any one, may it please Your Majesty, of the chiefs now present." The king again hesitated, and in the intervening time, the messenger whom all must obey was gaining entrance to the death-chamber; from the effort to provide for the future rule of the kingdom he relapsed into unconsciousness, and passed away without having named his successor to the throne.

The foremost candidate for the vacancy was undoubtedly the king's first cousin, Prince William Lunalilo; and in the matter of birth nothing could be said adverse to his claim. His mother was Kekauluohi, niece and step-daughter of Kamehameha the Great; he was popular, and of an amiable, easy disposition. But there were grave reasons why the choice was injudicious, and indeed hardly constitutional; for Prince William's personal habits even at this time were such that he was under the guardianship of Mr. Charles R. Bishop, the banker, his property being out of his own control, while he received from his guardian an allowance of only twenty-five dollars a month as spending money. His selection was chiefly due to the influence of the representatives of the single island of Oahu, but having once been announced, was accepted with the usual cheerfulness and good faith displayed by the Hawaiian people, who have always been loyal subjects to any one of their own acknowledged chiefs.

His cousin, Kamehameha V., had such advisers as Mr. R. C. Wylie, Mr. C. C. Harris, Mr. F. W. Hutchinson, Hon. S. H. Phillips, and others, all men of ability, but not associated with what is known as the missionary party. On the accession of Lunalilo, this latter party showed a determination to control the king, and by subjecting his weakness to their strength, to influence the fate of the Hawaiian people and the destiny of the Islands. They succeeded in securing the following cabinet: Hon. Charles R. Bishop (Foreign Affairs), E. O. Hall (Interior), R. Stirling (Finance), A. F. Judd (Attorney-General); two out of these four were from families who landed upon our shores with the single intention to teach our people the religion of Christ. The policy of the new cabinet was distinctively

American, in opposition to that which may properly be
called Hawaiian ; the latter looking to the prosperity and
progress of the nation as an independent sovereignty,
the former seeking to render the Islands a mere depen-
dency, either openly or under sufficient disguise, on the
government of the United States.   Then, as at the
present day, the entering wedge was the concession of
a harbor of refuge or repair at Pearl River.   The proposition created great excitement, and was vehemently
opposed by those of native birth ; for patriotism, which
with us means the love of the very soil on which our
ancestors have lived and died, forbade us to view with
equanimity the sight of any foreign flag, not excepting
the one for which we have always had the greatest respect, floating as a matter of right over any part of our
land.   There is a gentleman still living at Honolulu
whose boast is that he was the father of the project to
annex Hawaii to the American Union.   It may, therefore, be perfectly permissible to mention here that the
Pearl Harbor scheme of 1873 is declared with good
reason to have originated with him, — Dr. John S.
McGrew, — and was then openly advocated by him as
a preliminary to the obliteration of the native government by the annexation of the whole group to the
United States.   But in the midst of the discord produced by the agitation, the king's health began to fail
rapidly ; and at his express wish the project of the missionary party at that time to enter into closer relations
with their own country was laid aside until a more convenient season.   A change was recommended to Lunalilo ; and arrangements were made for a trip to the

largest island, Hawaii, noted with us for its high mountains and the favorable influences of its climate on the health.

By the advice of Dr. Trousseau, the king's physician, it was decided to go to Kailua; and thither went the royal party. Besides Dr. Trousseau, the king's chamberlain, Mr. Charles H. Judd accompanied us; then there were Kanaina, the king's father, Queen Emma, Princess Likelike, Mrs. Pauahi Bishop, Kapiolani, afterwards queen by virtue of marriage with my brother Leleiohoku, my younger brother, some others perhaps — and myself. The Hawaiian Band of native musicians also were with us; and every attempt was made to divert the mind of the king from his malady, and insure a favorable change. During our stay we were often visited by emissaries from Honolulu, urging upon the king the appointment of a successor, or praying him to return to the capital for the consideration of the subject, to all of which suggestions he appeared to be at least indifferent, if not absolutely opposed. In fact, he said openly enough that he himself owed his sceptre to the people, and he saw no reason why the people should not elect his successor. I suppose it is no secret, but really a matter of history, that the person most ambitious to succeed him in the rule of the Hawaiian nation was Emma, the widow of Alexander Liholiho, Kamehameha IV. She and a number of her retainers were with us during our entire stay, although she had taken advantage of residence there to make some excursions in the neighborhood. Amongst these I especially recall a trip she made to the mountain,

Hualalai, to visit the celebrated temple of Ahuaumi. This place once devoted to our ancient worship is a wonderful pile of rock, built by one of the kings of past centuries, and its construction was comparatively a short work, and yet each single stone must have been raised by a multitude of strong hands and muscular arms, passed from one set of laborers to another until it found its location in the structure; and the whole building thus completed was consecrated by Umi to the gods, and used for purposes then deemed most sacred. Visitors usually make this one of the celebrities to be seen if they are near enough to its location; but I regret to say there must have been those in the vicinity who had no respect for sacred antiquities, for a number of these stones, so laboriously erected, have been torn down, and from them a goat-pen has been built.

It was not long, however, that any of our party could indulge in recreation, for the rapid failure of the health of the king rendered it necessary for some one of us to be always watching with him. When it came to be the turn of Queen Emma, she urged him in plain language to nominate her to assume the reins of government at his decease; but his determination appeared to be unchanged to leave the selection to the people. Even when I was by his bedside, doing my duty as one of those chosen by birth to stand near during his dying hours, Queen Emma did not cease from her persistency, but again broached the subject of succession, and spoke to the king of the great importance to his people of naming an heir to the throne. The indelicacy of this persuasion from a Hawaiian point of view

will be understood by those who have studied our national customs. He made her no reply, but turned
from her as he lay on his bed. It was considered
best that he should return to Honolulu, to which re-
luctantly he consented; so, accompanied by the chiefs
and their attendants, we returned with him home. As
long as he retained consciousness he insisted that the
selection of a successor should be left to the people,
and even his ministers were powerless to change his
determination; and with a full intention of allowing
the succession to be settled by ballot rather than by
his constitutional right of appointment, he passed away,
apparently without pain. Indeed, so peaceful was his
end that the appearance of death began long before its
reality, and the marshal of the realm, supposing the
king to be dead, undertook the draping of the palace;
scarcely had the long festoons of crape been hung upon
the outer walls when it was discovered that the king
was living. It was not thought best to remove these
emblems of mourning, for their use might be appropriate at any moment; so an attempt was made to cover
or conceal them, and they were really in position about
two days before the final scene.

Although Queen Emma was not named by the king
as his successor, it was found that he had liberally remembered her in his will. A most important proviso
of that instrument was the fund left for the founding
of the Lunalilo Home for aged and indigent Hawaiians.
This institution admits those of both sexes, the men
being in one department and the women in another.
It is well managed, and its inmates are happy and con-

tented, so much so, indeed, that they often conduct themselves as if youth and hope were still their portion, and from the sympathy of daily companionship they wish to enter the closer tie of matrimony. This they are permitted to do without severing their connection with the institution, and there is a separate department provided for those who have thus agreed to finish the journey of life together.

BERNICE PAUAHI BISHOP MUSEUM

CHAPTER VII

QUEEN EMMA

THE contest for the succession which resulted in the elevation of my family — the Keaweaheulu line — to royal honors is of course a matter of history. Since the king had refused to nominate his successor, the election was with the legislature. It must not be forgotten, however, that the unwritten law of Hawaii Nei required that the greatest chief, or the one having the most direct claim to the throne, must rule. The legislature could not choose from the people at large, but was confined to a decision between rival claimants having an equal or nearly equal relation in the chiefhood to the throne.

Queen Emma's claim was not derived through her own family, but as the widow of Liholiho, one of the Kamehamehas. The great-grandfather of Kalakaua (the other claimant), and Kamehameha I. were own cousins; and, as I have already noted, it was to this ancestor and to other chiefs of our family that the late dynasty had owed its succession, and the uniting of the kingdoms of Hawaii under one government.

Now, it is not denied that Queen Emma had a rightful candidacy. It has already been seen that the king hesitated, and finally failed to decide between her rights

and those of our family to succession.   It was now the
duty of the legislature to determine the question.

From the fact that Queen Emma was a resident of
Honolulu, the capital, and the immediate scene of the
election, has arisen the impression that she was the real
choice of the Hawaiian people. She naturally had about
her a considerable personal following, scheming for
office, and a large body of retainers, all within the city
and environs ; and hence could there make a formidable
showing. She had also, of course, partisans here and
there throughout the Islands. Her canvass was, however, limited almost exclusively to intrigue within the
city, while Kalakaua and his friends sought the suffrages of the country people and their representatives.
Each party was vigorous in its own way, and there was
great excitement. It cannot be said that either party
felt much assurance as to the result, until the vote was
actually declared. But Queen Emma herself seems
never to have doubted that she must be the chosen
sovereign ; and it was policy for her advisers to flatter
her expectation, upon which their own fortunes hung.
For this she should rather have our sympathy than our
reprobation. Her active candidacy was legitimate, and
compatible with public spirit. But for her subsequent
course there is little justification. Her disappointment
assumes too personal a manifestation to be excused in
the representative of royal responsibilities. It is therefore because of its political consequence that I deem it
proper to record here what will doubtless seem to the
public, from any other point of view, a mere detail of
feminine pettiness.

It is a fact that Queen Emma ardently desired and hoped to succeed King Lunalilo, and that during the time that he lay unconscious, with life barely perceptible to those of us who stood nearest him, she was busily whispering among her friends the details of her plans. I was presently informed that she purposed to supersede General Dominis by Mr. F. S. Pratt as governor of Oahu, and that various other government positions had been promised. But if our party attended with its eyes to the intrigue, it at least maintained silence until the king died, and his remains were removed to Iolani Palace, and laid in state in the Red Chamber on the royal feather robe of Princess Nahienaena, the sister of Kamehameha III.

The legislature assembled in the old court-house, now the merchandise warerooms of Hackfeld & Co., the shipping merchants. At the first and only ballot it was found that David Kalakaua was elected, receiving thirty-nine votes to the six votes cast for the rival candidate, Queen Emma.

The vote, no doubt a surprise to Honolulu, being declared to the people who surrounded the legislative halls, was received with acclamation, mingled with shouts of disapproval. Naturally, the partisans of Queen Emma, being residents of Honolulu, and some of them inspired with liquor, were easily incited to riotous action. They were re-enforced by her own dependants, who came to their assistance from her residence. This was between three and four o'clock of the afternoon of the 12th of February, 1874.

An attack was made by the mob on the legislature ;

furniture was demolished; valuable books, papers, and
documents which belonged to the court or to the attorney-general's office were scattered abroad or thrown
from the windows. Clubs were freely used on such
unlucky members of the assembly as could be found
within the walls, and some were thrown through the
open windows by the maddened crowd. Many men
were sent to the hospital for treatment of their broken
heads or bruised bodies. But this was not an expression
of the Hawaiian people; it was merely the madness of
a mob incited by disappointed partisans whom the representatives of the people had rebuked.

In the mean time, the newly elected King Kalakaua,
the Princess Likelike, and myself were quietly awaiting
returns in the house which had been the residence of
Queen Emma while her husband was the reigning
monarch. At this date she resided in the house of her
mother, Mrs. Fanny Rooke, and we were the only occupants of the mansion of Liholiho. There was complete
tranquillity also at Iolani Palace, where the late king's
remains still lay in state, a few soldiers only being on
guard about the chamber in which rested all that was
mortal of the deceased monarch.

Presently a lady, Miss Hannah Smithies, came into
our presence, and abruptly told my brother that he was
the king of the Hawaiian people. He could not believe
the matter already settled, and leaving us, walked out
a little distance with an idea of meeting some one to
confirm or deny the report; he soon returned, closely
followed by Mr. Aholo and Mr. C. H. Judd, who not
only brought him the same news, but informed him of

the disturbances at the court-house, from which they said they had but just escaped with their lives. These two friends were followed by Hon. Charles R. Bishop, Minister of Foreign Affairs under the late king, who warmly congratulated my brother on his accession to the throne, and confirmed the statement that a most serious riot was in progress in the business part of the city. No dependence could be placed on the police nor on the Hawaiian Guards; these had proved unfaithful to their duties to preserve order, and had in some cases joined the partisans of Queen Emma in their riotous actions. So Mr. Bishop asked the king's advice as to whether it would not be wisest to appeal at once to the foreign vessels of war, of which there were three in the harbor, that they might land their forces and restore tranquillity to the city.

In view of the fact that a riot was in progress, that the halls of justice were in possession of a mob rendered irresponsible by the use of liquor, and that night was approaching, when incendiarism might be feared, my brother, the king elect, my husband, the late Governor Dominis, and Hon. Charles R. Bishop, Minister of Foreign Affairs, united in a request to Hon. Henry A. Pierce, the American Minister, that armed men might be landed from the American ships Tuscarora and Portsmouth, to sustain the government in its determination to preserve order, and protect the lives and property of all residents of the city of Honolulu. A force was also landed from the British man-of-war Tenedos, whose commander, Captain Ray, being absent on shore, the responsibility was assumed by his executive officer, Lieu-

tenant Bromley. Commander Belknap and Commander
Skerrett of the United States forces took possession of
the square on which the court-house is built; and on
seeing this, the mob melted silently and entirely away.
The armed marines subsequently, at the request of the
Hawaiian authorities, guarded the treasury, arsenal, jail,
and station-house. The British marines were marched
to the residence of Queen Emma, and, after dispersing
the rioters assembled there, they occupied the barracks
and guarded the palace itself. There was no permanent damage done by the disturbance. The Hawaiian
people are excitable, but not given to bloodshed or
malignant destruction of property.

I may here remark that the action of United States
Minister Henry A. Pierce has been quoted as furnishing a precedent for that of Minister John J. Stevens.
Nothing could be more incorrect. When the town was
in danger, and the lives and property of all classes in
peril, even then, until written request was made by the
king, by the governor of Oahu, and by the Minister of
Foreign Affairs, no interference was made by foreign
war-ships. When armed forces were landed it was to
sustain and protect the constitutional government at a
mere momentary emergency from a disloyal mob. The
constitutional government of 1893 and the governor of
Oahu not only made no request to Minister Stevens,
but *they absolutely protested against his action*, as an
unwarranted interposition of foreign forces in a dispute
which had arisen between the queen and a few foreign
residents. It was on the request of these *latter* that
Minister Stevens's acts were based, at a time when, save

for differences of political opinion, the city was perfectly tranquil. Even had there been a disturbance, no one but the government could have authorized the employment of alien troops.

Governor Nahaolelua of Maui, one of her trusted adherents, had left the house early to carry to Queen Emma the news of Kalakaua's election. When she learned the result from the lips of one of her own friends, she could no longer doubt its truth, though it was unexpected and unacceptable. On the day following the riot she sent for Mr. Nahaolelua, and demanded of him if it were not possible to ask for another vote in the legislature on the question of the succession. What might have been the result had he consented to this, cannot be told; for while the matter was in discussion at Queen Emma's residence, there broke in upon their deliberations the booming of the salute of twenty-one guns, indicating that my brother Kalakaua had taken the oath of office. This would have made any further opposition nothing less than treason, and the matter was consequently dropped.

Queen Emma never recovered from her great disappointment, nor could she reconcile herself to the fact that our family had been chosen as the royal line to succeed that of the Kamehamehas. All those arrested for disturbing the peace the day of the election were her own retainers. Two days after the trouble she came to the palace, and used her influence with King Kalakaua to have them released. As the king went to the audience chamber to receive her, he spoke to the queen and myself, asking us to be present and assist at the

reception with himself; but before we could comply
with his wishes she had seen him, made her request,
and then withdrew hastily from the rooms without
awaiting the entrance of Queen Kapiolani or myself.
Why she should cherish such bitterness of spirit against
the queen is past my comprehension. Queen Kapiolani had been aunt to Queen Emma, having been the
wife of her uncle Namakeha, and had nursed the young
prince, the son of Alexander Liholiho, although her
rank not only equalled, but was superior to, that of
Queen Emma, the child's mother.

The sweet disposition and amiable temper of Queen
Kapiolani never allowed her to resent in the least the
queen dowager's bitterness, nor would she permit herself to utter one word of reproach against the mother
of the child she had herself so dearly loved. In this
respect my brother's wife showed her truly Christian
character, and there were occasions when the lack of
courtesy on the part of Queen Emma became something very like insult. For instance, it is the custom
with the members of the highest families, the chiefs of
the Hawaiian people, at such time as it is known that
any one of their rank is ill, to go to the house of the
chief so indisposed, and remain until recovery is assured, or to be present at the deathbed, if such should
be the result. On these occasions, if Queen Emma
met Queen Kapiolani, who, of course, from this date
became, as my brother's wife, the lady of the highest
rank in our nation, she would studiously avoid recognizing her. Many and many a time did Kalakaua make
the effort to bring about a reconciliation between the

HIS MAJESTY KING KALAKAUA

two ladies; but although Queen Kapiolani would have
assented to anything consistent with the dignity of
womanhood, Queen Emma would not make the least
concession.   Even in the very residence of my brother,
visiting the palace at the invitation of the king, if the
queen were present she avoided recognizing her, and
would at times rise and leave when Queen Kapiolani
entered, saluting no one but the king as she retired;
although this was an outrageous impertinence to the
queen under her own roof, it was through Christian
charity ignored by its recipient.   Notwithstanding this
persistent anger, my brother-in-law, Hon. A. S. Cleghorn, prevailed on his wife, the Princess Likelike, to
continue the acquaintance.   I confess that my own
patience with such displays was not equal to a like forbearance; and, as I would not stoop to court her favor,
nor could accept, without proper and dignified notice,
her overbearing demeanor towards myself, Queen Emma
never forgave me my own rank and position in the
family which was chosen to reign over the Hawaiian
people.   It did not trouble me at all, but I simply
allowed her to remain in the position in which she
chose to place herself.

Kalakaua never forgot to invite Queen Emma to all
the entertainments given at the palace, and on state
occasions he strove to do her the highest honor.   At
the opening or closing of the legislature a seat was
reserved for her appropriate to her rank as queen
dowager, but she never showed the king in any way
that she appreciated his courtesy.

CHAPTER VIII

KING KALAKAUA

My brother's reign began on Feb. 12, 1874; and on the fourteenth of the same month he appointed, by the consent of the nobles under the twenty-second article of the constitution of 1864, our younger brother, William Pitt Leleiokoku, his successor to the throne. The prince became regent during the first absence of Kalakaua from his kingdom, on a tour abroad of which I shall soon speak. He was a very popular young man, about twenty years of age, having been born on the 10th of January, 1854. But the amiable prince was not to live to ascend the throne, or even for any extended enjoyment of those social pleasures in which he bore so prominent a part. He died on the 10th of April, 1877, having been in the position of heir apparent for about three years. He had the same love of music, the like passion for poetry and song, which have been so great a pleasure to me in my own life, as well as to our brother, King Kalakaua. He had a taste for social pleasures, and enjoyed the gay and festive element of life. During the absence of the king, there were three separate clubs or musical circles engaged in friendly rivalry to outdo each the other in poetry and song. These were the friends and associates of the prince regent, those of the Princess Likelike, and my own friends and admirers. Our poems and musical compositions were repeated from one to another, were sung by our friends in the sweetest rivalry, and their respective merits extolled : but candor compels me to acknowledge that those of Prince Leleiohoku were really in advance of those of his two sisters, although perhaps this was due to the fact that the singing-club of the regent was far superior to any that we could organize ; it consisted in a large degree of the very purest and sweetest male voices to be found amongst the native Hawaiians. They were all fine singers ; and these songs, in which our musical circles then excelled, are to be heard amongst our people to the present day. And yet it still remains true that no other composer but myself has ever reduced them to writing. This may seem strange to musical people of other nations, because the beauty and harmony of the Hawaiian music in general and of these songs in particular have been so generally recognized. But as soon as a popular air originated, it was passed along from its composer to one of his most intimate friends ; he in turn sang it to another, and thus its circulation increased day by day. It was not long before every one had the same knowledge of the new melody as happens in communities where a new and favorite air is introduced by an opera company. With other nations music is perpetuated by note and line, with us it is not. The ancient bards of the Hawaiian people thus gave to history their poems or chants ; and the custom is no different to this day, and serves to show the great fondness and aptness of our nation to poetry and song.

I will now return to the date of the departure of my brother, King Kalakaua, to the United States. Yielding to the wishes of those residents of his domains who were from American or missionary stock, my brother had organized the negotiation of a treaty of closer alliance or reciprocity with the United States; and even before leaving home he had commissioned Judge Allen and Minister Carter to submit such a treaty to the American government. To advance the interests of this movement by his personal presence, he accepted passage for himself and his suite on the ship-of-war Benicia, and sailed for San Francisco in the autumn of 1874. My husband, the late General J. O. Dominis, and United States Minister Henry A. Pierce accompanied him on his travels. One of the officers of this steamship was Lieutenant Whiting, who received permission to accompany King Kalakaua to Washington. He is now a commander, and has since married Miss Afong, one of a large family of children, all girls, whose mother is one of our people, but whose father was a rich Chinese resident, now returned to his native land. From the moment of landing my brother made friends, and was treated with the kindest consideration by the American people of all classes. There was a very strong feeling of friendship between the king and the late General U. S. Grant. It amounted almost to recognized fraternity.

The result of this visit is well known. It secured that for which the planters had gained the endorsement of the king; it resulted in the reciprocity treaty of Jan. 30, 1875. So this, one of the first official acts of King

Kalakaua, was very satisfactory to the party in power; but even then there were a few who protested against the treaty, as an act which would put in peril the independence of our nation. The impressions of the people are sometimes founded upon truth; and events have since proved that such was the case here, — that it was the minority which was right in its judgment of the consequences of the Hawaiian concession of 1875 to the power of the foreigner.

On Oct. 16, 1876, at the house on Emma Street, was born to Princess Miriam Likelike (Mrs. A. S. Cleghorn) the child now known to the world as the Princess Kaiulani. She was at once recognized as the hope of the Hawaiian people, as the only direct heir by birth to the throne.

Kaiulani was only six months old when my brother, Prince William Leleiohoku died; and it was evident that the vacancy must be instantly filled. The Princess Ruth, daughter of Pauahi and Kekuanaoa, who had adopted Leleiohoku, asked of the king if she herself could not be proclaimed heir apparent; and this suggestion was placed before the king's counsellors at a cabinet meeting, but it was objected that, if her petition was granted, then Mrs. Pauahi Bishop would be the next heir to the throne, as they were first cousins. At noon of the tenth day of April, 1877, the booming of the cannon was heard which announced that I was heir apparent to the throne of Hawaii.

CHAPTER IX

HEIR APPARENT

FROM this moment dates my official title of Liliuokalani, that being the name under which I was formally
proclaimed princess and heir apparent to the throne of
my ancestors.   Now that this important matter had
been decided by those whom the constitution invests
with that prerogative, it became proper and necessary
for me to make a tour of the islands to meet the people,
that all classes, rich and poor, planter or fisherman,
might have an opportunity to become somewhat acquainted with the one who some day should be called
to hold the highest executive office.   The first journey
undertaken was that of encircling the island on which
the capital city of Honolulu is situated; we therefore
started from our home to make the trip around the
coast-line of Oahu, a tour of nearly one hundred and
fifty miles, following the roads which wind along on the
brink of the ocean.   This we proposed to do on horseback; although my carriage, where I could rest if required, accompanied the party.   Our cavalcade was a
large one; my immediate companions being my husband, General J. O. Dominis, governor of the island,
and my sister, the Princess Likelike, wife of Hon. A. S.
Cleghorn, who was attended by her personal suite.   But

large numbers are no discouragement to Hawaiian hospitality, especially under the additional inspiration of
love and loyalty to their chiefs ; so the people opened
their doors with an *"Aloha nui loa"* to us in words
and in acts, and wherever we went a grand reception
awaited us on arrival.   Our route was first to the eastward, past Diamond Head, Koko Head to the point of
Makapur, then turning to the northward and around to
Waimanalo, where we found ourselves the guests of Ah
Kau, a very wealthy Chinaman, who owned a large plan-
tation there devoted to the cultivation of rice.   Intelligence of our approach must have travelled faster than
we had ridden ; for as soon as our cavalcade drew near
to this estate we were greeted with a discharge of fire-
crackers and bombs, let off to do honor to the presence
of the heir to the throne and her companions.   There
was no cessation of the salutes during the feast of good
things which had been spread by Ah Kau for our refreshment, to which and to the professions of loyalty
on the part of our host, we did ample justice.   From
thence we proceeded to Maunawili, the beautiful residence of Mr. and Mrs. Edwin Boyd, whose doors were
already opened for our reception ; and here we spent the
night and remained an entire day, enjoying the entertainment prepared for us, which can be described in no
better terms than by saying that we received a royal
welcome indeed.   Our progress continued on the day
following through Kaneohe, our noonday rest being at
the house of Judge Pii, where a generous lunch awaited
us on the moment of our arrival.   The people of that
entire district had congregated to do us honor, and

showed to us in every way that there was no doubt nor
disloyalty in their hearts.   Yet, while still at Kaneohe,
a letter was received by the Princess Likelike from her
husband, in which that gentleman advised his wife to
return to Honolulu, and stated it as his opinion that if
it was the purpose of my tour to meet the people and
cultivate their love, the time spent on the route would
be wasted, because they were all zealous partisans of
Queen Emma.   My sister acquainted me with these
views of her husband, and asked my advice as to her
course.   I did not wish to influence her in any way, and
therefore left it to her option to continue the journey
with me, or to take Mr. Cleghorn's advice.   But we had
already advanced far enough on our pathway amongst
the people to prove that her husband had made a great
mistake, for no heir to the throne could have been more
royally received by all than I had been.   The princess
had not failed to notice this, and as we proceeded it was
still more apparent; the most zealous of Queen Emma's
people, now that the question had been officially decided, hastened to do us honor.   So, after due consideration, Princess Likelike decided that she would not
return.   A decision she had no after occasion to regret,
and was one which made me very glad; for she was welcomed and showered with marks of favor by the very
adherents of Queen Emma, of whose disappointment
she had been warned by her husband.   It would be
tiresome to others, perhaps, should I go on and describe
with minute particulars the steps of our party as they
passed around the island.   From place to place the reception was the same, cheerful, hearty, and enthusias-

tic, — Kahuku, Waialua, Makahao, Waianae, and so on to our latest stopping-place, which was with Mr. James Campbell and his sweet wife at Honouliuli. He had the advantage of a little more time in his preparations for our reception than was possible to some of our other places of rest, and had spared no pains to give us an ovation in every way worthy of himself and his amiable companion. The result was a manifestation of kind feelings and generous hospitality such as, even at this distant day, cannot, no, nor ever will be, effaced from my memory. From thence we started for Honolulu; and as it was noised abroad that the party would enter the city, there was scarcely space for our cavalcade to pass between the throngs of people which lined our way. From Leleo to Alakea Street it was a mass of moving heads, through which only slowly could our carriages, horses, and outriders pass. It was understood and accepted as a victorious procession; and out of sympathy for the disappointed dowager queen, our people refrained from noisy demonstrations and loud cheering, and instead the men removed their hats, and the women saluted as we passed.

I have been thus careful in reviewing this my first trip as heir to the throne, both because it is a pleasure to recall the memory of that epoch in my life, and further that I may speak with pride of the continued affection, of the unshaken love, of these my people. In some nations the leaders, the chief rulers, have gone forth through districts conquered by the sword, and compelled the people to show their subjugation. Our progress from beginning to end was a triumphal march, and might well be described as that awarded to victors; but there were no dying nor wounded mortals in our track. We had vanquished the hearts of the people; they showed to us their love; they welcomed me as Hawaiians always have the ruling chief; and to this day, without the slightest appeal on my part, they have shown that their love and loyalty to our family in general, and to myself in particular, have known no change nor diminution, even under the circumstances, now so different from those of twenty years ago.

CHAPTER X

MY FIRST VISIT TO THE UNITED STATES

In the early part of the year 1878 I was not in the enjoyment of my usual good health ; and my physician, Dr. Tisdale of Oakland, Cal., advised a trip to that coast, trusting that the change might be of benefit to me.   At this date steam communication was not as frequent nor as convenient as has since been established ; yet we had very comfortable and pleasant accommodations on the steamer St. Paul, on which we departed.   I was accompanied by my husband, General Dominis ; and amongst the agreeable company on board were Mr. and Mrs. Wm. F. Allen, Mr. Nott, who married Miss Mary Andrews, and Mr. C. O. Berger, who married a daughter of Judge Weideman.   Besides these, I recall the names of Mrs. J. I. Dowsett and her son, J. I. Dowsett, both deceased, and Mrs. C. B. Wilson.   The trip was made in nine days ; and at its termination I obtained my first view of the shores of that great country, the United States, of which land I had heard almost without cessation from earliest childhood.   If first impressions be accepted as auspicious, surely I found nothing of which I could complain on this visit ; for many prominent citizens of the great city of the Pacific coast came to do us honor, or entertained us during our stay.   Amongst

these were my husband's old friend and playmate of
earlier days, Governor Pacheco ; also Mr. Henry Bishop,
brother of Mr. Charles R. Bishop, who married my
sister Bernice ; Mr. H. W. Severance, at that time in
the consular service of the Hawaiian government at
San Francisco ; Mr. R. S. Floyd and wife, the gentleman being connected with the great observatory established through the munificence of the late James Lick ;
Mr. and Mrs. Toler of Oakland ; Mrs. Haalelea and
Mrs. Coney (at this time residing at Oakland with the
children of Mrs. Coney) ; and many others, who united
to give us a delightful introduction from the islands of
the tropics into that land with whose history we have
been so intimately connected. The first welcome of
strange shores is not often forgotten by the traveller,
however numerous may be the subsequent experiences ;
so these flattering attentions were most sincerely appreciated then, and have never ceased to awaken emotions
of gratitude in my heart.

While we did not travel extensively through the
State, yet our visit to Sacramento must not be passed
by without a word ; for many were the visitors who
called to welcome us while staying at the Golden Eagle
Hotel. Amongst these I recall the name of Mr. H. S.
Crocker, a prominent citizen ; then there was Mrs.
Charles Crocker, whose home we visited. She occupied a most elegant mansion ; and in its pleasant surroundings, and the generous hospitality with which we
found ourselves entertained, the welcome there was not
unlike that I have noticed in my account of our tour
around our island home. Where all are so perfect, it

seems scarcely possible to distinguish one feature above another ; yet her art-gallery made a great impression on me at the time, and I can see again, as I recall the past, the many beautiful paintings by prominent artists with which it was adorned. They were works of genius indeed, so true to nature and so lifelike ; but they were far too numerous for me to try at this day to recall them by name. The least detail of her grand and beautiful residence was nothing less than perfection. The floors were paved with artistic designs in tiles of white, of blue, and other colors. There were apartments devoted to the several branches of natural history ; and the cabinets of stuffed and mounted birds, as well as of quadrupeds and animals in great variety, interested and amused me as if I had been a child taken to a museum of curiosities. The whole collection must have been of great value, and it has given me pleasure to learn that since my visit it has been turned over to the State of California for the delight and information of future generations.

From thence we returned to San Francisco, and after a month's absence prepared for our homeward voyage, which was made on the steamer Wilmington, Captain Fuller, now harbor-master by commission of the present rulers of the port of Honolulu. The ocean air, charming company, that cordial welcome of friends which so quickly dispels the sense of loneliness one feels when a stranger in a strange land, all had combined to prove the wisdom of my physician's advice ; and I returned in most excellent health and my accustomed good spirits.

During the summer of that year, 1878, my husband

and I visited the island of Maui, and while General Dominis was for a brief time recalled to Oahu, my brother,
His Majesty Kalakaua, came to Maui especially to have
an interview with me.   He was always kind enough to
seek my opinion on questions of public interest, but this
trip was undertaken for the special object of consulting
me about some appointments to official positions then
under discussion.   It was at Wailuku, where my husband had left me at the residence of Hon. H. Kuihalani,
that the king arrived with a few attendants.   I recognized his great consideration for me in this act, and his
deference to my opinion; for had he so wished, these
appointments could have been made without the least
consultation and the names of his selection would have
been known to me only through the regular channels of
information to all, and the king would have been spared
a trip from his capital to another island.   He spoke
to me about the appointment of Mr. Charles H. Judd,
whom he proposed to nominate to the office of chamberlain, and further to that of special agent for the management of the crown lands.   Both of these offices were
held by my husband at this time.   That of chamberlain
was only temporary, but the other had been his official
position since the days of Kamehameha V.; and under
his administration of the leases and revenues of these
lands, both during the reign of that monarch and ever
since, all things had been considered very satisfactory.
The king's proposition to withdraw both these appointments from General Dominis in order to confer them
upon another caused me much anxiety, and I must confess no little indignation.   But I restrained these feel-

ings, and replied to the king with proper meekness, telling him as my sovereign that whatever seemed best to him ought to be done, and that it was clearly his privilege to act upon his own views of what was right in the matter. He then asked me in plainer terms if I had no opinion to offer to him, to which I replied that I had; and then went on to inform him that this Charles H. Judd, whom he was now to bring into favor by public office, and by placing him nearer to his person, had worked against him, and had opposed his nomination to the throne of the sovereigns of the Hawaiian Islands. Mr. Judd had not been content with silent opposition, but had gone over to Koolau and openly canvassed that district in the interest of Queen Emma. When he heard that my brother had received the majority vote of the legislature, he then with soft words returned to try the arts which we call " *to malimali*," to ingratiate himself into the royal favor. My honest opinion having been demanded of me by the king, it was given in the above terms; and I added, "I see that Mr. Judd has been successful; he schemed for favors at your hands; he has obtained what he coveted, and procured of Your Majesty the displacement of my husband, although General Dominis has been faithful to every trust, a constant and true friend of yours for years, and a loyal follower to this very day of his removal." My husband's absence gave me the right and the courage to speak thus plainly to the king. "Well," he replied, "say that I have made my appointments, what is there remaining that I can do for you, my sister?" To this I answered that I would be pleased if

he would appoint Governor Dominis to be governor of
Kauai and of Maui in addition to the office he held, the
governorship of Oahu. The king most cheerfully consented, and I wrote at once to my husband telling him
just what had been said and done; my letter not only
met his approval, but he showed it to Hon. C. C. Harris,
who commended me in the highest terms for the stand
I had taken in the discussion of this delicate and difficult matter.

It was with good reason that I had selected the
office of governor of Maui as a token of the king's appreciation of the constant loyalty of my husband. Independent of his fitness for the position by reason of
his long experience on the island of Oahu, it was well
known that the ruling governor, Moehonua, could not
live for any length of time; he was dropsical, and the
disease was approaching its final stage; so I could indicate my preferences without feeling that I was asking
that any person should be displaced to please me. The
very next mail from the island brought the intelligence
of the governor's death. He was a most estimable man,
far superior to many of a corresponding rank, which was
not of the highest; yet he was a good specimen of the
Hawaiian race, of noble birth and patriotic sentiments.
On the confirmation of the appointment to General
Dominis, he appointed Hon. Mr. Aholo as his secretary
and lieutenant-governor of the island, to which we immediately proposed to make a visit; for we had heard
that the people were extremely contented and even enthusiastically pleased with my husband's appointment.
The experience of this visit would seem to most abun-

dantly prove the wisdom of the king's choice of General
Dominis.   Our people feel that in honoring their chiefs,
in respecting those who are legitimately their rulers,
they are doing not only a duty, but a pleasure to themselves.   It was only needful to let it be known that the
governor of their island accompanied by the heir to
the throne was to be with them, to give the signal for
the opening of every door, and the most cordial greeting
by every wayside.   Consequently the unremitting attentions shown to us by all classes of the people, the many
tokens of kindness received by us on that journey, are
still and always will be gratefully cherished in my heart.
It may be interesting to some to read the names of
those who at that time, nearly twenty years ago, were
residents of this island.   There were the Hon. and
Mrs. Aholo, Mr. and Mrs. Hayselden, Mr. A. Fornander, Mr. and Mrs. Nahaolelua, Hon. Adam Kakau, Mr.
and Mrs. Kuihalani, Mr. and Mrs. John Richardson, Mr.
and Mrs. Everett, Mr. W. H. Corwell and his family
to two generations, Mr. and Mrs. W. H. Daniels, Mr.
and Mrs. James Makee, Mr. and Mrs. Henry Turton,
Mr. and Mrs. Unna, and representatives of the distinctively missionary families of the Alexanders and the
Baileys.

To go over in detail the steps of our tour would be
to repeat that which has been written of my trip around
the island of Oahu ; so I will only say that the above
families, and many others not mentioned by name, absolutely vied with each other in making us welcome, and
providing a generous hospitality for our entertainment.
The mere mention of these names recalls to me with

sadly interesting vividness the past in my native land, when those of Hawaiian and of foreign birth were united in a common love of country, and only too eager to compete with each other for the privilege of showing to us their loyalty and love.

CHAPTER XI

MAUNA LOA

In the year 1880 Miss Helen Aldrich of Berkeley, Cal., made me a visit. She was the daughter of Mr. W. A. Aldrich, a banker, who had married a first cousin of my husband, Elizabeth, the child of Mr. R. W. Holt. Shortly after her arrival we took a trip to the largest of our islands, Hawaii, on which is situated that volcano called with truth one of the greatest natural wonders of the modern world. I was attended by my retainers, and after a short and pleasant voyage we arrived at the port and chief city, Hilo. As though to illuminate in honor of my visit, on the night preceding our ascent of the mountain a bright glow was seen on the top of Moku-aweoweo. This was the portent which preceded that great flow of lava which soon commenced from Mauna Loa, and took its course down the sides of that mountain towards the city of Hilo. We were thus witnesses from the very beginning of one of the most extensive and long-continued eruptions which has ever been recorded in history, for it was protracted over a period of eleven months. Early on the morning following we started on horseback on our journey to the crater of Kilauea, where we arrived about five o'clock the same evening. This is not, as some strangers suppose, a mountain by itself,

totally distinct from the general volcanic system of
Mauna Loa.   That word in our language signifies the
great long mountain, and the nature of the elevation
well deserves the term ; for in height, 13,700 feet, it is
exceeded by few in the world, while in extent it includes
about one-third of our largest island.   The eruptions
are not usually from the summit, but generally through
fissures in its sides.   One of these is the crater lake of
Kilauea, a region of perpetual fire, of an activity more
or less pronounced, yet never entirely extinct, and situated some twenty miles or so east from the summit, at
an elevation of about four thousand feet.   It is one of
the few, if not the only one, of the volcanoes in the world
which can be visited at the periods of its greatest displays without the least danger to the observer ; because
it is always possible to watch its bubbling fires from a
higher point than their source.   It is not the lava from
the burning lake which makes its way down the mountain, but that from other places where the concealed
fires of Mauna Loa burst forth.

There is now a modern hotel at a spot commanding
a good view of the points of interest ; but at the date of
this visit we were received and made very comfortable
in a large grass house with thatched roof, under which
some forty persons could have been accommodated.
Here we were most hospitably received, our tired horses
were cared for and sheltered near to our resting-place,
and we did ample justice to the evening meal which had
been provided for our company.   After our refreshment,
darkness quickly succeeded the setting of the sun (there
being no long twilight, as in more northern climates) ;

so we spent the evening in watching the fiery glow in
the crater, the brilliance of which seemed to be spread-
ing along the level floor or surface of the pit. From a
flooring of light and heat the surface changed at times
to billows of actual fire ; then jets burst up or fountains
played high in air, standing by themselves a moment
like burning columns ; then steam intervened to stifle
the flames. Mist following this, the crater was for a
while hidden from our sight, and nature's gorgeous fireworks suspended. At one of these intervals we retired
for the night ; but at two o'clock we were all awakened
by our host to see an exhibition such as has seldom been
furnished for the inspection of any of the many tourists
who visit that region. This was a most brilliant illu-
mination at the summit of Mauna Loa itself ; and far
from lessening, its manifestation seemed to render more
vivid, the fires of the crater of Kilauea. The mists
had cleared away in that direction, and we thus had
the good fortune to watch on one and the same occasion the outbursts of light at the summit and the jets
of dancing flame in the sides. It was a night never to
be forgotten by any of our party, and well worth the
time and labor of the journey, were there no more to be
enjoyed. That which was nearest to us, the rising,
boiling sheet of liquid fire, seemed to show no abate-
ment by reason of the vent at the mountain-top, but in
its agitations disclosed each moment sights more and
more wonderful to our gaze. The next day was spent
by our party in descending the crater to the very limits
of its seething fires, but I remained at the hotel. They
were all provided with some offerings to Pele, the an-

cient goddess of fire, reverenced by the Hawaiian people. This custom is almost universal, even to the present day. Those born in foreign lands, tourists who scarcely know our ancient history, generally take with them to the brink of the lake some coin or other trinket which, for good luck, as the saying is, they cast into the lava. Our people, the native Hawaiians, have no money to throw away on such souvenirs of the past; but they carry wreaths of the pandanus flower, *leis*, made like those seen aboard the steamers at the departure of friends, necklaces, and garlands of nature's ornaments, which are tossed by them into the angry waves of the basin. As I have mentioned this incident, my thoughts have gone back to that paragraph wherein I wrote of the overthrow of the superstitious fears of the fire-goddess through the brave acts of my aunt, Queen Kapiolani, when she defied the power of the elements at this very spot. So, to prevent misunderstanding now, perhaps it would be well to notice that this propitiation of the volcano's wrath is now but a harmless sport, not by any means an act of worship, very much like the custom of hurling old shoes at the bride's carriage, or sending off the newly wedded couple with showers of rice; usages which form a pleasant diversion in the most highly cultivated and educated communities. After a day spent in watching the activity of the crater, the party returned to our hotel, weary, hungry, and ready to enjoy the refreshment and repose of which they were in need. One night more was spent at the volcano house of the olden time, and then we all started on our ride down the mountain for the city of Hilo.

The display had not diminished in extent nor in its strange, wild beauty. The lake in the crater was still boiling, and over Mokuaweoweo the location of the opening was easily distinguished by the brilliant glow of light. But turning our backs on these natural wonders, nature was perhaps more lovely in the charms by which she lined our pathway towards the sea; for this road is justly considered to be one of the most beautiful exhibitions of the scenery of the tropics in Hawaii, and our cavalcade passed between lines of verdure or flowers enchanting to the eye and fragrant to the sense; there were the bright blossoms of the lehua, both yellow and red varieties, and other plants or trees shading and pleasing each of us as we advanced. Although we did not arrive at our destination until about five that afternoon, and were quite fatigued with our long ride, yet it had been an excursion of great enjoyment, and I am sure no one of the company was other than satisfied with it.

The great increase in the lava flow which subsequently took place had not at this time threatened the peace of the city; so our return to our friends was made the signal for a round of social pleasures. A grand entertainment in honor of the visit of the heir to the throne was given by Mr. and Mrs. Luther Severance; and it afforded me much satisfaction to show to my California cousin some examples of the generous style of the hospitality of those days, in which those of foreign or of native birth vied with each other in a friendly rivalry of good things. Judge F. S. Lyman was then lieutenant-governor of the island, and with his

amiable wife showed us all the attention in his power;
then there were Judge Akao and his wife, Mr. and Mrs.
Governor Kipi and their agreeable family. The family of Mr. D. H. Hitchcock, especially his wife and
daughters, were also most kind and attentive to me
and those who accompanied me. If, in these reminiscences, I should fail to name those who have made
such occasions pleasant, it must be accepted simply as
an unintentional omission, the names I have given being
but examples of that universal kindness received by me
from all. Just as we were leaving our kind entertainers, Sir Thomas Hesketh arrived in the port on his own
yacht for a visit to the island; he was accompanied by
Hon. Samuel Parker, whom he had invited to be his
guest during this excursion. The regular steamer of
passenger service between Hilo and Honolulu received
me and my company for our return to Oahu, where we
arrived in safety; and not long after my cousin, Miss
Aldrich, took her departure for her home, with, I am
sure, some very pleasant memories of the natural beauties and social pleasures of life on the Hawaiian Islands.

A VIEW ON THE ROAD TO THE VOLCANO KILAUEA

CHAPTER XII

KALAKAUA'S TOUR OF THE WORLD

In the early part of the month of January, 1881, a message through the telephone reached me at my private residence at Washington Place, that my presence was required immediately at Iolani Palace. I answered the summons at once; but on my arrival the king was not to be found at the palace, but I eventually discovered him in a long building adjacent thereto, in which were kept some of his favorite boats. He was selecting some oars for the boat named the Kanoelani, and while still engaged on this work he communicated to me his wishes and instructions. He notified me that he expected soon to sail on his trip around the world, and that he desired me to assume the control of the government, and the charge of public affairs as regent, during his absence. He then went on to inform me that he had already held a meeting of the cabinet council on this matter, at which it had been proposed by the members that there should be a council of regency, of which I should be the head; but that the action of the council should be required for the full exercise of authority. This is an important page in Hawaiian history, because it shows how persistently, even at that date, the "missionary party" was at work to undermine at every point the authority of the constitutional rulers of the Hawaiian people.   As the king had sent for me with the express purpose of asking my opinion, I gave it in terms too plain to admit of the least misunderstanding between us.   I told him that I did not admit either the necessity or the wisdom of any such organization as that of a council of regency; that to my view, if intrusted with the government during his absence, I ought to be the sole regent.   I then proceeded to explain my reasons for this opinion, saying that if there was a council of regency, there would be no need for any regent.   In case such a body were to be commissioned to govern the nation, who, then, would be the chief executive? in fact, why was any such individual required at all?   To these considerations the king gave careful attention, and appeared to see that my views of the situation were founded upon reason and justice.   The result of this informal conference was, that before his departure I was appointed sole regent, with the functions of the reigning sovereign of the Hawaiian Islands during his absence. On the 20th of January, 1881, accompanied by Mr. C. H. Judd and by Mr. W. M. Armstrong, both from missionary families, amidst the salutes of the shipping and the booming of cannon, His Majesty Kalakaua took his departure, being the first of the sovereigns of the nation to undertake a tour of the globe.

In nothing has my brother been more grossly misjudged and even slandered by those whose interests he had at heart than in this journey.   Probably he did have some love for travel, some sense of pleasure in visiting foreign lands — who amongst us has not felt the desire to see the great and beautiful world which God made, and on which man has built so many magnificent cities and works of art? Why should he not have felt this interest? But the master motive for this enterprise was the good of the people of the Hawaiian Islands over whom he had been called to rule. I have already spoken of his visit to Washington for the purpose of assisting at the ratification of the reciprocity treaty. That negotiation successfully carried through by his commissioners created a new want in his domains. The sugar-fields demanded laborers, and at this time it was a problem to decide from whence these could be obtained. Soon after landing at San Francisco, the king first visited Japan; from there he proceeded to China; with the statesmen of both these nations, including the celebrated Li Hung Chang, my brother conferred upon questions of international interest, but more especially in regard to the emigration of their subjects from their territory to the sugar plantations of our islands. While he was thus working for the prosperity of the residents of his kingdom, and for an immigration which should result in the wealth of those of foreign ancestry or affiliations, they were accusing him of a reckless spending of money, and of the waste of time and revenues in foreign travel. From China the king went on to Siam, where he was most royally entertained by the ruling monarch; then to India, whose climate, resembling ours, caused him to be in favor of initiating an emigration thence to our cane-fields. Nothing, however, resulted from his examination of the chance of employing the coolies of India; but China and Japan have since then sent many laborers to our plantations. We know now what imported or contract labor means. It must be remembered that at this date the experiment was in its infancy, and the question was to find some class of laborers who would not suffer in our tropical climate at field labor. The conclusion cannot be avoided, that if my brother had indeed sought his own pleasure rather than the good of all residents under our flag, his family would be in their hereditary rights to this day. By his liberality to those of American birth he inaugurated the treaty of reciprocity; by his investigations and solution of the problem of labor he gave them the opportunity to raise sugar at an enormous profit; and he thus devoted the earlier part of his reign to the aggrandizement of the very persons, who, as soon as they had become rich and powerful, forgot his generosity, and plotted a subversion of his authority, and an overthrow of the constitution under which the kingdom had been happily governed for nearly a quarter of a century. This was accomplished by them in 1887, as will be seen when I reach that date in my recollections. After his studies of the labor question in the East, my brother made a tour of the chief countries of civilized Europe, returning by way of Washington, and in every place receiving from all classes many marks of personal attention or national courtesy. He arrived home on the 29th of October, 1881; and this was naturally followed by my immediate resignation of the office of chief ruler, which I had held for nine months and as many days.

CHAPTER XIII

MY REGENCY

BUT there are a few matters of interest during this time of which I must now speak. King Kalakaua had been gone but a few weeks when the startling news was in circulation that the small-pox had broken out in the city. It was supposed to have been introduced from China; but our past experience with the disease had shown us how fatal it might become to the Hawaiian people, and whatever the inconveniences it became necessary at all hazards to prevent its spread. Summoning the cabinet, I had all arrangements perfected to stay the progress of the epidemic. Communication between the different islands of the group was stopped. Vessels were absolutely prohibited from taking passengers. A strict quarantine of all persons infected or under suspicion was maintained; and so scrupulously and energetically were these regulations enforced, that when they were relaxed and quarantine raised, it was found that no case had been reported outside the place of its first appearance. But it was a serious thing to confine its ravages to the city of Honolulu, in which there were some eight hundred cases and about three hundred deaths.

After the privileges of travel were restored to all alike, I had a desire to visit Hilo again; and so, with a large company of retainers, as was fitting to my regency, I started on this excursion. Mrs. Pauahi Bishop, the Princess Ruth, Mrs. Haalelea, and their immediate attendants, had preceded me; and I invited the Royal Hawaiian Band of native musicians to form part of my retinue, not for my own pleasure especially, although music forms to me a great part of the enjoyment of life, but because I wished to bring with me, to my friends and my people on that island, a delight which I knew to them was quite rare, and in which I was quite sure all would find much satisfaction.

It was in the month of August, six months after I had watched the commencement of that lava flow which is now celebrated in the history of that region of wonders. I found Mauna Loa was still alarmingly active, and that three streams of molten fire were creeping down its sides, so that the good people of Hilo were living in daily apprehension that the fiery element would reach their doors, their houses be consumed, and their lives, perhaps, imperilled by the rivers of flame. It was a grand and beautiful sight, in spite of the suggestion of danger, as you rode along the borders of the lava stream, which had chosen the channels of the watercourses or filled the basins where these had formerly spread themselves out into pools of refreshing fluid; the molten masses retained the heat of the source of their origin, even when rolling along, or falling as a great cascade into some hollow, which was soon filled up with the melted elements of the earth's centre, making one level plain where had been channels or pits in the earth's surface.

In some directions it seemed to be miles in width and of a length up the mountain-side to the summit of which the eye could not reach; while at night the surface of moving fire resembled a plain on which was situated a large city in conflagration. It was a display of fireworks of nature's manufacture such as has been seldom seen in the world, and which never could be seen excepting at the base of Mauna Loa. There was intense excitement at Hilo, for it was not known how soon the on-coming rivers might reach the city; yet there was a fascination in the display, or in the danger, which drew thousands out to watch the streams of moving flame. Some of the spectators were doubtless attracted by motives of curiosity, others were prompted by their fears; but of one thing there could be no manner of doubt, all were vividly, even if painfully, interested. There have always been features peculiar to the flow of lava from this region which can scarcely be explained by natural causes; while this our grand volcano is capable of inspiring fears which cannot be concealed, yet it is no less a fact that it has never been destructive to human life, nor made havoc with property. At this very time, while the people of Hilo were flocking to the sides of the immense river of molten lava, as it steamed down the mountain-sides on its way to the sea, or watching from the banks bordering the seething mass the course of its flow, it would creep up sidewise on the rise of a hill, with no apparent cause for the action; or nearing a stone wall it would surge upward, filling in solidly the topmost crevices at an elevation of perhaps three feet from the soil, instead of running downward

and to the lower level, or pouring itself into the hollows
and lowest places. The residents of Hilo, who lived
in their handsome houses constructed of wood and so
easily inflammable, on finding that time did not abate
the extent or volume of the flow, lived in terror of los-
ing life and property, dreading at any moment to see
the fiery river turn its course towards their dwellings.
Consequently the churches were opened, meetings were
held, and earnest prayers offered to the Almighty Ruler
of the elements that he would spare the people from the
great misfortune which threatened to overtake them.
To one of these prayer-meetings I received a special
invitation, and attended with my suite. In the course
of about a week thereafter, there was no doubt in the
attitude of the volcano; its flow had been stayed, and
the volume of the lava was diminishing, although for
another week sparks of light or streaks of flame were
here and there to be seen, but the great danger was over.
Naturally, devout men remembered the days of fervent
prayer, and said that the God to whom they had cried at
the moment of peril had listened to the supplications of
his people, and delivered them from threatened evil.

On the next arrival of the steamer Kinau from
Honolulu, my sister, the Princess Likelike, joined me,
and by the same steamer we with our entire retinues
took departure, intending to visit Kau, where the people,
in anticipation of my visit had made great preparations
for a reception; but on arrival of the steamer at Kaa-
lualu, Mr. George Beckley, the purser of the steamer,
requested me earnestly not to land, assigning as his
reason that the stay of the steamer there would be very

short, not over a few minutes, and that she could not be longer detained. To my knowledge the people had already arranged for my promised visit with lavish hospitality, so I did not like to disappoint them, as there was to be a grand *luau*. I therefore requested the Princess Likelike to go ashore and represent me on the occasion, which she kindly did; but the assembled multitudes were excessively disappointed that I could not be present, and expressed to my sister their sentiments of keen and sincere regret. Leaving that landing-place, our steamer proceeded to Hookena, where corresponding tokens of welcome awaited our arrival, and where the people had come together to show to me their friendship. Here I was met with the same objections on the part of the purser, who would have prevented a landing if he had been able to do so; but the crowds on shore were determined not to be disappointed, and as for myself, I shared their intention that the grand preparations made for my entertainment should not be in vain. Besides, there were special causes for my resolution that this district should not be passed by. It was at that time distinctively Hawaiian. The pure native race had maintained its position there better than in most localities. There had been no introduction of the Chinese amongst the people, nor had any other race of foreigners come to live near their homes. The Hawaiian families had married with Hawaiians, settling side by side with those of their own blood. Thus it was that only on Hawaii, and in no other part of the group of islands, could there be found a district so thickly populated, where the population was so strictly of my own people, as this to which I was now a visitor. This made it peculiarly interesting to me; and my reception, and enjoyment of the welcome of the inhabitants, were all that one could have desired. From thence my progress continued, first to Keauhou, then Kailua, and last of all Kawaihae; of these, and in truth of all the districts at which we had touched in our progress from Hilo, it may well be said that each had vied with the other in friendly rivalry, each had striven to outdo its neighbor in the grandeur of its preparations made for my entertainment. It was not the flattery of words; their loyalty and love were expressed by everything which was done to render my stay attractive, each person assisted at the welcome, and the parting was a sorrow to all my faithful friends. Amongst the larger landholders who did all possible to make my stay on Hawaii pleasant was Hon. Samuel Parker, who with his family most cordially received and hospitably entertained us at his seaside residence there. He spared no pains in his efforts to furnish my table with all which the most fastidious taste could desire; there were fish from the sea in great variety and of delicious freshness, many of the other delicacies, such as "*opihi*" for example, being especially Hawaiian in use or origin. All these were furnished from the vast estates on the island owned by Mr. Parker or subject to his control, and time would fail to speak of the many other attentions or numberless kindnesses shown by him. Mr. Parker became my Minister of Foreign Affairs under the latest cabinet commissioned by the constitutional monarchy of the Hawaiian Islands. After a most delightful journey, and many happy days spent on the island of Hawaii, I returned to Oahu, glad, as most tourists are, to find myself once more at my own home, and to settle down to my domestic life at Honolulu.

Another necessary excursion, however, had already been planned for me; namely, a trip around the island of Oahu, at the very outset of which there arrived news of an event which stirred the world with horror; this was the assassination of President Garfield. The stores were at once draped in mourning, meetings expressive of sympathy for the family of the deceased president, and of regret at his untimely end (which we shared with the American people), were called at once by those of his nation, but were attended by both Hawaiians and foreigners. To one of these, which was to be held in the large Congregational Church on Fort Street, on the evening of the 6th of October, I think, I was especially invited to be present; but, as before the sad intelligence of his death was received all arrangements had been made for my tour, I did not feel that these could well be changed, and I therefore sent a note of regret, expressing to those in charge the assurance of my sympathy with the object for which the meeting had been called.

CHAPTER XIV

A SERIOUS ACCIDENT

THEN leaving Honolulu attended by some few of my retainers, I went first to the residence of Mr. J. A. Cummins, a gentleman who subsequently undertook a diplomatic errand for me to the city of Washington, and who in 1895 was suspected and even punished by the present rulers of Hawaii for participation in the attempt to smuggle arms for possible use by the people desiring a return to the monarchical form of government.

At that time the possibility that the monarchical form of government could be overthrown would have been incredible, and my visit to Waimanalo was simply the occasion of a renewal of that social welcome and hearty entertainment such as had attended me everywhere since my nomination to the Hawaiian throne. In fact, I might claim with reason that the future hopes of the Hawaiian people were with my party. I was accompanied by my sister, the Princess Likelike, who had with her the little child-princess Kaiulani, and that infant's governess, Miss Barnes; Mr. J. H. Boyd was of the number of our attendants. After a generous lunch at Waimanalo, on the estate of Mr. Cummins, we left for Maunavili, the country-place of Mr. and Mrs. Boyd, in whose hospitable mansion we passed the night, and left our gentle hostess regretting that our stay had been so short ; but events proved that my tour was not to be extended far beyond her residence, for we had proceeded on our way to Kaneohe but a few steps, when a singular accident happened to my carriage. My horses were driven by Mr. Joseph Heleluhe, and in some unaccountable manner the reins of one of the horses became entangled in the bit of another. We were descending the steep side of a hill, and the result was that the driver had no longer control of the animals. Consequently the carriage came down the hill with such velocity that I was thrown violently out, and landed between two rocks ; but fortunately there was a bit of marshy ground where I struck. It was a matter of immediate wonder that my life had been spared. Certainly no one could have been nearer to instant death. This had been witnessed from the homestead of our hosts ; and Mr. Cummins, arriving on the scene almost immediately, sent for a stretcher, which was sent at once from the residence of Mrs. Boyd. On this I was placed, and the litter raised upon the shoulders of four men ; thus was I carried all the way to Waimanalo. Mr. Cummins, having preceded the sad procession, met us at the foot of the hill with a wagon. It was a sorrowful breaking-up of what had promised to be a delightful journey. Messages were immediately sent to all the points on the island I had intended to visit, informing the people of the accident which had befallen me, and notifying them that it would be useless to go on with preparations for my reception, as it was the intention of those who had

charge to send me at once to Honolulu. So, under
the kind care of Mr. Cummins and Mrs. Kaae, the
wagon was driven to the wharf, where the little steamer
Waimanalo, belonging to Mr. Cummins, awaited me.
All that tenderest care and kindest heart could suggest
was done to make me comfortable by my kind hosts;
and the cavalcade of retainers, with which I had come
out so gayly, followed in demure silence. Despatches
had also been sent to Honolulu; and my husband, Governor Dominis, and the princess's husband, Hon. A. S.
Cleghorn, were acquainted with the particulars of the
accident. Mr. Cummins, Mr. Kaae, and Mr. Frank
Harvey, assisted by other friends, saw that I was put
on board the steamer with as little pain or inconvenience as possible. My sister and little niece were by
my side; and all the company were safely accommodated on board the Waimanalo, which at about three
o'clock that afternoon steamed out to sea. After a
smooth and uneventful run we drew near the wharf at
the foot of Fort Street, in the port of Honolulu. It
was nine o'clock at night when the little craft got
alongside the wharf, where crowds of people awaited
her arrival. The night was fine and clear; the moon
was shining brightly. As the boat was fast, I turned
my eyes toward the shore, and saw a line of soldiers
drawn up to receive me. When the litter was taken
from the deck and placed in a wagon, I discovered
that these men were to draw my carriage to the place
prepared for my reception. When all had been made
ready, the word was given to proceed, and the procession started. To me it was a solemn moment, one

which can never be forgotten, — the shops and houses of the merchants still draped with crape in memory of the fallen president at Washington, the crowds of native Hawaiian people which lined the way, their respectful silence broken only by their smothered sobs or subdued weeping, and with it all the steady, measured tread of the soldiers who were drawing the wagon on which I had been laid by my devoted friends. Although I had suffered much, was still in pain, and not out of danger, yet in it all there was the sweet assurance for which much can be borne, — the blessed consciousness that all this manifestation was because my people loved me. My husband was walking by the side of my wagon, and the tramp of the soldiers was growing shorter as we neared our home, while the throng of sympathetic followers who had attended our march grew less only when we reached our very doorway. My return thus to my people and my family from the very border of death left an impression upon me which is too sacred for any description.

On arrival I asked to be placed in one of the cottages on our grounds, preferring to occupy this small, one-story house rather than to be carried upstairs to the more commodious apartments of the great house known as Washington Place. My wishes were complied with at once by my kind husband and faithful attendants.

The nature of my injuries was such that a long rest was required. At first it was thought my back was broken by my fall; for when I endeavored to rise after recovering from the first shock, it was impossible to do so, nor could I change in any way my position until

assisted by my followers, Mr. Heleluhe being one of
the first to offer me aid. Even then, when depending
upon their strength of arm as they tried to raise me,
the least exertion or motion gave me the greatest pain.
My physician, Dr. Webb, arrived at the cottage at Washington Place about the same time as myself, although
he had been a long distance in search of his patient.
The moment he received news of the accident he had
ridden to Waimanalo, a distance of twelve miles by the
shortest route, and not finding me had at once returned.
He made a careful examination of my condition, and was
relieved to find that the injuries to my back were no
more serious than a very severe wrench and strain. He
was a homœopathist, and left some medicines to be administered, directions to be followed by my nurses; and
watches were to be regularly set, and relieved by night
and by day. At the end of three weeks I was not yet
able to raise myself, or even sit up in my bed; so finally
it was the opinion of my medical advisers that I should
make a great effort and persevere in spite of the pain,
lest I should become bedridden. These instructions
were followed out with a result which proved the wisdom of the course recommended; for I was soon able
to ride about in my buggy, still weak, but improving
slowly.

But the process of recovery was very gradual, and
only successful by the most constant care and great
patience of my attendants. These were divided into
watches of three hours each, and three persons were
always at my bedside. To one of these was assigned
the duty of waving the *kahili*, or long-plumed staff of

state, the insignia of royalty; to another that of using the fan for my comfort, both of these being women; while to the third, a male attendant, belonged the duty of doing any necessary errands, and of making my female attendants comfortable in whatever way their needs might require. Whenever I was lifted, or even turned, it was done by the strong yet tender hands of six men, three on each side. Had these been nurses trained by years of experience to manage the sick they could not have proceeded with more skill and gentleness; so quietly and gradually was my position changed that I could scarcely perceive the movements, which were such as to give me the least pain. It was the same when it was judged best for me to leave my bed. By the strong arms of my native attendants I was lifted in a sheet, then easily laid on an extended but movable chair, which was raised to an erect posture without the least strain on my muscular system. Even when I began to move about the room my dependence on my faithful retainers did not cease, and with one on each side it was almost impossible for me to fall. From the reclining-chair I was transferred without movement or strain to my carriage, and taken from it in the same manner, thus securing change and fresh air with no exertion to myself. My position was not without its amusing side, even at the most critical moments; for when I was supposed to be asleep or unconscious, conversations or little actions would take place in the sick-room which were perfectly understood by me, but of which I was supposed by my attendants to have no knowledge whatever. When scarcely able to sit up I was consulted about the mottoes with which it was the intention to crown the triumphal arches throughout the city at the approaching return of my brother, the king, from his tour around the world; and it was a great satisfaction to me to receive such marks of deference while I lay a helpless invalid.

All classes of adherents had been represented in the watchers about my bedside. There were Colonel C. P. Iukea, Colonel J. H. Boyd, Major Anton Rosa, Governor John T. Baker, Mr. C. B. Wilson, Captain Leleo, Mr. Joseph Heleluhe, Mr. Isaac Kaiama. These and many others had their watches in the invalid chamber, while Hon. Samuel Parker and Mr. Charles Williams were present from time to time. Most of these gentlemen were accompanied by their wives as assistants in their kind offices. Princess Ruth and my sister, the Princess Likelike, were daily visitors

KING KALAKAUA, HIS CABINET AND STAFF

CHAPTER XV

KALAKAUA'S RETURN

IT was during this period of convalescence that my regency was brought to a close. With that enthusiasm always shown by the Hawaiian people in doing honor to their sovereigns, the grandest preparations were made throughout the islands to welcome the arrival of the king. In Honolulu the joy was general, and the foreign element was well represented in the festivities. The streets were given up to the people, and were crowned with triumphal arches. Before the day of his expected landing at the wharf, the most elaborate preparations had been made to give him a royal greeting. The mottoes, in the selection of which numberless parties had consulted me, were displayed in every part of the city, and there was an especial arch designed for each district of the island of Oahu.

The long-expected day came; and there was a long cavalcade of horsemen in attendance on the king, who rode ahead, accompanied by the gentlemen of his personal staff. Outriders and aids were seen on every side. A week was devoted to the festivities of the reception. Iolani Palace was not available; for the old building had been pulled down, and the new one was not then completed, although in process of erection. So the king with his queen, Kapiolani, occupied a smaller building which is named Kinauhale. It was in this building that during my brother's absence I had conferred the order of Kalakaua on two persons distinguished in the Roman Catholic Mission, both of them now having passed to their reward, — Hermann, the Bishop of Olba, and Father Damien, the leper priest.

When the festivities of my brother's return were over, I moved to my Waikiki residence, accompanied by some of my retainers or attendants, amongst whom I might mention Mrs. Kapena and Miss Sheldon. In the course of a very few weeks, and under the beneficent influences of this change, I had recovered my strength, and was able to walk without assistance. Hamohamo is justly considered to be the most life-giving and healthy district in the whole extent of the island of Oahu; there is something unexplainable and peculiar in the atmosphere at that place, which seldom fails to bring back the glow of health to the patient, no matter from what disease suffering. In order to encourage the people who might be semi-invalids to resort there, I have always left open my estates on that shore, so that the air and the sea-bathing, the latter most essential in our climate, might be enjoyed without any charge by all who choose to avail themselves of the privilege. I have also caused trees to be set out, both those whose fruit might be of value and those of use for shade alone, so that the coast might become attractive to chance visitors. When it is the *malolo* season, the fishermen living in my neighborhood will go to my beach to launch their canoes, and push off two or three miles into the

incoming surf to catch the flying-fish ; it is a very exciting sport, and at the same time it is a means of livelihood to them.   Nor are they the only people benefited
by this free fishing-ground.   Most of their catch is taken to the markets of the city.   Some part is brought
in, and landed on the beach at " The Queen's Retreat,"
where whole families of visitors are often to be found
passing the day in rest or pleasure.   These have brought
with them an abundance of our national dish, the whole-
some *poi*, and perhaps have added bread and butter and
wine, and stores of other nice things ; to these they
may now, if they wish, join the sweet and toothsome
flying-fish.   Oftentimes they make a further purchase
of the latter to carry home for the family supper.
Political events have brought me leisure, and from the
view through the porticos of my pretty seaside cottage,
called Kealohilani, I have derived much amusement, as
well as pleasure : for as the sun shines on the evil and
the good, and the rain falls on the just and the unjust,
I have not felt called upon to limit the enjoyment of
my beach and shade-trees to any party in politics ; and
my observation convinces me that those who are most
opposed to my system of government have not the
least diffidence about passing happy hours on domains
which are certainly my private property.   To watch the
families of the Royalist and the Provisionalist mingling
together, sharing each the other's lunch-baskets, and
spending the day in social pleasures at the " Queen's
Retreat," one would never suspect that racial or political
jealousy had any place in the breasts of the participants.
While in exile it has ever been a pleasant thought to

me that my people, in spite of differences of opinion, are enjoying together the free use of my seashore home.

The king having resumed the executive office, affairs of state were no longer committed to my charge. But I was in a position to observe that our industries were moving along on the high road to prosperity, and that with a fair degree of harmony between the king and his ministers, our government was administered smoothly, and in a manner conducive to the welfare of all his subjects, whether native or foreign born. But there are a few events of the days of my regency which, ere I pass on to another era, may be worthy of mention.

During the king's absence, and while Mr. H. A. P. Carter was Minister of the Interior, he notified me one day that there was a death-warrant awaiting my signature. This was the first time it had been forcibly brought to my notice that the executive held the power of life and death, and it seemed to me a most terrible thing that I should be obliged to sign an order which should deprive one of my fellow-mortals of life. I simply could not do it, and so said to Mr. Carter. He regarded it as only an official act; but I asked the cabinet if they could not devise some other method of punishing the culprit in order to spare me the pain of signing the death-warrant. Minister Carter tried as best he could to convince me that in no event would I be held responsible, that any mistake or culpability would rest on the shoulders of the cabinet, and I need not feel in the least degree responsible. But he failed to convince me. I told him that I would take the matter into consideration, and notify him if, after thinking it over, I could conform to his views. Two weeks, perhaps three, went by, and I had never felt that I could in this case attend to my official duty. Finally Minister Carter again pressed the subject upon my attention; reminding me of the fact that the matter had been considered and judged, that the cause of justice was delayed, the sentence unexecuted, and that it was absolutely my duty to sign the warrant, which I finally did, but with the greatest reluctance.

In the month of July, while the king was absent, Chief Justice C. C. Harris, a man who in many ways had been prominent, died; there were some elements of peculiar sadness in the death of Judge Harris. His wife, a daughter of a former chief justice, Allen, was at the time under restraint in another room of the same house, being hopelessly insane. His death made it necessary for me to appoint some person in his place. The first associate was at that time Mr. Albert F. Judd, and the second Mr. L. McCully. At one of the public functions in the government building at which I was expected to preside, there occurred an incident which will suggest the eagerness for distinction and precedence manifested at the time by prominent representatives of the " Reform " party. At such state occasions there were seats assigned to the ladies of the cabinet at the right of the king's dais. The wives of ministers had the front row of seats. (In times of more ancient date the first seats of honor were always taken by the native Hawaiian chieftesses; but by " Reform " regulations, especially in the reign of King Kalakaua, his family were the only natives of rank present, so it became a very easy matter to provide for them.) Directly behind the seats of the cabinet ladies were placed those intended for the ladies of the justices of the supreme court. On this occasion, I being the regent, my sister Likelike stood at my right, my husband (who had a right to the title of prince although he never assumed it, but preferred to be called governor or general), accompanied by Hon. A. S. Cleghorn, father of the little Princess Kaiulani, were at my left.

As yet no appointment had been made by me to the vacant place on the bench of the supreme court, because I had consulted my brother, the absent king, and was awaiting a reply. But Mr. A. F. Judd had instructed his wife that she should occupy a seat with the cabinet ladies, and even to take the first seat, thus assuming precedence over all. It was a surprise to Minister Carter on entering to find the seat which belonged to his wife occupied by another person. After a little discussion betwixt them, the question was referred to me for decision. I immediately said that the seat belonged to Minister Carter's wife, and suggested that Mrs. Judd resume the place which belonged to her with the other ladies of the associate judges of the courts, adding that she was no more at present than the lady of the first associate justice. "But," expostulated her husband, "I am as good as chief justice already, as I am to be appointed to that office;" and then he proceeded to demand of me if I had not already received notice of his appointment. I replied that I had not, and that my decision of the question of precedence was announced. Then, as the assembly was in readiness to proceed with its duties, although Mrs. Judd obstinately refused to yield the place which belonged to the wife of Minister Carter, I turned my attention to other and more important matters.

While I was a prisoner in Iolani Palace, now called Executive Building, it seems that the little comedy of precedence was re-enacted under the " Republic " in the rooms beneath mine, at the assembling of the legislature. Minister Cooper arrived with his wife ; and to his astonishment and anger, there was Mrs. Judd again, seated in the place which should have been reserved for Mrs. Cooper.   In order to secure the coveted precedence, Mrs. Judd had arrived very early, secured for herself the seat of honor, and, as before, absolutely refused to leave it.   Words passed between the chief justice and the minister.   Mr. Judd claimed that he was the highest officer in the islands.   To which Minister Cooper retorted that he held no cabinet position, and was certainly out of place among cabinet ministers ; while he, Cooper, as the minister of foreign affairs, should be entitled to the first place in the government after that held by the president himself.   The disputants did not on this occasion send to me for an opinion on this perplexing question.   Had they done so I should have decided without a moment's hesitation that the position of Mr. Cooper was the correct one, according to the usages of nations, whatever may be the relative rank in republics as between the executive and judicial departments.   But it would seem from this second occurrence that the passion for dignity and place is not confined to courts of royalty or to those who sustain them.

CHAPTER XVI

CORONATION CEREMONIES

IN the early part of the year 1883, preparations were made to formally ratify the accession of the new dynasty to the Hawaiian throne by investing both His Majesty Kalakaua, and his queen, Kapiolani, with the crown and other insignia of royalty. To this end all needful articles had been ordered from Europe, excepting such as could be readily obtained in the nearer port of San Francisco, Cal. This was very properly intended by the king to be a jubilee year with his people, and at the grand celebration nothing was to be left undone which could contribute to the general enjoyment. All the people, high or low, rich or poor, from Hawaii to Kauai, were to be made welcome at Honolulu; and elaborate preparations were made for their reception. The two crowns were made in England, and were of gold studded with precious stones; from the same country came also the dresses of the queen and those of her sisters, the Princess Poomaikalani and the Princess Kekaulike. My toilets were furnished from Paris dressmaking establishments, and consisted of two complete costumes. The gown to be worn during the day at the coronation ceremony was of gold and white brocaded silk; that intended for the *soirée* and the royal ball was of crimson satin; each costume was perfect in itself, the lesser details being in harmony with the dress; both were heavily embroidered, and were generally considered to have been the most elegant productions of Parisian art ever seen in Hawaii on this or any other state occasion. My sister, the Princess Likelike, had sent to San Francisco for her wardrobe, which, like mine, consisted of two complete costumes, one of which was of white silk of figured brocade handsomely trimmed with pearls; her full evening dress was of silk, in color or shade styled at that time "moonlight-on-the-lake," and, with head-dress to match, it was very effective.

Even in the early part of January, from all parts of the islands, crowds began to flock to Honolulu, impatient for the promised ceremony; and from thence to the 12th day of February, 1883, the number of those visiting our capital city was daily increasing. It was an unusually rainy winter, and our streets were very muddy; but the good-natured multitude waded through the rain or mud to see what was going on, or to make their purchases at the stores, without complaint. Money was spent lavishly by the visitors; all the stores were thronged from morning to night by eager and easily satisfied purchasers. The principal establishments benefited by the money of the people were those of John Thomas Waterhouse, who had two places of business, B. F. Ehlers & Co., H. Hackfeld & Co., and T. H. Davies & Co. Besides these there were the jewelry shops, notably that of the Wenners; even the Chinese merchants came in for their share in the circulation of the money of the people.

The day to which all had been looking with eager
anticipation arrived. Iolani Palace, the new building of
that name, had been completed the previous year, and
a large pavilion had been erected immediately in front
of it for the celebration of the coronation. This was
exclusively for the accommodation of the royal family;
but there was adjacent thereto a sort of amphitheatre,
capable of holding ten thousand persons, intended for
the occupation of the people. In this building there
were assigned proper stations to all the principal officers
of the government, besides which the members of the
diplomatic or consular bodies had their appropriate
places; then there were the nobles and the delegates to
the legislative assembly, the chief justice, his associates,
and other officers of the court, while on the veranda
of the palace on the one side were seated the officers of
the vessels of war in the port, and on the other persons
of rank or position who had not been otherwise assigned
to stations.

Promptly at the appointed time His Majesty Kalakaua, King of the Hawaiian Islands, accompanied by
Her Majesty Kapiolani, his queen, made their appearance. I give the order of the procession to the royal
pavilion. Princess Kekaulike, bearing the royal feather
cloak, and with her the Princess Poomaikalani; then the
Princess Likelike, with the child-princess Kaiulani, and
her father, Hon. A. S. Cleghorn; Governor Dominis,
and myself; we were all attended by our *kahili* bearers,
and those ancient staffs of royalty were held aloft at
our sides. Then followed Prince Kaiwananakoa, bearing one of the crowns, and Prince Kalaniaanole bearing

IOLANI PALACE, FRONT VIEW

the other crown, succeeded by two others of noble birth
and lineage bearing insignia of royalty of either native
or traditional usage, the *tabu* sticks, the sceptre, and
ring. Then came Their Majesties the King and Queen,
attended by their *kahili* bearers, who stationed themselves just inside the pavilion. As the royal party entered, the queen was immediately attended by her ladies
in waiting, eight in number, all attired in black velvet
trimmed with white satin. The long and handsome
train of Her Majesty's robe was carried by two ladies of
high rank and of noble lineage, Keano and Kekaulike.

The ceremonies were opened with prayer by Rev.
Mr. Mackintosh; and then followed one of those coinci-
dences which are so striking on any such occasion, and
was certainly noticed as one of the most beautiful incidents of the day. In the very act of prayer, just as he
put forth his hand to lift the crown, before placing it
on the brow of the king, a mist, or cloud, such as may
gather very quickly in our tropical climate, was seen to
pass over the sun, obscuring its light for a few minutes;
then at the moment when the king was crowned there
appeared, shining so brilliantly as to attract general attention, a single star. It was noticed by the entire
multitude assembled to witness the pageant, and a mur-
mur of wonder and admiration passed over the throng.
The ceremonies proceeded with due solemnity, and the
whole scene was very impressive and not to be forgotten. At its close the company retired to the palace
in the same order as that in which it had come forth;
and the day ceremonies being over the crowd dispersed,
retiring to rest from the fatigues and excitements of the

day, so as to be able to enter with zest into the festivities of the evening, as a grand ball was to be given at the palace. Indeed, the entire grounds were given up to pleasure such as can only be fully imagined by those who have actually mingled with a happy people in the festivities of a tropical night.

Throughout the week one diversion followed another; until, with citizens and visitors almost surfeited with merrymaking, it came to an end, and Honolulu once more settled down to its every-day quiet and routine. Certainly the coronation celebration had been a great success. The people from the country and from the other islands went back to their homes with a renewed sense of the dignity and honor involved in their nationality, and an added interest in the administration of their government. Honolulu had been benefited in the mean time financially, the merchants and traders of every degree reaping a bountiful harvest from the free expenditure of money by every class. The king has, however, been blamed for expending the public revenues for such a purpose, and this festival is still cited as an instance of his "reckless extravagance." A considerable contingent of the people of New England objected, if I have read correctly, to the building of the Bunker Hill Monument. In my own view the expenditure in either case was quite justified by the end sought. The Saviour himself was once accused of extravagance, or at least of permitting it, not, however, by a truly loyal disciple. The men who "carry the bag" are not always the best judges of royal obligations. It was necessary to confirm the new family "*Stirps*" — to use the words of our constitution — by a celebration of unusual impressiveness. There was a serious purpose of national importance; the direct line of the "Kamahame-has" having become extinct, it was succeeded by the "Keawe-a-Heulu" line, its founder having been first cousin to the father of Kamahameha I. It was wise and patriotic to spend money to awaken in the people a national pride. Naturally, those among us who did not desire to have Hawaii remain a nation would look on an expenditure of this kind as worse than wasted.

CHAPTER XVII

PRINCESS RUTH AND MRS. BERNICE PAUAHI BISHOP

In the spring of 1884 the Princess Ruth completed a handsome residence on Emma Street, and gave a grand *luau* to celebrate the event. This was followed by a splendid ball in the evening, which was attended by all the best society of Honolulu, whether of native or foreign birth. But after this festivity the princess was taken suddenly ill, and left for Kailua on Hawaii in hopes that the journey would restore her health. She was accompanied by Mrs. Bernice Pauahi Bishop, her own cousin, and also by Mrs. Haalelea. She received every attention, but notwithstanding this, did not recover; and on the twenty-fourth day of May her remains were brought back to Honolulu, and laid in state in the handsome new house, Keouahale, which she had just erected. Keouahale has recently been purchased for school purposes by the present government of Hawaii. While lying there in state, the usual native ceremonies attending the death and obsequies of a high chief were accorded to her remains. There were the daily attendance of watchers, the waving of *kahilis*, and singing of the chants of the departed. To explain the latter I might add, that whenever a child was born into one of the families of the high chiefs, it was customary to compose a chant, not only in honor of the event, but further rehearsing the genealogy of the infant, the deeds of its ancestors, and any daring acts of wonderful valor and prowess in which they had participated. These chants were committed to memory, and passed along from mouth to mouth amongst the retainers of that chief. At the death, as at the birth, they were intoned in honor of the one for whom they were composed. I have my own chant, which has been sacred to me all my lifetime. Any child of noble birth who had no such record, were it possible to suppose such a case, would be judged unworthy its rank It was a further custom observed amongst us for all chiefs of rank parallel to that of the deceased to remain at the house which contained the remains whilst the body was lying in state. So on this occasion Queen Emma, Mrs. Bishop, the Princess Likelike, and myself, all took up our residence at the mansion so recently occupied by Princess Ruth. The celebration of the last rites of interment did not take place until three weeks after her death. When all the honors which her royal rank required had been accorded to her remains, and these had been laid in the mausoleum, it was found that her sole heir was Mrs. Bishop, her nearest living relative, who not only inherited the beautiful residence, but further, all the property of her cousin. Not long after these events it was found that Mrs. Bishop was in failing health ; and on consultation with Dr. Trousseau, she was told that the nature of her malady was so grave that she should lose no time in taking advice from the best physicians in San Francisco, to which city he counselled she

should go at the earliest opportunity.   She accordingly
went.   On her arrival, she was informed by Dr. Lane
that her disease was of the nature of cancer, and that
immediate surgical treatment was the best course.   She
submitted to an operation, and on her recovery from
this, returned to the islands.   My sister, the Princess
Likelike, was in San Francisco at the same time, and
returned to Honolulu with her towards the end of that
summer.   Mrs. Bishop went to her Waikiki residence ;
and when I called to see if there was anything I could
do for her, she besought me to come and stay with her,
which I did until the day of her death.   It was here
that I first noticed the great change which had come
over the mind of Queen Emma, and which was more
plainly noticed at or just after Mrs. Bishop's decease.
About two weeks before the close of her life, it was
thought best to remove Mrs. Bishop to Keouahale ; but
she failed rapidly from the day of the change until the
16th of October, 1884, when she was released from her
painful experience.   Then there followed a repetition
of those rites and ceremonies customary on the death
and burial of the high chiefs, such as that house had
but just witnessed in the case of Princess Ruth.   It
was at this time more especially that Queen Emma
showed plainly by her peculiar actions that she was suffering from some malady.   As time passed away the
progress of physical disorder seemed to go on ; she
grew nothing better, but rather worse, and in the month
of April, 1885, she died.   Then followed a queer proceeding on the part of her agent.   At first the remains
were laid in state at her own house ; but Mr. Cart-

wright and a few of his friends took it into their heads
to have the casket removed to Kawaiahao church, the
apology being that her house was not large enough to
accommodate such a gathering as would come together
on the day of the funeral. This was accordingly done,
much to the wonder and displeasure of those who had
charge of the church, and of the friends of the departed
queen. Queen Emma was not an attendant there. On
the contrary, she had been chiefly instrumental in the
founding of the Anglican Mission, and was an Episcopa-
lian. Why, then, supposing it had been at all necessary
to select a church for her funeral, did they not select
the Episcopal church? That was her own church, and
she should have been buried therefrom ; for while living she had shown strong attachment to it, and an
equally strong feeling of opposition to other denominations. The persons selected by her agent to guard her
remains showed no regard for the sacredness of the
place. They smoked, feasted, and sang songs while
awaiting the last solemn rites due to the dead. However, when the day of burial came, Bishop Willis of the
English Church adapted himself to the circumstances,
and officiated from the Congregational pulpit with the
ritual of his own church ; after which, with all the pomp
and splendor due to her state as a queen amongst the
sovereigns of the Hawaiian people, she was borne up
the Nuuanu Valley, and laid by the side of her husband, Alexander Liholiho, or Kamehameha IV.

When the will of Mrs. Bernice Pauahi Bishop was
read, in which she disposed of her own estate, I did not
happen to be present ; but her husband, Hon. Charles

R. Bishop, informed me that I had been duly remembered, that his wife had bequeathed to me the lands of Kahala, island of Oahu, Lumahai on Kauai, Kealia in Kona, Hawaii; besides which he sent to me a pair of diamond wristlets, a diamond pin with crown which had once belonged to the Princess Ruth, and a necklace of pearls beautifully chased and set in tigers' claws. But nevertheless I must own to one great disappointment. The estate which had been so dear to us both in my childhood, the house built by my father, Paki, where I had lived as a girl, which was connected with many happy memories of my early life, from whence I had been married to Governor Dominis, when he took me to Washington Place, I could not help feeling ought to have been left to me. The estate was called Haleakala, or House of the Sun, and the residence received the name of Aikupika; but both these are forgotten now in that of the Arlington Hotel. This wish of my heart was not gratified, and at the present day strangers stroll through the grounds or lounge on the piazzas of that home once so dear to me. Yet memories of my adopted parents still cling to that homestead, and rise before me not only when I pass its walls, but as I recall in a foreign land the days of my youth.

CHAPTER XVIII

BENEVOLENT SOCIETIES

ANOTHER provision of the will of Mrs. Bishop may be noticed here. It was found that she had made ample provision for the education of the people of her race; and an educational and industrial institute was to be erected, specially limited in its mission to young Hawaiians. The privileges of this commendable charity were likewise restricted by the benefactor to those of the Protestant faith. The Presbyterian churches in Hawaii may profit by this devise; but those of the English Catholic or Roman Catholic Missions are excluded because of their religion, which scarcely makes the institution a national benefit.

In the early part of the year 1886 His Majesty Kalakaua designed and established an organization for benevolent work amongst his people; it was called the Hooululahui. The first meeting of the society having been appointed at Kawaiahao Church, there was a good attendance of the first ladies of the city, not only those of Hawaiian families, but also of foreign birth. It was my brother's intention that the society should have as its head Her Majesty Kapiolani, his queen; but to make it more efficient and systematic in its work, the society was divided into three departments. Of these, the first embraced the central part of the city of Honolulu, and this was under the presidency of the queen. Next came the lower part of Honolulu, Kaumakapili, extending as far as Maemae, and embracing all the district beyond Palama, which was assigned to my management and presidency. In like manner the third division, Kawaiahao, extending through Waikiki and Manoa, Pauoa, and a certain portion of the city, was assigned to my sister, the Princess Likelike. All denominations, including the Roman Catholics, were invited to co-operate in the good work. The Princesses Poomaikalani and Kekaulike, neither of whom is now living, gave their aid to the queen. The former was made governess of Hawaii, and the latter governess of Kauai. These two ladies did all in their power to assist Queen Kapiolani in her work of charity, and my sister and myself were equally interested to attend to the needs of our departments; but the responsibility for the general management was really upon the king, who not only had to assume the financial burden, but gave to the work the weight of his official influence, and always responded cheerfully to our calls upon him for advice, giving to us with liberality the advantage of his own good judgment. The people responded with good-will from other parts of the islands, and the work has gone on for over ten years since it was first established by my brother. Of those then interested, Queen Kapiolani and myself are the only two of the managers now living. As Princess Likelike and the other two princesses died, their departments came more under the personal management of the queen. Like many other enterprises of charity, the original intentions of the founders have been improved upon ; and the society is merged in other good works, or its purposes diverted to slightly different ends. The organization is now consolidated in the Maternity Home ; the charitable funds which used to be distributed amongst the poor, the amounts contributed by the people everywhere to carry out the designs of the king, are still doing good through this institution, of which the Dowager Queen Kapiolani is the president, assisted by a board of managers consisting of notable Hawaiian ladies, and by others of foreign descent.

In the year 1886 I organized an educational society, the intention of which was to interest the Hawaiian ladies in the proper training of young girls of their own race whose parents would be unable to give them advantages by which they would be prepared for the duties of life. As no such association had ever existed, although there had been frequent cases of private benevolence, it seemed a good time to interest those who had the means in this important work. Therefore I called a meeting, notifying all whom I thought would be likely to attend. The response was very gratifying, and on the appointed afternoon a goodly number of our best ladies assembled in the Kawaiahao church. The meeting was opened with prayer ; after which I arose, made a short address, and explained to the audience my purpose in requesting attention to the moral and intellectual needs of those of our sex who were just beginning life. These remarks seemed to meet the approval of all present ; but yet, in looking around, it was evident to me that

the society would be more prosperous in two divisions,
as there were those in attendance who could not work
well together. My sister, the Princess Likelike, was of
our number ; so I suggested that she should be the head
or president of one division, and I would take the other.
Names were then taken, those who announced their
willingness to work for the subject were enrolled, and
the association was called "The Liliuokalani Educational Society." At our second meeting a constitution
was drawn, submitted for approval, and adopted. Both
branches then began their work, which went on with
results that at one time appeared to be most encouraging.   But my sister did not live a year after this
movement had begun, and on her death circumstances
operated to impair the efficiency of the society.   However, her branch of it came under my personal direction ;
and the object for which I had called the meeting was
never forgotten, nor was the education of the young
girls of Hawaiian birth neglected either by myself or
by those I had interested in its importance, until the
changed conditions of January, 1893, obliged me to live
in retirement.

On the twenty-fourth day of September, 1886, by request from the king, a charter was granted by the privy
council to the *Hale Naua*, or Temple of Science. Probably some of its forms had been taken by my brother
from the Masonic ritual, and others may have been
taken from the old and harmless ceremonies of the
ancient people of the Hawaiian Islands, which were
then only known to the priests of the highest orders.
Under the work of this organization was embraced

matters of science known to historians, and recognized
by the priests of our ancient times. The society further held some correspondence with similar scientific
associations in foreign lands, to whom it communicated
its proceedings. The result was some correspondence
with those bodies, who officially accepted the theories
propounded by the *Hale Naua;* and in recognition of
this acceptance medals were sent from abroad to the
members highest in rank in the Hawaiian society.
Unworthy and unkind reflections have been made on
the purposes of this society by those who knew nothing
of it. Persons with mean and little minds can readily
assign false motives to actions intended for good, and
attribute to lofty ideas a base purpose or unholy intention. That some good has been done by this organization the members themselves could readily certify.
It had been the custom before the days of His Majesty
Kalakaua (it is the usage even to the present day) for
the chiefs to support the destitute and to bury the dead.
This society opened to them an organized method of
doing this; it cared for the sick, and it provided for
the funerals of the dead. Had the king lived, more
good would have been done, and the society would have
been in a more flourishing condition; yet the money contributed for its purposes while he lived was invested in
stocks, and many persons have drawn benefits from the
dividends. Although it was small, it was a beginning.

CHAPTER XIX

On the second day of February, 1887, died the Princess Miriam Likelike, wife of Hon. A. S. Cleghorn, leaving one child, an interesting little girl of eleven years of age, to begin the serious business of life without a mother. She is now the Princess Kaiulani, and has been receiving her education abroad since her fifteenth year. I was tenderly attached to my sister, so much so that her decease had an unfavorable effect on my health. It was, therefore, with satisfaction that I received from my brother, the king, a most unexpected proposition. This was that I should accompany the queen to the grand jubilee at London, in honor of the fiftieth year of the reign of the great and good Queen of Great Britain. It was on a Saturday night early in April that I received this invitation, which I at once accepted. As I was at that time living at my Palama residence, early on Sunday morning I sent a despatch to my husband, who was with his mother at Washington Place, asking him to come to see me immediately, which he did. I then told him of what had transpired between His Majesty and myself, and that it was my wish and intention to accept. He cordially agreed with me, and said that he would like to be of the

PRINCESS KAIULANI
Reproduced, by permission, from a photograph by Elmer Chickering, Boston

party, of which I was very glad. But I was still better
pleased when, acting under my advice, he consulted the
king, and returned as quickly as he could to tell me
that it was all settled that he should go with us. Only
a few days of necessary preparation were left to us;
and by the 12th of April we were ready to embark
on the steamship Australia, by which we had taken
passage for San Francisco.

But I could not think of leaving without saying farewell to some little girls, five in number, the charge
of whose education I had assumed, and who were at
Kawaiahao seminary. So on the day of departure, at
about eleven o'clock I stopped at the schoolhouse. At
my coming all the pupils were gathered together into
the large room, where I made them an impromptu address, telling them of my intention to sail immediately
for foreign lands, encouraging them to be faithful to
their duty to their teachers, and warning them that it
would distress me more than could be expressed should
I ever hear that any of them had done other than right
during my absence. After these few farewell words I
left the institution, I must confess with some fears in
my heart, some misgivings as to the future of some of
the girls whom I had addressed. But these doubts
were set at rest by their letters, and it made me very
happy while I was abroad to hear accounts of their
progress and continued good behavior.

The next call after leaving the seminary was upon
my mother-in-law, Mrs. Dominis, to whom, at her home
in Washington Place, I bade an affectionate adieu.
Then, accompanied by my husband, I proceeded directly

to the steamer. Queen Kapiolani and her attendants were already on board; the king was awaiting us there to bid the party farewell. When this was over, and His Majesty had gone ashore, the word was given to get under way, and the steamer took her departure in the presence of one of those immense crowds which throng the wharves on such occasions. On the seventh day out we were boarded by the pilot off the Golden Gate; it was early morning, but by nine o'clock of the same day we were steaming toward our berth at the wharf. On the third day at sea my husband was attacked with rheumatism, which rendered him perfectly helpless, so that he had to be carried ashore on a stretcher. Kind friends succeeded in taking him to the Palace Hotel without occasioning him severe pain, for which attentions they earned my gratitude.

We remained in the city of San Francisco about one week, during which the health of General Dominis improved so that we took one of the northern routes for the city of Washington. While at San Francisco the queen improved every moment to see what she could of the city, this being her first visit to any foreign country. In this pleasure I was unable to participate, my husband's illness having rendered me a watcher by his bedside. But I made the acquaintance of two very charming princesses from Tahiti. They were lovely ladies; one was the Princess Moetia, the other the Arii Manihinihi.

From San Francisco our party pursued its journey across the continent. At Sacramento we received some pleasant attentions, and there were peculiarities of nature in scenery and changing seasons which were most interesting to those from a land of perpetual summer. When we arrived at Summit, for example, there were the lofty peaks covered with their snowy mantles. This was similar, but more extensive, to what we could witness on the tops of the highest mountains on Hawaii; but here it was universal, and the valleys were also filled with snowbanks. Then, when we passed through the long snow-sheds the train came to a stop for a few minutes while some members of our party got off to examine the snow, which blew through the cracks or crevices in the boards on to the railroad track. Taking it up and rolling it in their hands, they made snowballs, and pelted each other with it, quite ordinary sport for cold climates, but a rare opportunity for those born in the Hawaiian Islands, and to be always remembered as a novel experience. After coming forth from the sheds again into the light of day, we descended gradually until we reached the Great Salt Lake; and at the city of the same name, the capital of Utah, we stopped a few hours, meeting not only many of the prominent elders of the Mormon Church, but quite a number of our own people who were living there. These were naturally much delighted to meet visitors of their nation so far from home. After a short rest we resumed our eastward course.

The next principal place of which I have a vivid recollection is Denver, which was an infant city then, comparatively just springing into being; there were but a few scattered houses, quite distant from the line of the railway, and not very suggestive of such a thriving city

as is now, I hear, on the site of those humble begin-
nings. But that which had interested us most along our
line of travel was the trees without a sign of leaves or
blossoms, since with us the verdure is perennial; and the
sight of shrubs or bushes, or even lofty trees, standing
out bare of foliage or flower, struck us very strangely.
We made no stop in Chicago, and the oil regions of
Pennsylvania were the next natural wonders to interest
us as we passed through them on the train. Here
there were signs of the coming of the summer, the
tree-tops being covered with opening foliage, and the
grass growing greener. There were some few spring
flowers to be seen in bud or blossom by the waysides,
and Nature welcomed us with a display of her beauties
akin to those of which we had taken farewell in our
own beautiful islands.

We arrived safely at Washington, and found comfortable quarters at the Arlington Hotel. Our party
consisted of the following individuals: Her Majesty
Queen Kapiolani, wife of my brother, the reigning
king; Lieutenant-General J. O. Dominis, governor of
the island of Oahu, and myself; Colonel C. P. Iaukea,
Colonel J. H. Boyd; besides which each of us had our
attendants, the queen having four, and each of the
others at least one attendant or valet.

CHAPTER XX

WASHINGTON — THE WHITE HOUSE — MOUNT VERNON

A few days after our arrival the Queen signified her wish to call on the President, so we all attended Her Majesty to the White House. President Cleveland and his beautiful young bride most cordially received and hospitably entertained us; and a more recent experience of my own would prove that neither one of them has ever forgotten that their position required them to be really the first lady and the first gentleman of the land.

At two o'clock in the afternoon of the same day our call was returned by Mrs. Cleveland, accompanied by the ladies of the cabinet. No person could have shown in her presence a fairer type of youth and loveliness than the wife of the President, and her manner was graceful and dignified in a rare degree for so young a lady. She impressed us with a conviction, since most abundantly justified, that she was well chosen for the duties and responsibilities of an exalted position. On the day following her call we were invited to dine at the executive mansion. The Queen occupied the seat of the guest of honor at the right of President Cleveland; the Secretary of State, Mr. Endicott, attended me to my seat on the President's left; the Hawaiian Minister, Hon. H. A. P. Carter, was assigned to a seat on Mrs. Cleveland's right; while General Dominis, my husband, waited upon Mrs. Endicott, and was at Mrs. Cleveland's left.   The remaining members of the Queen's party were disposed of in proper order, and the dinner passed off with cheerfulness and in due form; it was a grand affair, and arranged with the best of taste. The apartment where it was held had been decorated to do honor to the occasion.   The toilet of Her Majesty Queen Kapiolani was of white silk brocade of the choicest Japanese manufacture, artistically embroidered with heavy raised and richly worked designs; it was cut in Hawaiian fashion, a loosely flowing robe of a pattern or mode very becoming to our women, whether made of inexpensive calico or print, or of the finest of silks or most lustrous of satins.   A description of this dress was given by all the newspapers, and attracted so much attention that on our arrival abroad the Queen was requested to wear the dress at court, with which solicitation she was happy to comply.

Next to the courtesies extended by the President and the ladies of the executive, perhaps the consideration shown to us by dignitaries of the Masonic order most deserves my notice.   General Albert Pike, accompanied by thirteen members of the Supreme Council, thirty-third degree, Scottish Rite, called on the Queen and myself.   He was a person of most impressive appearance, a venerable gentleman with long flowing beard and silky white hair resting on his square shoulders, and with the kind, benevolent character and charming manners so appropriate to his official position as the head of

SCENERY ON THE ESTATE OF PRINCESS KAIULANI

THE FISH POND

the order of fraternity and charity. He greeted us with dignity and cordiality, and left with Queen Kapio-lani and myself written evidences of the consideration with which we were regarded by his order. These were certificates, of which mine is always carried with me, giving us the privilege of an appeal to the brethren of the fraternity in any part of the world wherever or whenever they could be of use to us. Both General Pike and the members of his staff were well acquainted with my husband, because General Dominis was of the same Masonic rank, and had maintained frequent cor-respondence with them on subjects of interest to the world-wide and useful society. While it has now been a joy to me to find my husband still remembered by the Masons of Washington, and to receive from them on my own part evidences of continued interest, I have sorrowed to find some places vacant in the number of those who greeted me so cordially ten years ago, notably that of General Pike.

Many other visitors and social attentions caused the time to fly past most agreeably ; several entertainments where the Queen and her party were the guests of honor having been arranged for by the Minister of Ha-waii to the United States, the Hon. Henry A. P. Carter. On one of these we were taken to the barracks, and in-vited to a careful inspection of the quarters for the officers and men. We were received with honors by the commanding officers and their wives, and taken all over the buildings, while the numberless comforts and conveniences of the establishment were exhibited and explained to us. After this an artillery drill was ordered for our special benefit, and we had the pleasure of seeing how expeditiously both men and horses could work the great and destructive field-pieces. After a few hours pleasantly spent in this manner, we returned to our hotel, intending to visit the great historic spot of the American Union on the day following.

So, at as early an hour as was convenient for Her Majesty to be ready, carriages were taken for the wharf, where a boat was awaiting us, placed at our disposal by the courtesy of the United States government. A number of prominent ladies and gentlemen were already on board to be our companions and entertainers, amongst whom I recall the names of Mr. John Sherman, then senator, now Secretary of State; Mr. Evarts, the celebrated lawyer; and many senators, whose names I do not now recall, with their wives. When we were all on board, the lines were cast off, and the little steamer started on her way down the river. It was in the beautiful month of May. The trees were out with their fresh green leaves, the early flowering shrubs were in blossom, and the banks at the riverside were lined with verdure.

The different points of interest, forts, monuments, and public buildings, were pointed out to us, and places we had often heard mentioned identified as we passed along. Near to the grounds, however, the band which had accompanied us, discoursing the sweetest of music, changed to more solemn cadences; and, as the edifices which mark the sacred spot came in sight, the American flag was lowered, the steamer's bell was tolled, the gentlemen removed their hats, and the air of the " Star

Spangled Banner" was rendered with impressive effect.
The steamer then came to a standstill, and boats were
lowered.   Into the first the Queen entered; and the
whole party disembarked, occupying in all five boats in
their transportation ashore.   There was but one vehicle
at the boat-landing, into which those of us who wished
to ride entered, and the party was conveyed to the
mansion house.

On arriving we were requested to register our names
in the book kept for that purpose in the great central
hall; from there we were conducted to the banquet-
hall, passing through a smaller room where there was a
little, old-fashioned square piano, said to have been the
property of General Washington.

The rooms which had been used by General Washington, General Lafayette, and by Martha Washington
were opened to us; and we were permitted to enter,
and, further, to pause in the lady's bedroom to listen
to the story of her constancy to the memory of her husband, whose grave she watched, as she sat daily at her
window, from the day of his interment to that of her
own death.   This story, with the scene of its happen-
ing around me as I listened, was most touching to my
heart; the simple four-posted, old-fashioned bedstead,
with its chintz curtains, the arm-chair with valance
and chintz-covering, the well-worn steps descending to
a lower floor, — these homely souvenirs all spoke to
me of the sister woman who had sat and reflected over
the loss of that heroic life which it was her privilege
to share, and rendered the visit almost too sadly interesting for the accompaniment of a pleasure tour.   Why

is it, by the way, that she is now "Martha Washington," when even in that day she was always mentioned as "Lady Washington"? Is it a part of the etiquette of the new woman's era, or of the advancing democratic idea?

Another change I noticed in a recent visit was that bars are now placed at the doorways where then we were allowed to enter with perfect liberty to examine everything in the rooms. As time has passed, and the means of visiting the sacred shrine have become more available to the many, it has been found necessary to exclude the crowds that go to Mount Vernon; for the relic-hunter shows no respect to that which is the common property and the priceless heirloom of the people of the United States. So the ladies of the association having the care of this estate are obliged to protect the antique furniture and ancient ornaments from too close inspection.

After spending many interesting moments in the examination of the house and its contents, we went out upon the lawn, and had our photographs taken in a group, Mr. Sherman being the Queen's escort, and Mr. Evarts performing a like gallant duty for me. The next point of interest was the tomb where lie the mortal remains of that great man who assisted at the birth of the nation which has grown to be so great. Although it is but an humble resting-place for one so honored in the remembrance of mankind, yet the sight of the sarcophagus of the general and his wife as they lay side by side, the fresh, warm sunlight streaming through the iron bars which formed the gateway or entrance to the tomb, made a great impression on me; and although the Queen's party were silent, and exchanged no comments, it seemed to me that we were one in our veneration of the sacred spot and of the first President of his country. After this lull in the conversation, the party turned as if by common consent to retrace their steps toward the river, where our boats awaited us.   The wild-flowers were blooming beside our footsteps, the birds were chirping in the budding trees, or chasing each other through the branches.   Mount Vernon was at its loveliest.   There was more of the real face of nature there then than is found to-day, for now the wild flowers are notably absent.   We returned to the city with the consciousness of taking with us the pleasantest of memories of our excursion, and a renewed appreciation of the hospitality of the nation whose capital city we were visiting.

CHAPTER XXI

BOSTON AND NEW YORK — EN ROUTE FOR ENGLAND

LEAVING Washington, we next visited the city of Boston, where on arrival we found that apartments had been engaged for us at the Parker House. We considered these the pleasantest rooms we had seen, and enjoyed excessively the liberality and good taste with which the city council had arranged for our comfort and pleasure. A committee from that body waited upon us, and did everything possible to make our visit a success. Receptions were given to us by His Excellency Governor Ames, and by His Honor Mayor O'Brien, to which cards of invitation were sent to well-known and prominent citizens. But besides these there was a general reception held at the Mechanics' Pavilion, an audience chamber capable of holding some twelve thousand persons; and it seemed as though everybody came, for it was packed with dense masses of people of either sex, to its farthest corner. We shook hands with multitudes. They seemed to enjoy it; and I know we took its fatigues most good-naturedly, as a delightful experience of democratic good-will.

Many pleasant excursions were arranged for our party while in Boston; amongst these was one to the Waltham Watch Factory, in which we were very much interested. To see each part of so delicate a piece of mechanism as a watch made from its very beginning until the perfect timepiece was ready for the wearer, afforded us much pleasure, and gave a new enjoyment to the possession of these indispensable articles.

We were shown the harbor or port of Boston, by means of a trip to Deer Island, and made visits to the city institutions for the care of criminals and paupers, and to other localities of interest. A small steamer was provided for our party and the invited guests of the city ; refreshments were served on board, and everything was done to make the afternoon pleasant for us. Queen Kapiolani was much interested in the quarters assigned to the women at Deer Island, and went through them with careful inspection. There was one inmate with whom the Queen spoke most kindly ; she was a woman said to be over a hundred years old, and was yet in the possession of her faculties.

Mr. and Mrs. Benjamin Keola Pitman, formerly residents of the Hawaiian Islands, accompanied us that day. From Mr. Benjamin Pitman, Sr., we had already received a visit at the Parker House. Which sudden reversion to personal friends leads me naturally to say, that, apart from the hospitalities received from the city of Boston, a day was reserved in which we received the relatives of my husband in a family gathering. At the hour appointed we descended to the reception room, and I found myself indeed amongst friends. There were the Lees, the Snellings, the Joneses, the Jacobses, the Emersons, and others whose names I cannot at this moment recall. I also remember one most welcome guest, not of our own family, Mr. George W. Armstrong.

There were a hundred or more, old and young, relatives of whom General Dominis had often spoken to me, and even some whom he himself now met for the first time, but all cordially happy to recognize their relations from those distant Sandwich Islands of which they had so often heard.   There were kisses, affectionate embraces, and many other expressions of regard, which made me feel that I was at home with my own family rather than with strangers in a foreign land. The day passed speedily and pleasantly away.

But the time arrived when we must bid adieu to our hospitable entertainers, and depart for the city of New York.   In New York we remained eleven days before sailing for England; but I was ill during this time, apparently from a severe cold, and obliged to rest quietly in my rooms at the hotel.   During my illness Mrs. James B. Williams was very attentive to me, often calling to see me, accompanied by her husband and daughter. She even sent her own family physician.   The Queen and the rest of the party improved the time in the great metropolis, seeing as much as possible of all there was to be seen, and receiving many attentions from prominent individuals.   Admiral Gherardi's ship was lying in port, to which Queen Kapiolani and her party made a visit, being received by the gallant sailor with all the honors due to her rank and station.   She was also much interested in her visit to the Metropolitan Museum, the mummies exciting her curiosity and wonder, as speaking of the people of a remote antiquity.

My interest was also aroused, and in spite of illness I accompanied the party. I recall a queer little mummy, centuries old, of whose history we learned some most peculiar details. After yards and yards of linen cloth had been unrolled, there was exhibited to us a prettily formed little hand; it was very lifelike, dark-colored, but appearing as that of a person who had but recently died; we were told that the mummy was of a woman, and that the writings with it signified she had been the mother of three children. It was very wonderful how perfectly everything had been preserved by the embalmer's art, even the cloth in which the form had been wrapped being in a perfect state of preservation. But the naturalness of the hand made the curiosity almost too startling for enjoyment, and I turned away from the sight because it spoke too plainly of death and burial.

We met many pleasant people in the city of New York, yet it is natural that I should recall best those of whose history I knew something in my own country. We visited Mrs. Kaikilani Graham, a lady of Hawaiian birth, who had married a resident of this city. She and her husband received us very cordially in a convenient little suite of rooms, or "flat," just cosey enough for the newly wedded pair. She took great pride in showing to us their child, a pretty baby; and she was happy in the fact that it was born on American soil.

But our eleven days' visit was drawing to a close, and the steamer by which we were to embark for our destination was ready for our reception. This was the City of Rome, the largest steamship I had ever seen, and

at that time about the largest afloat in the world. As
we stood on the deck to bid farewell to the land, it was
very amusing to me to see the four little steamers ply-
ing about our slowly moving hull, pushing the bow this
way and that, so that our course might be directed towards the broad ocean; finally it would appear that their
purpose was accomplished, and drawing away from us,
they allowed the huge ship to make her own way down
the harbor and off to sea.

She was crowded with passengers, at least a thousand souls being on board, all sorts and conditions of
men and women. There were a large number of musical people — well-known singers or musicians — going
abroad for study, or leaving for their homes after profes-
sional engagements in America; the usual number of
health seekers; those tourists who may be found everywhere intent on seeing the world; then a few like ourselves, to whom the Queen's Jubilee was the grand
attraction abroad. A strange mixture of humanity, and
just at the place where one has little to occupy the mind
save to study those by whom one is surrounded. It was
interesting to see the different methods by which each
person sought to pass away the time; to me it was natural to turn to music, my usual solace in either happy
or sad moments, so I composed songs, one of which certainly was written in anticipation of meeting in the person of the good queen all that was greatest and noblest
in a woman or a sovereign. These hopes were fully
realized during our stay in London.

Many of the passengers had recourse to the ship's
library, which was well supplied with books from the

best authors; and with these they beguiled the time
away reading, while reclining in their steamer chairs
on the decks.   Some with less of literary taste played
games; while there were also the languid or lazy, who
did nothing but lounge about the decks and wish the
time away.   By the kindness of the musical part of our
company, some two or three concerts were given in the
main saloon of our great ship, and were well attended.
Through them quite a sum was raised for sundry charitable objects.   Although the names of the performers
have passed from my memory, yet I remember that it
was asserted at the time that these voices, of which
they made a gift to the cause and a pleasure to us, were
of great value in the musical or operatic world.

There was one purpose for which an entertainment
was given which was peculiar to this ship and this voyage.   It was for the benefit of a shipwrecked crew we
had on board.   Just outside of the port of New York
there had been a frightful collision, and the City of
Rome had been fortunate enough to rescue a goodly
number of those who otherwise might have found a
watery grave.   Their condition, however, was pitiable;
for they had saved nothing of their effects, and in the
confusion of the wreck had lost husbands, wives, or travelling companions.   After their rescue some were lying
in pain and suffering on board our ship, uncertain what
had become of those dear to them.   Their desolate condition appealed to all hearts, and we were only too glad
to attend the concert and contribute our share to their
relief.   Then there was the regular concert which is held
aboard all the steamships which ply the Atlantic route,

that for the British sailors, whose widows and orphans look to the multitude of tourists for funds to aid them in the hour of need.

There was but one hinderance to our enjoyment of the passage across, and this was not to be avoided. For a few days the weather was thick and misty, so that the dismal sound of the great fog-horn of the City of Rome never ceased by day or night. But, after all, the delights and troubles of the trip were soon over. In about five days we were told to prepare to see the coast of Ireland; in another twenty-four hours we had landed the mails at Queenstown, and were on our way from thence to our port of destination, Liverpool.

CHAPTER XXII

ARRIVAL — LIVERPOOL — SOME ENGLISH TOWNS

OUR earliest greeting came from Col. George W. Macfarlane, who sent off two magnificent bouquets, one for Queen Kapiolani and one for myself. These were received in the stream, because our steamer was of such immense size that she did not proceed immediately to the dock, but lay off a distance of about five miles. But while we were at lunch a small steamer was seen approaching our vessel; and as we were told that this was intended to transfer us to the shore, we at once made preparations to leave the City of Rome. But there was to be quite a state reception before we were permitted by our friends to land. For by the "tender," or steam-tug, there came many passengers to greet us, and these had been conducted to the grand saloon. It was the intention of Queen Kapiolani to go there in order to bid the captain of the ship farewell, but on our arrival we were met by quite a company. Amongst these were the Hon. Theodore H. Davies, the British Consul to Hawaii ; Mr. R. H. Armstrong, the Hawaiian Consul at London ; Rt. Rev. Bishop Staley, formerly Anglican Bishop of Honolulu ; Mr. Janion of the mercantile house of Janion, Greene, & Co., long in mercantile relations with the Hawaiian Islands. These all bent

the knee, kissed the hand of the queen, and saluted
the rest of us with proper form; after which the conversation became general, and some most pleasant moments
passed in cordial greetings with these our friends.   Finally we were transferred to the little steamer, and
started towards the shore.   On our way we were much
interested in the great stone piers, the walls, the fortifi-
cations, — all of which were pointed out and explained
by those who welcomed us.   On passing the forts we
were told that the salutes to the royal party had been
fired, as was ordered the moment it was telegraphed
that we were safely across the great oceans of the Pacific and Atlantic.

A half-hour's sail brought us to the pier selected
for our landing.   The little steamer was made fast, and
we prepared to disembark.   Looking up the wharves
all along the piers, just as far as the eye could reach,
on the right or on the left, could be seen thousands of
heads ; the populace generally had heard of the expected landing of Her Majesty the Queen of the far-
off Sandwich Islands, and there had been a grand rush
of the curious of the city to meet her and her suite.
As we landed from the steamer, directly on our left
was a military escort which consisted of about one hundred of the soldiers of Her Majesty Queen Victoria.
These had arrived from Southampton that very day,
and were specially detailed to do us honor.   They were
a splendid body of men ; and as we passed along in front
of them to our carriages, they presented arms and saluted the queen, while the band which was with them
played the well-known strains of the British national

anthem, "God Save the Queen." Then the party
moved up the dock, at the gateways of which, or entrance to the city, we were met by the lord mayor
of Liverpool, with his attendants. He was decorated
with the insignia of his office, and welcomed us to the
city of which he was the official head.

Here our party was increased by the addition of a
larger number of our friends, amongst whom I recol-
lect Mrs. Janion with two young nieces; Mr. John Macfie, son of Mr. R. A. Macfie; Mrs. R. H. Armstrong;
and also an official representative of Her Majesty
Queen Victoria, who was assigned to us during our
stay. This was Mr. R. T. Synge, a gentleman of the
Foreign Office, whom Lord Salisbury, then Premier of
England, had intrusted with the charge of our party.
I think our retinue consisted of five carriages with outriders on each side. Queen Kapiolani and I occupied
the coach in which was the lord mayor. My husband,
Colonel Iaukea, and Colonel Boyd had a carriage to
themselves, attended by one of the city officials. As
I looked through the windows I could not refrain from
remarking on the splendid appearance of the cavalry by
which we were escorted. The men were all tall, square-
shouldered, muscular looking fellows, of equal height
and similar appearance. The horses, too, were just as
carefully matched, being alike in color, a rich brown,
splendidly caparisoned, and with all their accoutrements
of the neatest and most carefully burnished materials.
They rode along proudly by our sides; but, although it
was scarcely the season for it, I remember noticing
that the steam came from the nostrils of the horses

as if it were cold weather. I was told that the peculiar
atmosphere of the city of Liverpool, damp to saturation,
made this phenomenon quite usual.

Arriving at the Northwestern Hotel, we were conducted from our carriages to the quarters which had
been reserved for us. After rest and dinner, the queen
and most of the party went to the theatre; but I had
not fully recovered from the severe cold taken in New
York, and did not consider it prudent to go out.

About eleven that night the queen's party returned
from the theatre, and the next morning there was an
elaborate breakfast given to us by the lord mayor; he
himself escorted the queen. Lord Derby was assigned
to me; he was a most agreeable gentleman. There
were many other persons of prominence present, and the
entertainment passed off very delightfully. Later we
were taken to an organ recital given for our enjoyment
by a gentleman who was said to be the best organist in
all England. On the day following we took a train, intending to go to Norwich to visit a country gentleman
by the name of Stewart. On our way we passed by
fields covered with the richest blossoms of yellow gold;
the display extended over acres and acres of fertile
lands, and was indeed lovely to the sight, even had there
not been an element of usefulness connected with it.
We were told that these were mustard fields, from
whence the seed is raised that is ground and used so
extensively on our tables the world over. We also
passed through pretty villages, their neat dwellings surrounding the parish church with its tall steeple; in fact,
we were charmed with our introduction to the country

life of a land of which we had always heard, Old England.

Finally, there was pointed out to us a picturesque castle which had been owned by some celebrated family somewhere about the sixteenth century. But the family to whom it had descended becoming extinct, or unable to maintain there a proper state, the estate had been purchased by Mr. Stewart, who was a man of great wealth, and it had been made a most attractive country-seat. The grounds were extensive, and taken care of with the utmost attention. The occupant had but one child, a son, heir to not less than a couple of millions on his attainment of majority, and the probable successor of his father to this great and beautiful estate. Prior to our arrival at the mansion, while we were at Ipswich, the mayor of the city came forth to welcome us; he was clothed with the robes of office, and was attended by others bearing the insignia of power. He gave us a most cordial greeting; and in his company we met our host, who, with his amiable wife and only son, did all that was possible to make us at home in his magnificent castle.

A dinner was arranged for that evening, and all the prominent people of the immediate vicinity were invited to be present to meet us. During the evening the mace of Queen Elizabeth was exhibited to us by the lady in whose charge and keeping it was; her name has escaped me for the moment, but she fully realized the importance of the trust. She told us that it had been handed down in her family from the time of Queen Elizabeth; that it had been delivered to her by her father, whose proud privilege it had been to have especial care of it, and that since he resigned the charge it had never been suffered to go out of her keeping. Others had aspired to its possession, amongst them members of the royal family itself; but she had maintained that, as it was originally delivered to her family, none had a better right than they to its care and custody. We were also conducted outside the house, or castle, and shown its beautiful and spacious grounds. Here the queen was requested to plant a tree. A silver spade with ebony handle was given to her, and she cheerfully complied with the request of our host. Near by there was one of the most perfect trees that could have been imagined; it was a beech with dark brown glossy leaves. It was celebrated far and near for its beauty, and was certainly one of the handsomest trees which it has ever fallen to my lot to behold.

Bidding our genial hosts adieu, we passed on to the next town, where we were handsomely entertained at another old castle to which the people of prominence in the neighborhood had been invited. Amongst these were the dean and his wife from the neighboring cathedral, and Mr. Colman, the celebrated manufacturer of mustard; he was also a member of parliament. The people of the district, hearing of our arrival, came in crowds to meet us, and were much interested in all that was going on. Amongst the guests at the Castle was an elderly lady who appeared to be particularly interested in the Anglican or Episcopal Church at Honolulu, and made special inquiries in regard to Mr. Gowan, one of the preachers there, who then was one of the youngest of our clergymen and quite a favorite, but who has since married and settled at Victoria, Vancouver's Island. The next place of interest visited was St. Peter's Church, the chimes of which were rung for our enjoyment. It was a new harmonic experience, and very delightful; although I noticed that the men who rang seemed to do it with the greatest effort, but in chiming one man is assigned to each bell-rope. The method of ringing the bells by playing upon keys, very much as one would produce the tones from a piano or organ, may be less fatiguing, but a more metallic sound is produced, and it is far less artistic and melodious to the lover of music.

After visiting many other points of interest, at all of which everything was done for our entertainment, we prepared for our departure to London, arriving there a few days prior to the 20th, the day of the celebration, which was also Monday. The whole city was in commotion in view of the coming great event, — the Jubilee of the sovereign. Rooms were assigned to us at the Alexandra, where there were many other members of the royal families of the distant world. Amongst these were Prince Komatzu of Japan; the Siamese Prince, brother of the King of Siam; the Prince of India; and the Prince of Persia. At other leading public houses were quartered the princes and princesses of the nations of Europe.

CHAPTER XXIII

SOVEREIGN OF ENGLAND AND INDIA

IMMEDIATELY after our arrival Queen Kapiolani sent messages of congratulations to Her Majesty Victoria, Queen of Great Britain and Empress of India; and arrangements were made for us to present our felicitations in person at Buckingham Palace on Monday at one o'clock in the afternoon. At twelve precisely of that day, Queen Victoria and her suite entered London, coming from Scotland where she had been residing for some time. The streets were thronged with people anxious to catch a glimpse of their beloved sovereign. Strange it seemed to me at the time to learn that many who had grown from youth to age in London during a whole lifetime had never seen their queen. Accompanied by her favorite daughter Beatrice and her husband, Prince Henry of Battenberg, the queen was driven to Buckingham Palace, preceded by a detachment of her celebrated Life Guards, outriders from the same regiment being detailed for each side of Her Majesty's carriage.

When the hour approached for us to go and meet her, an officer came from the palace; and Queen Kapiolani and I, attended by Colonel Iuakea and Mr. Synge, took our departure for the hall of the reception. We

HER MAJESTY QUEEN KAPIOLANI

were shown into a large room, where some of the princes had already arrived; and our first greeting came from the Premier, Lord Salisbury. He was then a fine-looking gentleman of imposing presence. He seemed to me to be some sixty-eight years of age, tall and large, with a slight stoop at the shoulders, but with fire and brilliancy in his eyes which spoke of an active mind. I could not help being impressed with the man, the scope of whose mind must command the vast widely spread problems of the government of the empire of Great Britain. Mr. Gladstone has been called "The Grand Old Man," yet this thought was strongly emphasized to me also in the presence of Lord Salisbury. He has always appeared to me to be the greater man of the two. If his rule has been less popular and more conservative, it has required no less devoted patriotism and lofty abilities. I attribute the present prosperity of the British Empire very largely to the consummate wisdom and stanch loyalty of Lord Salisbury.

While Lord Salisbury was entertaining with his conversation the royal guests, two ladies entered the room where we were, and courtesying to me, stood by my side a little in the rear of my chair. I hinted to them that the queen was sitting at my side; but they pleasantly acknowledged the information with a bow, and said that they were sent in to attend me, to which I responded with a salutation. While this was going on we saw a trifling occurrence, which, however, proved to us that human nature is about the same in the palace as in the cottage. Several of the ladies of the royal household passed through the hall, and stopped just long enough, as they went by the door, to get a peep at the strangers from over the sea. So it would appear that even royalty can forget strict etiquette under the impulse of feminine curiosity.

We were not kept waiting much longer; for Lord Lathom, accompanied by the Honorable Secretary Ponsonby, appeared, and led the way to the audience chamber. They carried their batons of office. Queen Kapiolani arose, greeted, and, with her suite, followed them. We were perhaps twenty-five feet apart as we entered the reception room, the queen attended by Colonel Iaukea, and I by the Hon. Mr. Synge, the two ladies-in-waiting following me. At the end of the hall there was an official whose business it was to open and shut the door of the audience chamber. As it was now open, he held his baton of office across it, but at the approach of Queen Kapiolani and Colonel Iaukea he removed it, and allowed them to pass in; then I entered alone, and our party stood in the presence of the British Queen.

The room was of very moderate size, with a sofa at one end on which Her Majesty sat; besides this there were only two chairs, all the other furniture, if ever there were any, having been removed. At a farther window stood H. R. H. the Duke of Connaught and T. R. H. the Prince and Princess Henry of Battenberg. Her Majesty Victoria greeted her sister sovereign, Kapiolani, with a kiss on each cheek, and then, turning to me, she kissed me once on the forehead; we were asked to be seated, the two queens sitting together on the sofa and engaging in conversation, which was translated by

Colonel Iaukea.   In the mean time I occupied one of
the chairs.   Queen Kapiolani expressed her congratulations on the great event of the day, and her gladness
that the Jubilee found Her Majesty in good health, and
added her expressions of hope that she might live many
years to be a blessing to her subjects.   The Queen received her good wishes with a like spirit of cordiality,
thanking her for coming so far to see her, and then
went on to speak with enthusiasm of the pleasure she
had taken in meeting her husband, my brother, King
Kalakaua.   She said she had been much pleased with
him, and had never forgotten his agreeable visit.   In
the mean time the Duke of Connaught was at my side,
and we exchanged a few pleasant words.   Next came
the Princess Beatrice, who, after an expression of kindly
interest, returned to her former station.   Queen Victoria then entered into a little conversation with me,
confining her remarks chiefly to educational matters,
and asked me with some detail about the schools of the
Hawaiian Islands.   We then rose to make our adieus.

The two queens exchanged kisses as before, and the
Queen of England again kissed me on the forehead; then
she took my hand, as though she had just thought of
something which she had been in danger of forgetting,
and said, "I want to introduce to you my children;" and
one by one they came forward and were introduced.
After this I hesitated a moment to see if she had anything further to say to me, and finding that she had
not, I courtesied to her and withdrew.   By the time I
had reached the door of the audience chamber, Queen
Kapiolani had arrived at the farther end of the hall,

and thinking I was alone, I hastened my steps to rejoin her; but soon I was conscious of the presence of the ladies-in-waiting by hearing the whispered words, "Their Majesties." On looking about me I saw at the door to my left two very fine-looking gentlemen standing side by side in the doorway, one in a gray suit and the other in black, both carrying canes. They acknowledged my presence by a most gallant salutation, as I slightly bowed to them in passing; then they resumed the subject of their conversation. These were His Majesty the King of Denmark, and His Imperial Highness the Crown Prince, father of the present Emperor of Germany. On finding myself again with my sister-in-law, we prepared to enter our carriage and return to our hotel. Thus terminated my first interview with one of the best of women and greatest of monarchs.

CHAPTER XXIV

THE RECEPTION AT THE FOREIGN OFFICE

THAT evening an entertainment was given at the Foreign Office at which we were expected to be present. I expressed a wish on leaving the hotel to go in a carriage with my husband, which naturally placed the duty of escort to Queen Kapiolani on Colonel Iaukea and Hon. Mr. Synge. According to etiquette, by taking this step I was obliged to ride in one of the carriages belonging to the legation of Hawaii; and, as only the royal carriages could go to the principal entrance, the carriage in which I was would be obliged to present itself at the side entrance. But when we got there, and Colonel Boyd, our attendant, was asked whose carriage it was, he replied, "It is the carriage of the Crown Princess of Hawaii." Then the officer said that we had made a mistake by coming to that entrance. However, we passed in, and I was conducted to the waiting-room which had been assigned to the royal ladies for their exclusive use, while my husband and Colonel Boyd were taken to the room assigned to the use of the generals.

In the room I entered, what was my surprise to see my sister-in-law, Queen Kapiolani, standing almost alone and unattended, as though she were at a loss what to do next. Near me was a fine lady, a Grand Duchess from

one of the small German principalities. She had entered the room about the same moment with me; and
comprehending the situation at once, and knowing that
I spoke English, while the queen did not, she turned
to me and said, "Why does not the queen sit down, so
that we may all be seated?"   Upon receiving from
me a hint in our native language, the queen complied
with this wish, and we were all soon at our ease.   Then
there entered several gentlemen of royal blood, — the
King of Hanover, and princes and princesses of European countries, — and we adjourned to the grand reception room.   We were ushered into a large hall, well
filled with ladies of rank, and all of them most magnifi-
cently dressed to do honor to the occasion.

It would seem that each of these had brought out
the family heirlooms in precious stones.   There were
duchesses with shining tiaras, marchionesses with coro-
nets of flashing stones, noble ladies with costly necklaces or emerald ear-drops, little women who seemed
almost bowed down under lofty circlets of diamonds over
their brows, tall women bearing proudly off their adorn-
ment of stones of priceless value.   I have never seen
such a grand display of valuable gems in my life.
There was such a profusion of brilliant and handsome
jewels before my eyes, that to compute its worth would
be to lose one's self in a maze of confusing calcula-
tion.   Yet there was amidst the shining throng one
young lady, tall and of commanding presence, whose
sole ornament was a single glittering star fixed in her
hair.   It shone forth more brightly, attracted my gaze
more quickly, and its elegant simplicity excited my

admiration above all others. She was a lady of high rank, and it is a matter of regret to me that I did not learn her name.

While conversing with some of the duchesses who advanced to speak with me, Lord Salisbury made his appearance; and approaching Queen Kapiolani, offered her his arm, leading the way to the centre of the room, my husband and I following. Very soon we were joined by H. R. H. the Duke of Connaught, with Lady Salisbury. As this couple came up I waited a moment with my husband that they might pass in front of us; but the prince motioned to me to assume the precedence, and seeing him pause for us, we passed on, while he and his fair companion followed in our wake. Passing thus through the crowds, who made way as we approached, we were conducted to a side room, where refreshments were served. Here Lord Salisbury placed the queen on his right, and I was notified to be seated on his left, my husband standing behind my chair. The Duke of Connaught addressed him, and asked him to be seated, using as the form of salutation the title of governor. At first Governor Dominis declined, but on being urged by the prince, complied with his polite invitation. This is worthy of mention, because on this occasion the position of honor in the very centre of the room was assigned to our party. On the left of my husband was Lady Salisbury, and by her side the Duke of Connaught; then the Maharajah, Prince of Indore; and so on. The moments sped by very agreeably in general conversation; but as the Duke of Connaught glanced across the apartment, his eye caught sight of

Lady Aylesbury, who was at one of the more remote
tables. The prince very politely arose, went across the
room, and greeted her most gallantly, informing us as
he did so, that she was the only one of the ladies of
rank now living who had been present at the coronation of his royal mother, whose Jubilee we were then
celebrating. She was an elderly lady, with little curls
each side of her brow; and this act of courtesy and
gallantry to her impressed me as one of the prettiest
and pleasantest things seen that evening. From her
cordiality to the prince, I doubt not that it was highly
appreciated by Lady Aylesbury. After we rose from
the tables, we mingled in social conversation with the
guests of the evening for a few minutes, and then retiring from the rooms returned to the hotel.

CHAPTER XXV

THE JUBILEE — AT THE ABBEY — AT THE PALACE

On the following, or great day of the Jubilee, we were to be present in the morning at the historic church of Westminster Abbey; and the hour of half-past ten had been appointed for General Dominis and Colonel Boyd to take their positions there.   Our party, consisting of the members of royal families, left at eleven o'clock, the procession being led by the Japanese Prince; then followed the Prince of Persia, the Prince of Siam, and then the Indian Prince.

Succeeding these came the Queen of the Hawaiian Islands with myself, and to us was accorded the most unusual honor of an escort drawn from the Life Guards of Her Majesty Queen Victoria.   This was scarcely expected, but we were told that it had been especially granted to the Queen and Crown Princess of Hawaii. When we spoke of the high appreciation we felt of this and all the attentions we had received, we were assured in response, that, as we had come such a long distance to do honor to the occasion, Her Majesty had thought that the least she could do was to provide for us special honors.   We were given one of the queen's own carriages, with horses and drivers, during our stay in London. Our drive to Westminster Abbey was a short one. We passed through crowds and crowds of people, both sides of the street being thronged, but there was perfect order; besides which, the Life Guardsmen were on each side of our carriages. Detachments from the British navy, and members of the metropolitan police, were stationed at every point. But it was a happy, good-natured crowd (eleven millions, so I heard it estimated), assembled in the great city of London to congratulate the sovereign on her semi-centennial anniversary. As we passed from the Alexandra to the beautiful Abbey, cheering could be heard on every side; the fronts of the houses were a living mass of humanity. Benches were placed along their fronts, on which the people stood or sat, and every party that passed received enthusiastic salutations.

On reaching the doors of the Abbey, our party was met by Lord Lathom and Sir Henry Ponsonby, as representatives of Queen Victoria; and by them we were conducted to the seats reserved for our use. Colonel Iaukea and Hon. Mr. Synge disappeared at once as though swallowed up in the vast crowd which had been gathering in the place since the early hours of the morning. As the people arrived, they were arranged by the ushers in charge according to their rank. As delegation after delegation came in, each was quietly and properly assigned to its appropriate station.

In the centre of the great edifice, there was a raised platform, or dais, to which we were conducted. Soon after us a most prominent party arrived, and were also seated on the dais. We found them to be the kings, queens, princes, and princesses from several of the Eu-

ropean countries. There was a little lady who made
her appearance accompanied by her husband, who was
blind; she seated him on a bench back of that we occupied; then she proceeded to adjust his necktie, she
pulled down his coat and smoothed it out, and arranged
other parts of his uniform to suit her own taste. Finally, when his appearance seemed to her satisfactory,
she left him, and coming towards us took a seat directly
between Queen Kapiolani and myself. This lady was
none other than the Grand Duchess of Mecklenburg-
Strelitz, whose royal cousin, Queen Victoria, was celebrating the Jubilee of the day. On the left of my sister-in-law sat the Queen of the Belgians.

While we were awaiting the opening ceremonies, the
grand duchess turned to me and said, "*Parlez vous
Français?*" Upon my response in the negative, she addressed to me a similar question, only this time asking
if I spoke English; to which I replied, "Yes, a little."
Then, much to my amusement, she motioned to the princesses opposite to us that her companion understood
English, and we were very soon in a most agreeable
and animated conversation on the topics of the day.
Soon the band began the grand and solemn strains of
"God Save the Queen," and all but a few arose under
the impression that it announced the entrance of Her
Majesty Queen Victoria. The little duchess inquired of
me why I was rising, and without awaiting a reply volunteered the information, that the anthem was probably
in honor of the arrival of some members of the royal
family. And this proved to be the fact; for almost
immediately there appeared a company of ladies, these

being the daughters, granddaughters, and daughters-in-law of Queen Victoria. They advanced, and took their seats on the left side of the dais.

Their entrance was followed by another blast from the bugles and a further measure of the national anthem, to which there responded a company of the sons and grandsons of the reigning sovereign, led by His Royal Highness the Prince of Wales. These took their seats on the right of the dais, and thus we were surrounded by the royal household. After all was tranquil, there followed a final flourish of the trumpets; and for the third time the band gave us "God Save the Queen," and at this salutation there appeared Her Majesty Queen Victoria, preceded by the Archbishop of Canterbury and four other bishops. Slowly they proceeded to the stations which had been reserved for them, in the centre of the great church at the end farthest from the people, but quite near to where I sat, so that I could watch them to my perfect satisfaction.

Queen Victoria ascended the dais, and advanced to her seat at its very centre, where there was a plain-looking, old-fashioned armchair, said to have once belonged to St. Peter himself. She stood at a spot just opposite to this seat. All the rest of us had risen, and remained standing during her approach. Before seating herself, she made a little courtesy, which salutation was returned by all those who had awaited her coming from the opposite dais or platform. She was simply attired in a neat, black dress, wearing a bonnet very small and unobtrusive, while about her neck she wore a handsome necklace composed of single stone diamonds.

After she was in her seat, and the rest of us had followed her example, the religious services were begun, and most impressive they seemed.

The Archbishop of Canterbury opened the ceremony with prayer. Then followed the *Te Deum;* and the music must have had an especial charm of tender regret for the queen, for it was the composition of the Prince Consort, her deceased husband. Thus the grand pageant of religious worship proceeded; and while uprose the prayers of the vast assembly, invoking the blessing of the Almighty upon the head of the great British Empire, a gleam of God's sunshine penetrated through one of the windows, and finding its way from the casement across the grand temple, illuminated with its radiance the bowed head of the royal worshipper. It was a beautiful emblem of divine favor, and reminded me of the coincidence of which mention has been made that occurred at the moment of the coronation of my brother in Hawaii.

The inspiring anthems, as they were so grandly and harmoniously rendered by the great choir, lifted all hearts up to the Ruler of the Universe, and the solemn tones of the great organ hushed every thought inconsistent with the devout worship of the occasion. When this part of the ceremony came to a close, Her Gracious Majesty received the homage of her daughters and granddaughters, tenderly kissing each one in turn. They responded by a respectful kiss on the royal hand. The sons and grandsons next went through a similar manifestation of affection and respect, after which the procession began to form for leaving the Abbey. Its order in departing was exactly the reverse of that at the entrance, those preceding who had been last to arrive; finally, the last of the lords and ladies, dukes and duchesses, princes and princesses, kings and queens, were out of doors and on the way back to Buckingham Palace. The crowds had never left the streets and sidewalks, but had remained in position so as to get another view as we passed along.   The sea of heads on both sides of the royal party had not diminished perceptibly by so much as one individual, the gay decorations were all in place, and flags and streamers floated from every point. Never could there have been a day when London was more lavish of its holiday attire.

When we arrived at Buckingham Palace, I was waited on by the Duke of Edinburgh, whilst Queen Kapiolani was under the escort of the heir to the British throne, the Prince of Wales.   In the banquet hall was a long table through the centre, which took up the entire length of the room; this was assigned exclusively to the visiting kings and queens from every part of the world, many of whom had travelled long distances to be present at this Jubilee.   Two smaller tables were attached at each end of the long one, and these were set apart for the princes and princesses who were also the guests of the nation.   To one of these tables, and towards its centre, my escort, H. R. H. Prince Alfred, Duke of Edinburgh, and now of Saxe-Coburg, conducted me, and gave me a seat; on my right was the present Emperor of Germany, who proved to be a most sociable neighbor, and an agreeable conversationalist, so that we kept up quite an animated flow of words.   Truthfully speaking, I think the Duke of Edinburgh was not quite easy in his mind. He was the Lord High Admiral, and was naturally thinking of the long line of officers and men which had been drawn up to do honor to the royal visitors, and who could only be relieved from guard duty by his order. He excused himself to us a few minutes, probably to give some preliminary command to this effect, but soon returned, and still appeared as though he were anxious that the lunch and its ceremonies should be over. I suppose it was the natural uneasiness of the sailor, and a sense of the responsibility he felt for the comfort, and release from duty, of those under his authority.

During the course of the lunch, Prince William of Prussia asked me if I recognized a gentleman sitting opposite to us. I responded that I thought I did, and went on to say, that, to my remembrance it was Prince Henry of Prussia. He said that I was correct, and complimented me warmly on my strength of memory. This was the same prince who had once visited our Islands many years before this date, and whose delightful visit was unexpectedly shortened by the death of his brother Waldemar.

The naval forces were drawn up in a line a short distance from the palace, and as soon as possible after the repast they received the thanks of their royal commander; the officers and the men were assured of the queen's appreciation of their loyalty and devotion, and then all were permitted to retire, each body to its own vessel. I am confident that not a man there was more relieved at the change than the sailor-prince himself,

who then became more animated, and more like the
duke of whom I had such delightful reminiscences when
he visited me in Hawaii, — as I have said in a previous
chapter of these memoirs.

From the banquet hall Her Majesty, followed by her
royal guests, adjourned to a larger room in the palace,
commanding a fine view of the streets and squares
about us.   Here from the windows we watched the
marines and the naval forces as they filed past on their
way back to the ships from whence they had come.
They were a superb body of men, of whom their royal
commander, and indeed all England, might well be
proud.

After they had marched away, we were shown into a
side room where were displayed the presents which had
been sent to the queen in recognition of this her jubilee
year.   They were too many and too varied for me to attempt anything like an enumeration; yet there were one
or two pieces which I will mention.   Hawaii had sent a
unique frame placed on an easel, in the centre of which
was an embroidered piece, with the letters " V. R."
worked in the rare royal feathers, while the frame itself
was studded with diamonds.   Then there was a very
perfect representation of St. George and the Dragon in
the traditional form, but wrought of gold.   This had
been presented by the Crown Prince of Prussia, husband
of the Princess Royal of England, the daughter of
Queen Victoria, who was soon after this epoch left a
widow by her husband's untimely death.   At present
she is the Dowager Empress of Germany.   I now learn
that her afflictions have been increased by a loss sus-

tained in the recent conflagration at the Paris charitable bazaar, a calamity which put more than one household in Europe of royal connections into deepest mourning. After spending some time with us in the examination of her presents, Her Majesty Victoria retired. This was the signal for us to do likewise, so one by one we withdrew to our respective hotels.

As we drove homeward, and passed over the route by which we had come, scarcely a man or woman of all that vast crowd which had congregated there so recently was to be seen; the avenues of travel seemed to have been deserted. Yet the throng had dispersed in so orderly a manner that there had been no confusion, and no accidents were ever reported to mar the joy of the Jubilee.

CHAPTER XXVI

THE PRINCE OF WALES, "GRAND MASTER" MASON

WE were all too much fatigued to think of going out again that evening. Entertainment after entertainment followed in an endless variety, and on too grand a scale to think of enumerating them all, or even of mentioning the many ways in which the royal family of England showed its hospitality towards us. Amongst those who attended me personally, besides the Duke of Edinburgh, I must not forget to notice attentions from Prince Louis of Battenberg and the Grand Duke Sergius of Russia. One evening, after a grand reception, a ball was given at the palace, to which all royalty went to pay their respects to the first gentleman of England, the Prince of Wales, and his amiable wife.

Queen Kapiolani and I were conducted to seats on the dais, where the Princess of Wales, Princess Louise of Lorne, and other members of Her Majesty's household, were seated. It was an excellent point from which to see the dancing, which soon began. While watching the dance, I happened to glance down to the farther end of the hall, and saw the Marquis of Lorne bend his arm cordially about that of my husband, Governor Dominis, and pace to and fro with him about the hall, the two gentlemen seemingly much interested in each other as they engaged in prolonged and pleasant conversation. The entertainment went gayly on until a late hour, and as usual the first movement to retire was made on the part of the royal family; after which the guests began to take leave of each other, and we returned to our hotel.

There was one day set apart during the Jubilee for a Masonic Celebration; and from the grand crowd of visitors assembled in London to do honor to the occasion, invitations were sent to all members of that fraternity. The response was general, and at eleven o'clock of the day appointed the visiting brethren met at Prince Albert Hall. The arrangements were carried to such perfection that each person was conducted without the least confusion to a seat which had been assigned to him. My husband, Governor Dominis, wearing the regalia to which his rank as a Mason of the thirty-third degree entitled him, upon reaching the entrance indicated by the terms of the invitation he had received, found an usher in attendance to escort him to his place. After exchanging the signs and tokens of mutual recognition, he passed into the hall, and his guide conducted him through the vast assembly of the brotherhood. He had not the least idea as to what part of the chamber he was assigned, but followed in the footsteps of the gentleman in whose care he had been intrusted.

Soon they passed in front of the dais, or raised platform, commanding a view of the whole audience. On this was seated the Grand Master of the assembled representatives of the Freemasonry of the world, none

other than H. R. H., the Prince Royal, Albert Edward
of Wales. As Governor Dominis passed in front of
the Grand Master, still ignorant of his own position,
Masonic salutations were exchanged; and much to his
surprise my husband found himself conducted up to
the platform, where on the right of the Prince of
Wales the third seat had been assigned to him. His
astonishment was succeeded by emotions of pride.
Governor Dominis was always a most unassuming man;
not at all eager to put himself forward, never presum-
ing in the least to encroach on the rights or privileges
of others. But when he found himself thus placed in
one of the highest and most honorable of positions, it
was undoubtedly enough to make his bosom glow. But
he valued the honor as a Mason more than as a man;
for it was the recognition of his place in an organization
whose bond of union was that of brotherly love, and
whose ancient and noble rites these high-born or royally connected persons from every part of the globe had
assembled to celebrate.

In that great assembly over which the royal prince
presided, and into whose upturned faces my husband
had the joy of looking, were more than ten thousand
men of the different degrees of the order. Prayer was
offered by one of the grand chaplains; and the princely
Grand Master then rose and initiated the ceremonies
by giving out the national anthem, "God Save the
Queen," which was sung by all present with an ardor
and fervor seldom excelled. United in their bond of
affection and brotherly kindness, their hearts were also
filled with the spirit of the Jubilee which had allowed

them to meet in this grand assembly. It was an occasion to fill all present with a sense of its grandeur and importance; and when my husband returned to me his feelings and sentiments were too profound for expression, too lasting to allow him ever to forget. The usual forms and ceremonies of a Masonic gathering, known and understood only by those of the fraternity itself, had been, I was told, most impressively rendered, and gave great satisfaction to all.

My husband was always a most conscientious Mason, and fulfilled to the letter his duties as a friend and a brother to his order. Many a charitable deed towards the poor of the fraternity was done by him of which no one ever spoke, because no one knew anything about them at the time. Large sums of money have been contributed by him for the purpose of extricating brethren of the Masonic order from financial or other difficulties. These amounts were rarely returned to him; perhaps he had not expected that they would be paid. At any rate, nothing was said of them; but when his papers fell into my hands for examination at his death, they were disclosed to me, and I recognized what a great amount of good had been done, and what a true and faithful Free Mason Governor Dominis had been his life long. At this time the parties he had assisted had left Hawaii, and possibly had retained no thought of him or their obligation; yet a good action is never lost, and his many and beautiful deeds of generosity are precious to my remembrance, and remain a source of consolation to me to this day.

CHAPTER XXVII

ENGLAND'S HOMES AND HOSPITALITY

On one of the days when we were free of other engagements, the party of Queen Kapiolani took carriages, and drove out to the residence of Lady Aberdeen, where Mr. Gladstone was staying for a few days. We were received most cordially by himself and his good wife out under the trees on the ground. The weather was favorable, it was a lovely afternoon for social pleasure, and everything was done to make us feel at home in the society of the " Grand Old Man." As I remember his appearance, he was a tall, large-framed man, with broad, high forehead, dark, piercing eyes, and a nose which was the most prominent feature of a striking and intellectual face, — certainly a countenance and a presence, once seen, not easily to be forgotten. When he spoke, there was serious thoughtfulness in his remarks, and words of world-wide significance seemed as ready with him as those of common import are with any other. There were a number of visitors claiming the honor of an interview; he listened patiently to any one's questions, but directed his replies to all those by whom he was surrounded. Mrs. Gladstone was a tall, stylish woman of rather advanced years, of dignified mien and intelligent countenance; she stood by her husband's side during most of the time while he was conversing with his visitors, and from her attentive manner one could not but receive the thought that in the eventful life of the great statesman she must have been a valuable counsellor and a sympathetic confidant.

One Sunday soon after this interview, Mr. and Mrs. R. H. Armstrong called at our hotel, and took Governor Dominis and myself, attended by Colonel Boyd, on a little outing in their good company. Mrs. Newman, and her daughter, now Mrs. John Fowler, were also with us. Arriving at the railroad station, we entered the train, by which we were conveyed some distance out of town to a pleasant place called Richmond, situated on the banks of the river Thames.

There we were conducted to a house exhibited to us as the type of an English inn. I was much interested in the edifice; for I had always read from my earliest days glorious descriptions of English inns, where the pleasures of the chase culminated, and to whose doors the trophies of the hunters were brought. But on entering this house there was a little bit of disappointment, or at least wonder, as I surveyed its contracted quarters. The rooms were low-studded and of small size, so that probably no more than fifteen persons could have found accommodations therein. I could have almost reached the ceiling, had I stretched forth my arm and pointed it upward. Then, where were the banquet halls? Surely the inns of which the English novelists had told me must have been on a grander scale than this one to which I was conducted!

From the inn we went on board a steamer, which the forethought of Mr. Armstrong had secured for our comfort, and started out on an excursion which was to introduce a novel experience; for, after steaming up the river a short distance, we came to a lock; to pass it there were in waiting many other water-craft of all kinds, steamers and tow-boats, little vessels propelled by sails, or even small boats by oars and poles. When the gates of the lock were opened, that, and that only, was the moment when these could pass through; so there was such a scrambling in the water about us, such a jostling, such a pushing ahead to see who would get within the lock first, or, more important, that their boat should not be left in the outer waters when the gates closed. It was a lively contest, and often it appeared as though some of the craft would be hopelessly swamped; but the affair passed without accident, for indeed, with all their rivalry, everybody was good-natured, and the occupants of the boats took the matter very cheerfully when passed by a competitor.

But there was one phase of the exhibition which excited my attention, not to say surprise and wonder. This was the indifference of the men in the smaller boats, who lounged in the stern, cigar in mouth, book or paper in hand, while the poor girls with poles exerted their strength to the utmost to shove their boats along into the waters of the lock. Men smoking or reading while the women were doing all the work! Taking their ease, while from those called the weaker sex came the exertions necessary to get the boat into her place amongst the crowd of others. It was not a pleasant picture, nor did it speak of gallantry. I had never seen anything like it.

We all finally got through the gates of the lock, and steamed up the river until we came to a landing, where our attention was attracted by a very pretty sight; this was a house-boat, very nice in appearance, with an upper and a lower veranda, the upper being trimmed with curtains of a red material edged with white. Through the convenient folding-doors, which were opened above, we caught view of a large apartment, which I took to be the reception-room, and the lower room, also thrown open, was probably the dining-room. As we watched this neat home upon the water, there appeared a small skiff rowed by a man, but on the seat in the stern was another occupant, — a pretty little lady clad entirely in one prevailing color. On her head she wore a red hat; the parasol she held over it was red; she wore also red gloves and red shoes; but her fair face and golden hair made a contrast most lovely and striking with the tints of her costume and surroundings; and as she turned to look at us, the laughing blue eyes, which peeped out from under her rosy ensemble, made her indeed the picture of a charming Witch of the Thames. We watched her until she reached her house-boat, and disappeared from our gaze.

On landing, our party wended its way to another of the English inns. It had attracted our admiration from the water as it nestled prettily under the trees by which it was surrounded. On arriving we found a charming place. The long and well-kept walks of gravel and pebbles encouraging us to stray into its grounds;

and one by one we followed this inclination, while Mrs. Newman and some others, impressed with the same desire, climbed a neighboring hill. It was not a very difficult one, nor at all high; but it was a conspicuous object, because covered with tempting verdure and dotted with flowers, chiefly of the species of the rhododendron, whose vari-colored blossoms stretched out, all over the hillsides, in charming profusion.

But the wanderers were soon called to return, and the party reunited, because an omnibus had driven up by which we were to be taken to Clifton House, an estate owned by the Duke of Westminster. A short drive brought us to its doors, where we were welcomed, and shown through the apartments. This was nearer to my ideal of an English country-house; for here were lofty ceilings, and a spacious banquet hall, opening out on a lawn of richest and most luxuriant green. Looking out over this verdant foreground could be seen far away in the distance the blue line of the River Thames, winding in and out through the forest trees which rose along its border. The view was most beautiful, and I could well believe that in the past it had been the lordly estate of the Duke of Buckingham. With the aid of a lifelike portrait of a noble lady, which from its place on the walls of the manor looked silently down, I could picture to myself the days in which she had been the charming hostess of the reception-room in which we stood. I could see her doing the honors of this beautiful residence, and making guests welcome to her handsome estate, receiving the grand lords and lovely ladies who met there after the fatigues and excitements of the chase. The element of sport, and the thirst for pleasure, largely influenced the customs of that former epoch in English country life; and yet, with all their gayety, they were able to provide for the sustenance and happiness of a large number of retainers or tenantry without enormous expense. For these, their people, lived under their lords and mistresses with loving submission and loyal devotion, understanding the duties of their station in life, and therewith content; they looked to them for their maintenance and kind consideration, and asked for no more. The relation between master and retainer was one of love on both sides, of pure affection for a trusted and faithful vassal, of devotion and desire to please from the man to the master.

But at the present day all this has gone, the changes introduced by an entirely different civilization have made the former life impossible; the laws of trade, the demands of mercantile life, the advancement of commerce, of which London is the grand centre, have effected a revolution, which has entirely overthrown the relationship existing at other times between the country gentleman and his retainers. Now the lord of the manor rises early, and hurries away to the city, where important matters at the bank, or the shipping-office, or the lawyer's desk, are waiting for him; the places on his old-time estate, which long ago were filled with trusty retainers, are desolate, and often large halls stand permanently vacant. Walls are bare of ornament or picture because there is no one to keep up the establishment. Is England better and happier for the extinction of a style of life read of in history but not to-day existing ? At least, by such souvenirs as this manor house, are pictures brought back to one's mind of a past, that had much in it of sufficient worth to awaken emotions of sadness that it has gone forever.

We again boarded the little steamer which had awaited our return to her decks ; and when we were comfortably settled, she steamed away up the river. On the picturesque banks of the Thames we saw, as we passed, many pretty pictures of modern life. The water, too, was alive with moving craft, pleasure-boats and toiling steamers, while at several points were stationed bands of music, the strains of which came softly over the waters to our ears. All these sights and sounds added to the pleasure of our outing ; and yet most of the actors in this vivid pageant were, doubtless, only intent on the business of making a livelihood. We went about as far as the depth of the water allowed the steamer to ascend, and then turning, steamed back to the landing. I must not forget to notice that our enjoyment and understanding of the places we passed was increased by the presence of two entertaining young men of leisure invited as guests. They were strangers to us, but contributed much to our pleasure and information. One was a Mr. Skinner, but the name of his associate has for the moment escaped my memory. Disembarking from our steamer, we entered the cars, and were soon again at our hotel, and with the added happiness of having stored away the memory of a most delightful day on the celebrated River Thames, as well as of Mr. and Mrs. Armstrong's charming hospitality.

CHAPTER XXVIII

ILL NEWS FROM HAWAII — OUR RETURN

THE final entertainment, given to the party of royal
visitors from all quarters of the globe, was a garden
party, tendered by Her Majesty Queen Victoria, at
which she herself and all her good and beautiful children were present. Punctually at the appointed hour
the Queen of England, attended by the heir apparent
to the throne, H. R. H. the Prince of Wales, accompanied by the princess, his lovely wife, made their appearance ; following them came the other members of
the royal family. The procession moved along the
gravelled walks of the palace garden, led by the great
and good lady whose jubilee year we were celebrating.
It was made up of kings and queens, princes and princesses, from most of the reigning families of the world ;
on each side of us as we passed stood the crowds of
eager and respectful observers ; the greensward in the
gardens at each side of the walk was a solid mass of
people. These were of many ranks and conditions in
life, and principally persons of note. Among them
were well-known actors and celebrated actresses ; naval
officers, and other holders of official positions ; representatives of almost every class over whom the good
queen rules. Here and there, as we advanced, were

heard strains of music, tents having been erected for
the accommodation of the bands which were in service
for the day.   I think there were four of these at different points in our march, each composed of the best and
most skilful musicians that could be enlisted for the
occasion.

We finally paused before two tents which had been
assigned to the party.   Into one of these entered Her
Majesty Victoria, no one going into her tent, excepting
only the Prince of Wales.   Even the princess, his wife,
accompanied the other ladies into the tent which had
been provided for our reception.   Queen Kapiolani and
I had the honor of being directly with this accomplished
lady, while her husband, with a son's devotion such as
he has always so commendably shown, had gone to attend his royal mother.   Close to us was a table sumptu-
ously furnished with all that taste could desire; but
however attractive to the eye, I noticed its viands were
not liberally consumed.

As we had passed along in the light of day, I had
had an opportunity to impress upon my mind the appearance of the Queen of England, and to look at her
as a woman, under circumstances far more favorable for
permanent impression than in some of the pageants
where she had officially appeared.   She was sixty-eight
years of age at this time, and seemed to be in the best
of health.   In walking she carried a little ebony cane
on which she scarcely leaned.   She had been represented to me as short, stout, and fat, and not at all
graceful in appearance; but I did not at all agree with
the truth of this representation.   She was a well-pro-

portioned, gracious, queenly woman. I would not call
her handsome; yet she had a kind, winning expression
on her face which gave evidence of the gentle spirit
within. This was to be our final interview, and the
afternoon with its pleasures soon passed away; we bade
adieu to our royal hostess, wishing her with all our
hearts many, many more years of prosperity as a sovereign, and content and peace as the woman whose
name is respected and loved wherever the sun shines
throughout the wide, wide world.

Returning to our hotel, we received news which
changed at once the current of our thoughts. This was
of the revolutionary movement, inaugurated by those of
foreign blood, or American birth, in the Hawaiian Islands
during our absence. It was indeed a case of marked
ingratitude; for this rebellion against constituted authority had been brought about by the very persons
for whose prosperity His Majesty Kalakaua had made
such exertions, and by those to whom he had shown
the greatest favors. On receipt of the intelligence, we
decided that, instead of continuing our proposed tour,
and visiting the continent of Europe, we would return
at once to Honolulu. Mr. and Mrs. Armstrong proved
themselves faithful friends, and through their kindress
all was speedily arranged for the return voyage. They
were ably assisted in their hospitable work by Mr. and
Mrs. Sigismond Hoffnung and their son, Mr. Sidney
Hoffnung. The last-named had been *chargé d'affaires*
at Hawaii at one time in place of Mr. Abraham Hoffnung, who left him in that office during his own absence
in Australia. The Hoffnungs while we were in London

gave a grand entertainment and dinner in honor of the
visit of Queen Kapiolani, and we then had the pleasure
of meeting Lord Rosebery and his wife.   This lady was
a daughter of one of the Rothschilds, a large woman of
fine appearance and commanding presence, and of a style
which made her noticeable in company.   Then she wore
around her neck a string of single pearls which was a
wonder in itself, for I was told that its value was about
three hundred thousand dollars.   We had the pleasure
of meeting her again at an afternoon tea, which passed
off very charmingly, given to us at her residence, at
which there were many interesting people.

But after the news we received from home, our
minds would not be at rest to further enjoy the kind attentions which had been tendered us during the month
of our stay ; so we bade adieu to the beautiful city of
London, and took our departure for Liverpool.   There
we parted with Mr. and Mrs. Armstrong, and went on
board the Servia, Captain McKay, of the Cunard Line,
by which steamer we made a pleasant passage of nine
days to New York.   Resting only long enough to get
our accommodations on the overland train, in six days
more we were in San Francisco ; and six days' farther
travel, this time by water, found us nearing our home.
The weather on our westward way had been excessively hot ; for it was midsummer, and we had suffered
some inconvenience from the heat in crossing the continent.   Our own climate is so equal in temperature
that we feel extremes of heat even more than excessive
cold.

As our vessel was entering the harbor of Honolulu,

a smaller steamer came off to meet us; and being made fast alongside, we were transferred, and at once made for the shore. Here we found the people assembled to give us a royal welcome. The wharves were lined with throngs of men and women. The shipping, too, had been utilized for points of observation, and the decks and rigging of all the vessels were filled with those eager to watch the coming of the royal party. And yet, mingled with all the joy felt at our safe return, there was an undercurrent of sadness as of a people who had known with us a crushing sorrow. There were traces of tears on the cheeks of many of our faithful retainers, which we noticed, and of which we knew the meaning, as we passed by. They knew, and we knew, although no word was spoken, the changes which had taken place while we had been away, and which had been forced upon the king.

We were received by the members of the new cabinet of the king, by name Mr. Godfrey Brown, Minister of Foreign Affairs; Mr. L. A. Thurston, Minister of the Interior; Mr. W. I. Green, Minister of Finance; Mr. C. W. Ashford, Attorney-General, — all men of foreign birth; while of the ministry directly preceding, three members had been native Hawaiians.

Mr. Brown shook us warmly by the hands, and attended us to the royal carriage which had been waiting; and then, accompanied by the royal staff of His Majesty, we were quickly driven past the assembled multitudes to Iolani Palace, where King Kalakaua — my brother and the husband of Queen Kapiolani — was prepared to receive us. He appeared bright, and glad to welcome us back; yet we could see on his countenance traces of the terrible strain through which he had passed, and evidences of the anxiety over the perilous position, although this was only the commencement of the troubles preparing for our family and nation.

CHAPTER XXIX

"THE BAYONET CONSTITUTION"

IT is necessary now to briefly review the events which had taken place in our absence of about three months abroad. We arrived in Honolulu on the twenty-sixth day of July, 1887. A conspiracy against the peace of the Hawaiian Kingdom had been taking shape since early spring. By the 15th of June, prior to our return, it had assumed a no less definite shape than the overthrow of the monarchy.

For many years our sovereigns had welcomed the advice of, and given full representations in their government and councils to, American residents who had cast in their lot with our people, and established industries on the Islands. As they became wealthy, and acquired titles to lands through the simplicity of our people and their ignorance of values and of the new land laws, their greed and their love of power proportionately increased; and schemes for aggrandizing themselves still further, or for avoiding the obligations which they had incurred to us, began to occupy their minds. So the mercantile element, as embodied in the Chamber of Commerce, the sugar planters, and the proprietors of the "missionary" stores, formed a distinct political party, called the "down-town" party, whose

purpose was to minimize or entirely subvert other interests, and especially the prerogatives of the crown,
which, based upon ancient custom and the authority of
the island chiefs, were the sole guaranty of our nationality. Although settled among us, and drawing their
wealth from our resources, they were alien to us in their
customs and ideas respecting government, and desired
above all things the extension of their power, and to
carry out their own special plans of advancement, and
to secure their own personal benefit. It may be true
that they really believed us unfit to be trusted to administer the growing wealth of the Islands in a safe
and proper way. But if we manifested any incompe-
tency, it was in not foreseeing that *they* would be bound
by no obligations, by honor, or by oath of allegiance,
should an opportunity arise for seizing our country, and
bringing it under the authority of the United States.

Kalakaua valued the commercial and industrial prosperity of his kingdom highly. He sought honestly to
secure it for every class of people, alien or native, in
his dominions, making it second only to the advancement of morals and education. If he believed in the
divine right of kings, and the distinctions of hereditary
nobility, it was not alone from the prejudices of birth
and native custom, but because he was able to perceive
that even the most enlightened nations of the earth
have not as yet been able to replace them with a ruling
class equally able, patriotic, or disinterested. I say this
with all reverence for the form of government and the
social order existing in the United States, whose work-
ings have, for more than a century, excited the interest

of the world; not the interest of the common people only, but of nobles, rulers, and kings. Kalakaua's highest and most earnest desire was to be a true sovereign, the chief servant of a happy, prosperous, and progressive people. He regarded himself as the responsible arbiter of clashing interests, and his own breast as the ordained meeting-place of the spears of political contention. He was rightly jealous of his prerogatives, because they were responsibilities which no civic body in his kingdom could safely undertake to administer. He freely gave his personal efforts to the securing of a reciprocity treaty with the United States, and sought the co-operation of that great and powerful nation, because he was persuaded it would enrich, or benefit, not one class, but, in a greater or less degree, all his subjects.

His interviews with General Grant, his investigations into the labor problems, which the success of the Hawaiian plantations demanded, were all means to the same end, — an increase of domestic prosperity. He succeeded, and the joy of the majority was great. The planters were elated, the merchants were encouraged, money flowed into their pockets, bankrupt firms became wealthy, sugar companies declared fabulous dividends; the prosperity for which my brother had so faithfully worked he most abundantly secured for his people, especially for those of foreign birth, or missionary ancestry, who had become permanent residents of Hawaii.

The king did not accomplish these things without some native opposition; although it was respectful and deferent to his decision, as the ideas and customs of

our people require.   Some foresaw that this treaty with
the United States might become the entering wedge
for the loss of our independence.   What would be the
consequences should the Islands acquire too great a
commercial attraction, too large a foreign population
and interests ? would not these interests demand the
protection of a flag backed by a great military or naval
power ?   But Kalakaua, aware that under the provisions
of international law no nation could attack us without
cause, and relying on the established policy of our
great ally, the United States, fully assured that no colonial scheme would find acceptation there, boldly adven-
tured upon the effort which so greatly increased the
wealth and importance of his kingdom, — a wealth
which has, however, owing to circumstances which he
could not then foresee, and which none of his loyal
counsellors even dreamed of, now gone almost wholly
into the pockets of aliens and foes.

For years the "missionary party" had, by means of
controlling the cabinets appointed by the king, kept
itself in power.   Its leaders were constantly intriguing
to make the ministry their tool, or to have in its organization a power for carrying out their own special plans,
and securing their own personal benefit.   And now,
without any provocation on the part of the king, having
matured their plans in secret, the men of foreign birth
rose one day *en masse*, called a public meeting, and
forced the king, without any appeal to the suffrages of
the people, to sign a constitution of their own preparation, a document which deprived the sovereign of all
power, made him a mere tool in their hands, and prac-

tically took away the franchise from the Hawaiian race. This constitution was never in any way ratified, either by the people, or by their representatives, even after violence had procured the king's signature to it. Contrary entirely to the intent of the prior constitution drawn by a Hawaiian monarch (under which for twenty-three years the nation had been conducted to prosperity), this draft of 1887 took all power from the ruler, and meant that from that day the "missionary party" took the law into its own hands.[1]

It may be asked, "Why did the king give them his signature?" I answer without hesitation, because he had discovered traitors among his most trusted friends, and knew not in whom he could trust; and because he had every assurance, short of actual demonstration, that the conspirators were ripe for revolution, and had taken measures to have him assassinated if he refused. His movements of late had been watched, and his steps dogged, as though he had been a fugitive from justice. Whenever he attempted to go out in the evening, either to call at the hotel, or visit any one of his friends' houses, he was conscious of the presence of enemies who were following stealthily on his track. But, happily, Providence watched over him, and thus he was guarded from personal harm.

He signed that constitution under absolute compulsion. Details of the conspiracy have come to me since from sources upon which I can rely, which lead to the conviction that but for the repugnance or timidity of one of the executive committee, since risen very high

[1] See Appendix A.

in the counsels of the so-called republic, he would have been assassinated.[1]   Then they had planned for the immediate abrogation of the monarchy, the declaration of a republic, and a proposal for annexation to be made to the United States.   The constitution of the republic was actually framed and agreed upon ; but the plot was not fully carried out — more moderate counsels prevailed.   They therefore took the very constitution of which I have spoken, the one which had been drafted for a republic, hastily rewrote it so as to answer their ends, and forced Kalakaua to affix thereto his official signature.

It has been known ever since that day as "The Bayonet Constitution," and the name is well chosen ; for the cruel treatment received by the king from the military companies, which had been organized by his enemies under other pretences, but really to give them the power of coercion, was the chief measure used to enforce his submission.   They had illegally come out against him, bearing arms ; and it is openly stated that they had prepared measures to be a law unto themselves.[2]   Whatever the faults of Mr. Gibson, so long prime minister of Kalakaua, he was an able man, and his only public crime was his loyalty to his king.   And it was for this reason that he, and his son-in-law, Mr. Fred H. Hayselden of Lanai, were seized by a mob composed of the "missionary party" armed with rifles, and marched down the public streets to the wharves ;

[1] Chosen among five conspirators by lot to murder Kalakaua, he became horrified, and refused to act.

[2] See first part of Appendix B.

not an atom of respect being shown to the gray hairs of the old man who had occupied for years the highest position in the king's cabinet. Who was the man, and where is he now, who knocked off the hat, and struck the loyal old man, as he silently accepted his changed position?

So these two citizens were forced along into a small structure on the wharf, where hung two ropes with nooses already prepared, and a man of widely known missionary ancestry, led the outcry, vociferating loudly and lustily, "Hang them! Hang them!" Could it be possible, I thought, that a son of one of my early instructors, the child of such a lovely and amiable Christian mother, could so far forget the spirit of that religion his parents taught, and be so carried away with political passion, as to be guilty of murder?

Yet he was not the only one, by any means, who seemed to have forgotten those principles of our Lord, to teach which their parents had come to our shores. For while this was going on in the city, another missionary boy rode out to the country residence of Mr. Gibson, at Kapiolani Park, and entering abruptly into the presence of his daughter, Mrs. Hayselden, threw a lasso over her head, as though the gentle woman had been a wild animal, and avowed his intention of dragging her into town. While he held her, those with him searched the house, hoping that they might discover arms or some other evidence by which Mr. Gibson and the members of his family could be convicted and hung, but they were disappointed. After subjecting her to this brutality, which she bore most bravely, the ruffians left her to await the return from Honolulu of her natural protectors. But, alas! instead of their presence, what sorrow was to be hers! She received news of the manner in which they had been treated, and how doubtful it was whether they would ever be allowed to meet again this side of the grave; for after keeping their victims some days in terror of life, on the fifth day of July, 1887, the two men, against whom no charge, political nor criminal, was ever made, were placed on board a sailing-vessel and landed at San Francisco. The treatment received was too much for the elder sufferer; and although the conspirators had not directly assassinated him, he died soon after. His son returned to Hawaii, and became sheriff of Lanai during my reign. He was one of the first persons selected for dismissal by the present government; he had taken no part in public manifestations, but was informed by the attorney-general, Mr. W. O. Smith, that he was removed from office, " simply because you are a friend of the queen."

CHAPTER XXX

INVITED TO CONSPIRE AGAINST THE KING

Turning from this narration of the events which had transpired before the return of the queen's party from abroad, I will resume the thread of my personal narrative from the moment of meeting with my brother. After exchanging a few words of salutation and family greeting, we left the queen to listen to her husband's account of what had taken place during their three months' separation, and returned to our home, very glad indeed to be again settled at Washington Place.

There we found the good mother of my husband delighted to meet us, and filled with gratitude at our safe return. Her expressions of joy at once more meeting her son were but natural, for had he not always been devoted to her comfort? There was a little English lady who had been staying with Mrs. Dominis during our absence, and both my husband and I were glad to have the opportunity of expressing to her our sense of obligation for all she had done for his mother's needs while we were gone. She had been very attentive and considerate. Her name was Miss Davis, and she was a sister of Rector Davis of South Kona.

At this time, nearly a month after the revolution and change of constitution, everything seemed to settle

down into quiet again ; but appearances are deceptive,
and "the devil never sleeps." So, having achieved so
much of their desires, the conspirators worked day and
night to keep the city in a ferment. Plans were made,
and committees were formed ; the extreme views of
some of the members caused others, more scrupulous,
to retire, and to say that they could not willingly consent to be tools in the hands of wicked men, instruments of evil to their fellows. So these committees
were organized over and over again, without fixed purpose, without stability, until finally all other elements
had withdrawn from connection with the conspirators,
save a small number of agitators whose sole rallying-
point was annexation to the United States.

During the session of the legislature for the year
1888, Mr. James I. Dowsett, Jr., a young man, came to
my house at Muulaulani, Palama, to inform me that he
had been commissioned by those members who belonged
to the missionary party to inquire if I would accept the
throne in case my brother should be dethroned. To
my indignation at the proposition was added astonishment that the request should come from a mere boy
eighteen years of age ; and I responded at once to his
remark by saying, with some emphasis, that such a proposal was not to be considered. My answer would be
"No," and this final. He then, with an air of apology,
added, that he hoped I would not be offended with him
personally, because he had only been the bearer of the
message. Then he volunteered the intimation that,
since his errand had been unsuccessful, I might receive
a repetition of the same proposition in the course of a

GOVERNMENT BUILDING, HONOLULU

few days. I then asked him what was the intention of
the missionary party? what did they propose to do to
my brother? how was he to be dethroned? were they
going to murder him? To these interrogatories he replied that he knew nothing more about it, and bade me
adieu.

But, in conformity with his words, about a week
from that day my telephone was rung by Mr. W. R.
Castle, who wished to know if I would be at home that
morning; if so, he would like to call and see me on an
important matter, and would arrive in about half an
hour. He was told that I would see him, and at the
appointed time he appeared. He indicated that our
conference should be held in some place selected for
its privacy, where we would not be overheard nor inter-
rupted. I chose a side room, or corner, where I generally attended to my correspondence or did my literary
work. But in a room adjoining there happened to be,
at the moment of his visit, a party of girls who had met
to consult on a little social matter, — the arrangements
for a picnic. Just as soon as they heard me enter my
writing-room, and recognized from the conversation that
some one was with me, their voices hushed, and they
remained as still as mice; and so listened to every word
which passed between myself and Mr. Castle.

He announced to me that he had come to propose
that I should accept the throne, to which I should at
once ascend, and receive the support of the missionary
party. I demanded of him how my brother could be
dethroned. Did they mean harm to his person? He
denied that there was any such intent, but declared

that King Kalakaua must retire, and that I should
assume his position as the reigning sovereign.   Perhaps
they imagined at this time that I would be a willing
tool to carry out all of their projects.   It was true that
I was always an active member of all the associated
plans for carrying on missionary works, and was never
appealed to in vain by the missionaries to give money
or sympathy to all that was to be done in the name of
Christianity.   Whatever was to be undertaken by their
church, or by any of their societies, had received my
hearty co-operation from my earliest womanhood.   I
was about the first one to whom they went for subscrip-
tions, nor did they ever go empty away.   I was a member of the Fort-street Benevolent Society, also of the
Strangers' Friend Society ; and, at the very time of the
landing of the United States troops to overthrow my
government, was a member of the Woman's Board of
Missions.   In fact, I was concerned with the missionary party all my lifetime, in more measures of organized
benevolent work than I have the space to mention here.
Perhaps it was because I had gone hand in hand with
them in all *good* works that they thought I would cast
in my lot with them now for evil, — give my consent
to their plans, so frankly avowed, of conspiracy for my
brother's overthrow, and thus profit by their rebellion
against his lawful authority.   If so, they found themselves much mistaken.   I allowed Mr. Castle to explain
as fully as he pleased their designs, and then I told him
with firmness and decision that I would have nothing
to do with them in this matter.   Seeing that I firmly
declined the proposal, Mr. Castle retired ; and as that

was the last I heard about it, I infer that, having made
their plots, they lacked the courage, or the heart, to put
their plans into execution.   I will do the missionary
party the justice to state, that their confidence in my
aid for every good word and work was not destroyed
by my refusal to join in their conspiracies.   About the
time that the old Fort-street congregation was getting
settled in their new and beautiful building, now called
the Central Union Church, which is directly opposite
my residence known as Washington Place, I received
from my former instructor, Rev. E. G. Beckwith, a most
flattering letter ; and Mr. Charles Cook asked me to
take a pew there at five hundred dollars a year.   I was
pleased to know that the reverend gentleman, who had
known me throughout my whole life, — and at this time
I was some years past my fiftieth birthday, — should
entertain so favorable an opinion of his ancient pupil.
Although I was at this time quite a regular attendant
at the Kawaiahao church, yet I had this proposal of Mr.
Cook under consideration.   Just what I might have done
I cannot now say ; for the political events, which ulti-
mately led to the overthrow of my government by his
friends and his party, came upon me so thick and fast,
that I had little time for the consideration of anything
but the most important matters.

In the month of April, 1889, Mrs. Dominis became
very ill ; and one day the candle of life, which had been
flickering in the socket, went gently out.   But the
troubled political atmosphere was such, that even my
domestic sorrow was not respected.

For it had been proposed that the king should take

a trip to San Francisco, in regard to some commercial matter. It was a new scheme; some novel proposal to be made for closer relations with the United States, by which, of course, the missionary party was to be bene-fited, and of the terms of which my long-suffering brother was to be the bearer and the promoter. On Sunday, when my husband's mother was borne up the Nuuanu Valley to her last resting-place, the cabinet, not-withstanding the sacredness of the day, was in session, making plans and discussing means for the projected trip of His Majesty to America.

In the midst of our sorrow a message arrived directed to me. It was from Mr. Jonathan Austin, the Minister of Foreign Affairs, asking me if I would be one of a council of regency to take charge of the government during the expected absence of the king. I immedi-ately sent my husband, Governor Dominis, to inform His Majesty and his cabinet that I would accept the regency, but only to be sole regent in the king's place and stead; that the cabinet had full power to act upon all measures relating to the administration of govern-ment; that were I one of a council of regency there would be no executive; and that this was the second time I had been obliged to state my position and decline such an arrangement. While my husband was deliver-ing this message, the funeral ceremonies of his mother were suspended; and on his return the last sad rites of respect to her remains were rendered, and the proces-sion wended its way up the valley to her place of burial.

CHAPTER XXXI

THE KING THREATENED AND OPPRESSED

AFTER all, the anticipated trip was never taken. I am at a loss to explain the causes of its failure, but I understood that there was some friction in the cabinet. That body was now the absolute monarch of the kingdom of the Hawaiian Islands. Its members, Messrs. Austin, Damon, C. W. Ashford, with L. A. Thurston as its chief, defied the king to his face, and openly insulted him in his own palace. In one of their official documents they use to him the following language :—

" The government in all its departments must be conducted by the cabinet. Your Majesty shall, in future, sign all documents and do all acts which, under the laws of the constitution, require the signature or act of the sovereign, when advised so to do by the cabinet, the cabinet being solely and absolutely responsible for any signature of any document or act so done or performed by their advice."

As His Majesty very naturally demurred to such construction of even their own constitution, the cabinet appealed to the supreme court, who to the number of five justices, the first named being Albert F. Judd, and the last Sanford B. Dole, very consistently with the public record of these gentlemen, declared that the king was wrong, and that all power was placed in the hands

of the cabinet. It was by such acts as this that the
missionary party sought to humiliate my brother in the
estimation of his own people; so that it has well been
said by those conversant with the history of these days,
that His Majesty Kalakaua died in reality of a broken
heart, — broken by the base ingratitude of the very persons whose fortunes he had made.

On the 10th of May, 1889, the Princess Kaiulani,
being then in her fourteenth year, left Honolulu under
the charge of Mrs. Thomas Rain Walker, wife of the
British vice-consul, for England. It was the intention
of her father, Hon. A. S. Cleghorn, that she should remain abroad a short time for educational advantages;
but owing to the changes which have taken place since
her departure, she is still living with him in Europe.

In June, 1889, grand preparations were made for the
celebration, on the eleventh, of Kamehameha Day. All
who were interested in the races turned their steps in
the direction of Kapiolani Park. Twelve o'clock was
the hour appointed for the salutes to be fired, and
all was to be done to make the day one of enjoyment.
But a special invitation had been sent to me by the
committee of the Sunday-school of the Congregational
church to attend a picnic of the Sunday-school children, who were to assemble at the house and grounds
of Mr. John Thomas Waterhouse, Jr., up the Nuuanu
Valley ; so after the salute, or soon after twelve, I left
the gay company at Kapiolani Park, and with two lady
companions went up to the picnic, where I found myself most cordially welcomed, and made the guest of
honor of the pleasant occasion. Young and old seemed

to be very much gratified that I had willingly excused myself from other scenes of social enjoyment, to be present at the reunion of these interesting classes of children; and as for myself, I enjoyed the company, as I always take pleasure with children and in educational gatherings.

In the early part of July, 1889, I made a trip to Kauai; but before speaking of this journey, on which I was absent about a fortnight, I find it is necessary to go back a little, and give an account of my connection with Mr. Robert W. Wilcox.

Mr. Wilcox, in early youth, was sent abroad by King Kalakaua to be educated for future service to the state. But the revolution of 1887 compelled the king to cut off his income; and so he was recalled, arriving at Honolulu about the date of our return from the Victorian Jubilee. During his absence, however, he had met and married an Italian lady, the Countess Sobrero; and the young wife accompanied him on his return. For a while they were domiciled at the Arlington Hotel; but their means were nearly exhausted, and the party in power resolved to do nothing for them. Aware of the facts, in pity for their situation I offered them quarters under my roof until they could provide for themselves.

They were very glad to accept my proposal, and I gave them comfortable rooms in the long building attached to the main house at my Palama residence. I tried to make it as pleasant for them as I could, and devoted my attention especially to the newly married wife. She was excessively homesick, and was constantly making efforts to get together money sufficient to enable

them to leave the Islands. Through the kind assistance
of Mr. F. A. Schaefer, the Italian consul, and a few
others, after residing with me for two months, they
were at last able to leave Honolulu, and reached the city
of San Francisco. From thence I heard from her that
they were comfortably settled, that she had found pupils
in foreign languages, and that her husband had also
secured employment as a surveyor of lands. But early
in the year 1889 I received word from Mr. Wilcox that
he was again making up his mind to come to Honolulu;
that he intended to enter the political arena, and run as
a candidate for the legislature.

I wrote him at once, using all my influence to dissuade him from the very thought of it, telling him
plainly that he was far better off where he was. I
trusted that he had listened to my advice, but what was
my astonishment when he appeared at Honolulu. As
the rooms formerly occupied by him and Mrs. Wilcox
were not at that time used, and I was then living in
Washington Place, I told him that he was welcome to
go to Palama, and remain there until such time as he
should be able to provide for himself elsewhere. I could
not foresee that my kindness and hospitality to these
persons in need would be used by suspicious parties to
connect my name with a foolish and ill-organized attempt subsequently made by Mr. Wilcox to restore
some part of the authority of which the missionary
party had deprived the king. All unconscious of any
such scheme, I started on my journey to visit friends in
Kauai.

It was midsummer in 1889 when I arrived at the

island of Kauai, and at first took up my residence with
Governor Kanoa. He was one of the few chiefs of the
olden times and earlier manners who had not yet passed
away from earth. Although of lesser grade than some
of those mentioned in these memoirs, yet he was conversant with all forms of his duty, and observant of that
etiquette handed down from ancient days towards the
chiefs of rank superior to his own. It was, therefore,
natural to him to open his house to me, and to receive
my suite with that generous hospitality and cordiality
typical of the Hawaiian of high birth. After spending
a few days at his estate, he provided horses and carriages for my party, and accompanied by his wife, a good
Hawaiian lady, we proceeded to "Eleele," where I had
received an invitation from a young couple to be their
guest. From a brief but pleasant visit there, we went
on to Waimea, and took up our abode with Mr. and
Mrs. Levi Kauai. When it was known that the heir to
the throne was at their house, many people of that district called, and during my stay we received numerous
pleasant attentions. From here we made preparations
for retracing our steps, but stopped on our return to visit
at a pretty little estate, situated in a quiet valley just outside of Waimea, where resided Mrs. Gay and her daughters. Mr. Robinson and Mr. Francis Gay also made their
home with this amiable lady. All of these had ever
been noted for their patriotic attentions to any of the
chiefs who from time to time visited the district. This
reputation was ably sustained, and I retain the most
pleasing recollections of their courtesy and kindness on
this occasion. My regard for this family extended even

one generation farther back, their grandmother, Mrs. Sinclair of the island of Niihau, being also one of my warm friends.

On this visit I made careful inquiries as to the success of Mr. Gay's efforts to raise the " Oo " bird on this island. This is a bird about the size of a robin, under whose wings may be found the choice yellow feathers used in the manufacture of cloaks or collars exclusively pertaining to the Hawaiian chiefs of high rank. It is not the mamo bird, from which also feather capes and cloaks are made.

I had succeeded in getting from Hawaii, the largest island, some specimens expressly for their island. Twenty pairs had been brought as far as the island of Oahu. Of these, three pairs originally were sent to Kauai, but on making inquiry I found that only one pair was now known to be living there. These seemed to be thriving. Perhaps one cause of their content was a shrub or bush of the mimosa family growing near to the house, which bore fragrant blossoms very similar to those of the lehua, from which, in its own native island, this bird sucks the honey on which it subsists. They are true Hawaiians; flowers are necessary for their very life. This single pair of birds kept near to the house, and were often seen on this fragrant mimosa-tree. Ten years have flown by since I had the pleasure of looking at them there; but it is to be trusted that they have been thriving, laying their eggs year by year, and have by this time a flourishing colony. There is a bird on Kauai very similar in some points to the Oo, but they have a white feather under the wing instead of the much-prized yellow tip from which the celebrated *leis* and cloaks are made.

After the parting with this agreeable family we turned our steps toward Niumalu, the residence of the governor ; and having also exchanged with him our greetings and farewells, we took passage on the schooner James Makee for Honolulu.   I arrived in due time, refreshed by the journey, and with my party also delighted with the manifestations of kindly interest and loyal love which we had received throughout our trip.

CHAPTER XXXII

ATTEMPTED REVOLUTION

On returning to Washington Place, greatly to my regret I found my husband suffering much from the attacks of his old enemy, the rheumatism. But he bore his sufferings patiently, and was pleased to know that I had had so pleasant a journey. On the day following my return, I went to my out-of-town residence at Palama, in order to look over my garden, in which I have never ceased to take a keen interest. After satisfying myself that the faithful old gardener had given everything proper care, I turned my attention toward the house itself, and found matters there also satisfactory.

I had finished my examinations, and was just on the point of leaving, when I heard steps on the front staircase; and knowing that some person was without, I advanced to the door, which I did not open, but drew down the grating, and met the gaze of a young man with haggard, anxious countenance. It was Mr. Robert W. Wilcox who was standing before me, trying with all his self-control to appear calm, but evidently much excited. He told me in a few words that he was ready to release the king from that hated thraldom under which he had been oppressed, and that measures had

already been taken.   I asked him at once if he had
made mention of so important a matter to His Majesty.
He replied that he had not.

I then charged him to do nothing unless with the
full knowledge and consent of the king.   To this he responded that he had counted the cost, and would most
gladly lay down his life for my brother's sake.   He
then proceeded to inform me that it was on this very
night that the step would be taken; that every preparation had been made, and the signal for decisive action
would soon be given.   This was the first intimation of
any kind which had been brought to my knowledge of
the initiation of the movement.   At the time he was
speaking with me I had not the least idea of the use
which subsequent events proved had been made of my
Palama residence, and my old gardener had been kept
in equal ignorance.   Our lack of suspicion is easily explained; for the entire building can be traversed when
the shutters are kept closed, and no observer on the
outside would be any the wiser, whatever his position.
Knowing this as well as I, Mr. Wilcox and his associates had held their secret meetings there; and always
observing due caution, their occupancy or manner of
using the place was known only to themselves

It turned out just as I had been warned by my visitor; and on the very night of the disclosure the outbreak occurred, and Mr. Wilcox made his unsuccessful
attempt to overthrow the missionary party.   The king
that night was not at the palace, but at his boat-house.
I was in Washington Place.   As I have always been in
the habit of rising early, I awoke at my usual time, and

saw that my husband was quietly sleeping, and having a respite from his pain. I dressed without disturbing him, and strolled out into the garden, where I was in the habit of taking a morning walk before breakfasting.

I was not long there before I noticed that something unusual was transpiring. Members of the rifle companies were to be seen hastening from every direction; some of them fully dressed and carrying their arms in proper form, but some appeared to have left their homes in haste, so that they did not have the various parts of their uniform adjusted, but were dressing themselves as they ran past. They were all going in the direction of the armory on Punch-Bowl Street. Young Harry Auld, who was employed in the custom-house, went by while I stood near the gate to my grounds; and I asked him at once what was the meaning of the commotion at this early hour.

He informed me that Mr. Wilcox had taken possession of the palace, and was supported there by a company of soldiers. Naturally I connected this information with what I had heard the night before, and all became clear to me. Towards ten o'clock in the forenoon firing began, and soon shots went whizzing past our house. There were occasional outbursts of musketry throughout the day; but towards evening all became tranquil again, or nearly so. We heard that Mr. Wilcox had been deserted by his men, and had therefore surrendered. The rifle companies were stationed at the music hall opposite the palace; but their gallant commander kept out of harm's way at the Hawaiian Hotel, from whence he sent his orders by an orderly to his executive officer. Late in the afternoon Mr. Hay Wode-house, and the purser of the steamer Australia, climbed onto the roof of the hotel stables to have their share of the fun, taking with them a small mortar or other contrivance for firing bombs. They discharged these missiles into the palace grounds, aiming at the bungalow with such effect as to shatter the furniture of the Princess Poomaikalani, and do much other damage. This was the time when Mr. Wilcox sent word to Colonel Ashford that he would lay down his arms; and being arrested for the useless riot, he was led to the station-house. His punishment was a moderate imprisonment; and it has been said that he was released from the consequences of his act because he had in his power certain persons who would have been much terrified had he been inclined to tell all he knew. However this may be, it is evident that out of gratitude he had perhaps some plans or purposes for being of service to my brother, because the king had tried in the past to do something for him. His enthusiasm was great, but was not supported by good judgment or proper discretion. His efforts failed; and indeed, it is not easy to see how under the circumstances it could have been otherwise.

CHAPTER XXXIII

THE KING'S DEPARTURE — AGAIN REGENT

I HAVE spoken of the pleasant Sunday-school picnic of the 11th of June, 1889. My entertainers, it seemed, were sufficiently gratified with my presence not to forget me in their next invitations; and the year following I was invited out to Punahou, where the Sunday-schools of all the Congregational societies were to assemble. I first drove out to Kapiolani Park to see the races. These went on finely. The assembled multitude cheered on the winning horse, the sweet strains of the band floated out on the air of the beautiful day, and the people seemed inspired by their surroundings to forget all their political troubles or their domestic necessities. After I heard the salute denoting the noon hour, again, as on the previous occasion, accompanied by two lady companions, I proceeded to the picnic at Punahou. For some reason as yet not explained, the assembled worthies of the Congregational church did not seem as cordial as they were a year earlier. However, I did not allow any to know that I noticed the change; and besides, there were many sincere friends present who treated me most hospitably and kindly. While engaged in conversation with some of these, Mr. Albert F. Judd, the chief justice, approached me, and inquired if I could descry a vessel which was making her way slowly out of the port and gaining an offing. I replied that I saw the one to which he referred. Then he went on to volunteer the information that on board that craft was Colonel Ashford, who had escaped from prison, and was secretly taking his departure.

A few days prior to this celebration, in one of those turns of the tide of politics by which the Ashfords have more than once found themselves in strange company, Mr. V. V. Ashford, on some charge of seditious conduct toward the governing party, found himself in prison.

I mention this as but one amongst many instances I might recall where those charged with political, or, indeed any other offence, have, for reasons best known to the missionary party, been allowed or even constrained to leave the Islands. Of some of these, nothing more has ever been heard.

The 18th of November of that same year was celebrated with much display and many congratulations as the birthday of His Majesty Kalakaua. During the afternoon a reception took place at the palace, in which the societies organized by the king, the queen, or by myself had a general reunion. These were the Hooulu Lahui, the Liliuokalani Educational Society, and the Naua Society, the last named under the special patronage of the king. After paying their respects to His Majesty and the queen, the whole company adjourned to the wharves. As usual there was a fine regatta, in which many pretty water-craft took part. We are always favored with fresh and regular breezes, and the

little white-sailed yachts made a neat and inspiriting
picture as they contested for the prizes. Those who
won went home happy in their trophies of victory;
those who did not had, at any rate, a delightful sail.
The boat-houses were turned into places of entertainment, and fine lunches were given at that of the king
as well as at many others. My riding society had been
specially invited to take their refreshments at the boat-
house of Dr. Trousseau.

As we were all gayly going to lunch after viewing
the sport, general attention was attracted to a balloon
which was at the moment ascending from the foot of
Punch-Bowl Hill. Scarcely had the light globular object
reached the upper currents of the atmosphere, when it
was whirled away with fearful speed, for it was a very
windy day. On watching the car under the balloon, we
noticed that the man had cut himself adrift, and was
descending from mid-air in a parachute. He was coming down bravely; but what was the horror of all of
the spectators to observe that instead of landing on the
wharf, or even in the port, he was being carried far out
to sea, beyond the breakers, where the waters were alive
with sharks. Steamers and boats were immediately got
under way to effect his rescue, but he was never seen
again. The balloon from which he had made his fatal
leap also disappeared, and no trace of either was ever
discovered. The poor man probably met his fate from
the jaws of the monsters of the deep the moment he
touched the water.

In the evening there was a grand display of fireworks, and a procession of the fire companies of the

city.   There was also a new organization which paraded this evening, called the "Sons of Hawaii," at whose head was Mr. John Cummins.   It was to be reviewed by His Majesty Kalakaua.   The men were mounted on the finest horses which could be found in the city, and were manly fellows and good riders.   At eight in the evening Their Majesties, the king and queen, the members of the cabinet, with many who held office under the government, assembled in front of the palace to receive the organization.

I was not at that hour present, because I was making a tour of the city in order to inspect the decorations and see the fireworks.   But just as I finished my drive, and entered the palace yard, the "Sons of Hawaii" came up the avenue with their horses on the full gallop, making a most inspiriting display.   How well they sat their steeds, and how gracefully they rode!   Each man held aloft a lighted torch, adding much to the effect of the cavalcade.   They drew up in front of the king, and were most profound in their salutations.   I paid particular attention to their behavior, because amongst them were a number of the missionary boys, who seemed to act as though they would outdo those of native birth in their manifestations of loyalty and respect.   There was a sad interest to me afterwards in recalling this evening, because it was about the last celebration in which my brother made a public appearance.

The fatigues of this day, several sources of worry, and the responsibilities which I felt were approaching, brought on a slight fever ; and for three weeks I was confined to my rooms, at times not leaving my sick-bed.

Three days before his departure the king came to see
me, and told me of his intention to visit the United
States. I did all I could to dissuade him from the
journey. I reminded him of his failing health, and informed him that I was not in my usual vigor. Cold
weather, too, to which he was unaccustomed, was fast
approaching; and if anything should happen to him,
how would I, with my feeble health, be able to meet the
increasing burdens of my station. He replied that he
would leave those behind who would look out for the
government. His only errand at this moment was to
notify me that I was to be appointed regent during his
absence. He really did need change, after what he had
borne in recent years; and this consideration doubtless
entered into his resolution.

But the principal motive of his journey was to have
an interview with Mr. H. A. P. Carter, the Hawaiian
minister at Washington, in order to give him instructions in view of the McKinley Bill, which had just
passed the American Congress, the influence of which
was supposed to be dangerous to the interest of the foreign element at Honolulu, and destructive to the profits
of the sugar planters. So the king went cheerfully and
patiently to work for the cause of those who had been
and were his enemies. He sacrificed himself in the
interests of the very people who had done him so much
wrong, and given him such constant suffering. With an
ever-forgiving heart he forgot his own sorrows, set aside
all feelings of animosity, and to the last breath of his
life he did all that lay in his power for those who had
abused and injured him.

If ever there was a man who was pure in spirit, if ever there was a mortal who had perfect charity, he was that man. In spite of all the revilings uttered against him, he never once opened his lips to speak against another, whomsoever it might be. And so my poor brother said good-by to us all, and bade farewell to his beautiful Islands, which he was never to look on again.

Just before he sailed I went to the palace. There he called together his cabinet ; and addressing to the gentlemen a few pleasant words, he placed me in their charge, hoping for the best, and expressing the wish that under our care the burden of the government might be lighter than it had proved to him since he had been the reigning sovereign. At eleven o'clock he exchanged his last words with Queen Kapiolani and myself, and then hastened rapidly away to the wharf, where a boat from the United States man-of-war Charleston was in waiting to convey him on board that vessel. Crowds witnessed his departure, all the shipping was gay, the vessels saluted the out-going ship, a royal salute was fired, and he was gone.

CHAPTER XXXIV

THE KING'S RETURN — MY ACCESSION

THUS again began my regency. With only twenty-five soldiers to guard the palace, a feeling of uncertainty in the mercantile world, and many signs of domestic unrest, my husband thought it best for me to return to Washington Place every night; but each morning at nine o'clock I went to my official duties, and part of these was always the examination of some alarm or rumor which had come to the palace doors. Now it was the report of a secret meeting at some house up the Nuuanu Valley to debate upon an overthrow of my government, again the account of an assembling out on the plains for conspiracy. Often, even after I returned to my home, would come a telephonic message announcing that the palace was to be attacked, and the military must be called out.

On tracing these rumors, whenever there was any basis of truth in them, it was found that the agitation was always the work of that same clique who were never satisfied, always conspiring, always determined that they would either rule or ruin. Such men, having no covenant with their own consciences, suspicious even of their own shadows, in power or out of power, are always a menace to the peace of the community.

Nothing worthy of record transpired during the closing days of 1890, and the opening weeks of 1891, until in the city it was reported that the ship Charleston was in sight with yards cock-billed, in token of mourning. My ministers were assembled in the Blue Room of the palace ; and as I entered I could see on each countenance apprehension of the fate which we feared must have befallen the king, and to which we soon gave expression in words. On the arrival of the Charleston in port, we were officially notified. One of the cabinet went to the wharf to inquire what plans were made for the reception of the king's remains.

He brought back word that at five o'clock of that afternoon the admiral himself would come to the palace at the head of the party which was to escort the body of the deceased sovereign. Not wishing to leave the palace, I immediately wrote to my husband, who was at home suffering from rheumatism, to inform him of all that had been brought to my knowledge. On learning of my brother's death, in spite of his indisposition he came at once to the palace, so as to be near me at this critical moment. I was so overcome by the death of my dear brother, so dazed with the suddenness of the news which had come upon us in a moment, that I hardly realized what was going on about me, nor did I at all appreciate for the moment my situation. Before I had time to collect myself, before my brother's remains were buried, a trap was sprung upon me by those who stood waiting as a wild beast watches for his prey.

The ministers, who were apparently of one mind with the justices of the supreme court, called together the

members of the council, and when all had taken their
seats, sent for me.   I turned to Governor Dominis before entering the chamber, and inquired of him, " What
is the object of this meeting?"   He said that they had
come together to witness my taking of the oath of office.
I told him at once that I did not wish to take the oath
just then, and asked why such proceedings could not be
deferred until after my brother's funeral.   He said that
others had decided that I must take my official oath
then and there.

Few persons have ever been placed without a word
of warning in such a trying situation, and I doubt if
there was any other woman in the city who could have
borne with passable equanimity what I had to endure
that day.   I will scarcely limit the comparison to my
sex; I doubt if many men could have passed successfully through such an ordeal.   Ere I realized what was
involved, I was compelled to take the oath to the constitution, the adoption of which had led to my brother's
death.

After taking the oath of office administered to me
by the chief justice, Albert Francis Judd, the meeting
dissolved, and we adjourned to the Blue Room, where
all the members of the privy council came to pay to me
their mournful congratulations.   Of these the chief justice was the first; and as he shook my hand he said to
me, " Should any of the members of your cabinet propose anything to you, say yes;" and left me quite at
a loss to know what his words might portend.   But
it soon became apparent.   After the members of the
privy council departed, the cabinet remained.   Mr. Cum-

FUNERAL PROCESSION OF KING KALAKAUA

mins, Minister of Foreign Affairs, said that they wished
to notify me that they would have to continue in office ;
and then went on with a lecture, or apology, which I
could not understand, and the argument of which I do
not believe he had quite mastered himself. Mr. Godfrey Brown, the Minister of Finance, came to his relief
by offering the suggestion that no changes could be
made in the cabinet except by the legislature. The
only notice I took of their discussion was to say that I
could not understand the necessity of mentioning the
matter at all at such a moment. To this Mr. Peter-
sen, the Attorney-General, rejoined that I ought to understand the situation and accept it. I replied that
I had no intention of discussing situations or other
political matters at all at this time, and I would defer
all further notice of the matter until after the king's
burial.

At five o'clock the afternoon of the 29th of January,
1891, the solemn procession began at the boat-landing,
where the men from the Charleston had landed with the
king's remains, and from whence they took up the line
of their mournful march to Iolani Palace. It was a
gloomy, cloudy afternoon. As they moved slowly up to
the gates of the palace, there was a moment's pause ;
and just then a triple rainbow was seen to span with its
arch the entire structure, stretching from one end to
the other, and, as it were, embracing the palace. Crowds
of people thronged in, respectfully following the king's
remains, with hearts too full of grief to speak of the
deceased sovereign even to each other. When the *cor-
tége* arrived at the palace steps, the casket was placed

on the shoulders of the stoutest and best-picked men of the ship, and borne to a bier in the centre of the Red Chamber, which had always been the royal reception-room, where it was to lie in state.

The kind-hearted and ever-friendly officer who commanded the Charleston, Admiral George Brown, paid his respects to the widowed queen, and then, in company with his officers, returned to his ship. He had taken my brother as a guest of honor to San Francisco; he had shown to him the greatest courtesy and the most unaffected kindness during the passage; then, after the final scene, to him had belonged the sad office of conveying the remains of his late companion back over the same route, a silent passenger going to his final resting-place. The Hawaiian people are always grateful for tokens of respect shown to their chiefs, so on the proposed departure of the Charleston there was a general wish for a day to be given to the contributions of tokens of friendship to the admiral. On the day set apart for this grand expression of gratitude, men, women, and children crowded on board, each bearing some memento of Aloha to the gallant sailor. These consisted of curiosities of all kinds, — old-fashioned spears, calabashes, shells, necklaces, and countless other articles of native use or manufacture, each telling its own little story of our people, recalling to whoever might see it in any part of the world some tender memory of Hawaii.

CHAPTER XXXV

THE LAST SLEEP — LYING IN STATE

IN the meantime proper preparations were made for the funeral of His Majesty Kalakaua, than whom no king was ever more beloved by his people. The usual ceremonies were carried out as customary for the lying in state of a sovereign, or chief of the royal family. The casket was laid on a cloth of the royal feathers, which was spread over a table in the centre of the Red Chamber in the Iolani Palace, and guards were detailed for duty by day and by night. For this service twenty men are always selected, whose office it is to bear aloft the royal *kahilis*, which are never lowered during the course of the whole twenty-four hours. The attendants are divided into four watches of three hours each. Those relieving form a line, and take their positions as the stations are vacated by their predecessors, who, on resigning the plumes of state, return to their homes. The watchers are generally selected from men who can claim ancestry from the chiefs; of these there are quite a number still living, of well-known families, although now generally poor in worldly possessions. While in attendance at the side of the royal casket, some sang the death-wail or old-time *mèlès* or chants belonging solely to the family of the deceased chieftain; and in the meantime attendants of a younger race composed dirges which were more in accord with the lyrics of the present day. There was also detailed for my brother a guard of honor from the Masonic fraternity; two Masons always remained with the other watchers, and were relieved in a similar manner.

Three weeks constitute the period devoted to the obsequies before the burial, or the "lying in state," of the remains of a high chief of the Hawaiians. During this delay the cabinet and the privy council carried out the plans made for the details of the royal funeral. The death and burial of a sovereign is not a trivial matter in Hawaii. The people come from all parts of the islands to the funeral of the one whom they have known and loved as the head of the nation.

At last the morning for the final ceremonies arrived, and early in the day the sad exercises began with one of the most interesting and impressive ceremonies I ever witnessed. This was the honor rendered by the secret society of the Hale Naua to their head and founder. Prayers were offered, and they went through the different ceremonies, as is the custom with the Masonic or other similar fraternal organizations. The high priest, Mr. William Auld, officiated, two lay priests assisting during these parts of the ritual. Then entered twelve women with lighted candles in their hands; each one of these, bearing aloft her taper, offered a short prayer, the first words at the head, next at the shoulders, then at the elbows, then the hands, and so on to the thighs, the knees, the ankles, and the feet. There were six of the torch-bearers on each side; and after these forms they surrounded the remains, and all repeated in unison prayers appropriate to the burial of the dead. They then withdrew in the most solemn manner. This service, so far from being, as has been alleged, idolatrous, had no more suggestion of paganism than can be found in the Masonic or other worship. An excellent opportunity was given me to contrast the two on this occasion, and each seemed to me to be a most beautiful and impressive method of rendering honor to the memory of a deceased member.

At the hour appointed for the state services, each dignitary, according to his rank, took the place which had been indicated to him in the great Red Room. His Lordship the Bishop of Honolulu, wearing the robes of his office, then appeared, and began the service laid down in the Anglican ritual for the burial of the dead. At the proper time each person moved to the position which had been assigned for him in the procession which was to proceed from Iolani Palace to the royal mausoleum. And just at this point there was a slight hitch ; for the diplomatic corps declared that their members should be first after the carriages of the royal family, while the members of the cabinet claimed this position of precedence for themselves. After a brief discussion over the question, it was finally settled that the cabinet might take the first position, the diplomatic corps following, and in this order the procession moved onward On each side of the bier were the *kahili* bearers; and these plumes, some large, some small, of various colors, were borne aloft above the heads of the moving throng, who marched with slow step up the Nuuanu Valley towards the royal mausoleum. On arrival at Kawananakoa, the casket was placed in the centre of the tomb, and the final prayers were offered by the bishop and the clergy assisting his lordship, after which they retired. Then the Masonic brethren, embracing nearly all the members of the lodges in the city, who had marched in a body, filed in with slow and solemn step, and surrounded his bier. Clothed in the insignia of their order, they stood in saddest silence about the casket, on which was placed the regalia lately worn by my brother and their brother, and also a roll on which were the records of his rank as a Mason. Then the brethren marched around the casket, and each laid thereon a little sprig or branch of green pine as a final and personal token of his grief at parting with a brother Mason. When all had done this, they retired, leaving the members of the royal family alone with their grief in the silent recesses of the tomb. Lastly, the guns of the military escort gave the final salute to the departed, three volleys of musketry being successively fired above the grave; and the line of return was formed in proper order, the *kahili* bearers still waving aloft the plumes, those traditional accompaniments of royalty, and which now became the insignia of office appertaining to the former heir-apparent, who had now become the sovereign of the Hawaiian Islands.

BODY OF KING KALAKAUA LYING IN STATE

CHAPTER XXXVI.

MY CABINET — PRINCESS KAIULANI.

ON the day following the final ceremonies of the royal funeral my cabinet was called together; and one hour before the ministers were to arrive, Mr. J. A. Cummins, who was the Minister of Foreign Affairs, made his appearance, and asked if I had any plans or purposes in regard to the approaching meeting. In reply to this I advised him of my wish that he should resign from the cabinet, and accept the appointment of governor of Oahu, to which office I thought he would be better suited, as his duties would call him out amongst the people.

I felt sure he would enjoy visiting the outside districts; while the life of a minister in the cabinet bound him to official matters of a burdensome and responsible nature not so well adapted to his character and abilities. But to this offer of consideration for him, I was told by Mr. Cummins that he preferred to remain in the ministry. "But," I suggested, "the question is, will the ministry remain?" To this he replied that he had no doubt of that; in fact, he was sure that they would not be dismissed. I did not argue the matter with him, but simply said, "Are you, then, decided, and do you decline the appointment of governor of Oahu?" "Yes,"

he repeated ; "my determination is made, besides which
I may be of use here to the down-town party."

The hour of ten arrived and the cabinet met.   I inquired at the opening of the cabinet meeting what was
the business of the day ; to which reply was made that
it was necessary that I should sign without any delay
their commissions, that thus they might proceed to the
discharge of their duties.   "But, gentlemen," said I, "I
expect you to send in your resignations before I can
act."   My reasoning was, that, if they were *now* cabinet ministers, why should they appeal to me to appoint
them to the places which they already filled?   They
hesitated, and regarded each other.   "No," I continued,
"if you do not resign, I do not see how I can issue to
you new commissions."   This was a point to which they
did not think I would call attention, a suggestion which
they had not foreseen might come from me, and they
scarcely knew which way to turn.   They thought that,
while holding their former commissions, I ought to issue
to them new ones over my royal signature.   As this
did not agree with my views of the matter, I stated to
them definitely that it must be a question for future
consideration, and that it would be best to refer the
point for decision to the Supreme Court.   After a
lengthy period of the greatest anxiety to me, it was
announced by Chief Justice Judd that the decision was
in my favor, and that the commissions of the present
members of the cabinet expired with the death of the
king.

The ground on which the ministers had based their
scheme was, that the constitution distinctly stated that

no change of ministry should take place except by a vote of "want of confidence" passed by the majority of the legislature.   But while this was true, the document did not provide in any article for the continuance of the cabinet after the decease of the sovereign.   It was, therefore, held by the chief justice that the ancient custom in this respect remained in force, and that commissions held under the deceased monarch gave no authority under his successor.   Messrs. Cummins, Spencer, Brown, and Peterson, accordingly tendered their resignations, which I accepted, and then appointed: Mr. Samuel Parker, Minister of Foreign Affairs; Mr. C. N. Spencer, Minister of the Interior; Mr. H. A. Widemann, Minister of Finance; Mr. W. A. Whiting, Attorney-General; their commissions all bearing date of the 26th of February, 1891.   Besides these appointments the position of chamberlain, being vacant by the absence of Hon. George W. Macfarlane, was filled by Mr. J. W. Robertson, who had been his assistant, and who subsequently proved to be a most efficient officer.   Mr. Charles B. Wilson was appointed marshal.

While the matter was pending, arrangements were made for the meeting of the members of the House of Nobles for receiving the nominations of an heir apparent to the throne.   On the ninth day of March, 1891, Princess Victoria Kaiulani, Kalaninuiahilapalapa Kawekiu i Lunalilo, daughter of my sister, Princess Miriam Kekauluohi Likelike and Hon. A. S. Cleghorn, was duly proclaimed heir apparent, and her nomination recognized by the United States ship-of-war Mohican by a salute of twenty-one guns.

CHAPTER XXXVII.

MY HUSBAND MADE PRINCE CONSORT — HIS DEATH

In July I made the usual royal tour of the islands. I was accompanied by my husband, Governor Dominis, and by Hon. Samuel Parker and Hon. W. A. Whiting of my cabinet. I visited Hawaii, Maui, and Molokai. At all the places in these islands where we stopped we were most cordially greeted and royally entertained by the people. Returning to Honolulu, we started out again for Kauai, but with a larger party than on the previous portion of the royal tour. I was now accompanied by Prince Kalanianaole, Hon. Samuel Parker, Mrs. C. A. Brown, Mrs. W. A. Aldrich, Mrs. C. H. Clark, Mrs. P. P. Kanoa, attended by her husband, Mrs. C. B. Wilson and her son, J. H. Wilson, Hon. E. K. Lilikalani, Hon. John K. Richardson, Mrs. Ulumaheihei, Hon. W. P. Kanealii, Hon. D. W. Pua, Mr. J. Kekipi, and Mr. and Mrs. Joseph Heleluhe. Greatly to our mutual regret, illness prevented my husband from being one of the party.

At Kauai we were most hospitably received and royally entertained by Mr. and Mrs. W. H. Rice. They took us to their handsome private residence at Lihue, to which there came all the principal people of the islands to pay respects. It was a great pleasure to me to receive these greetings, because up to this visit I had never seen so large an assembly of the principal people of that island.   There were the Eisenbergs, the McBrides, the Wilcoxes, the Rices, the Smiths, some of these the living representatives of the oldest and best known of the missionary families.   It seemed to me to be more like an assembling together of our societies in the city of Honolulu.   Everything was done to make my arrival a most happy occasion to me by Mr. and Mrs. Rice, whose personal friends became my friends, and added their welcome to that of my genial hosts.   My visit to Hanalei was made comfortable through the energy and kindness of Mr. Rice.   In crossing from Hanalei through the sands of Hoohila, it was by reason of his personal guidance that the passage was made in safety, and that we reached the top of a high hill without accident.

Under the hospitable roof of Mr. and Mrs. Titcomb we spent a restful night ; and on the morning following, boarding the steamer James Makee, our party bade farewell to all the kind friends at Lihue.   From thence we proceeded to the island of Niihau, and landing, spent a very pleasant day on shore.   Every attention was rendered to us by the manager who had charge of the island under appointment from the Gays.   Horses and carriages were placed at our disposal, with which we rode through the country, and on our return found that we had been provided, by the forethought of this gentleman, with a luncheon of nice fat mutton ; and as we returned with excellent appetites and were a large company, it soon disappeared.   When evening came on we returned by the steamer to Kalapaki, where Mrs. Rice had preceded us and had a surprise in readiness. A grand sea-bath was proposed, to which we all gladly assented; and with scarcely an exception we refreshed ourselves in the cooling waters.

Then came the surprise, for under a grove of Hau trees growing back of their mansion-house was spread a most tempting table of good things. It was literally covered with the best of all that is produced in the whole extent of these islands. Nothing seemed lacking that could gratify the taste or tempt the appetite. Can it be possible that our genial host is the same man of whom, in narrating the events of the revolution of 1887, and the political troubles of Mr. Gibson, I have had occasion to speak, as showing later traits of an almost savage character? It is sad, but only too true. Moments sped quickly by, and time for departure came ere we were aware; so, bidding farewell to our entertainers and their numerous friends, we went on our way to Honolulu, where we arrived in the early part of the day following.

I found my husband somewhat better, but not yet able to leave his bed. He had not forgotten me during my absence, and had planned some surprises for me at our Waialua residence, which he desired to show to me himself. But he was too ill to undertake the journey. I was loth to leave him, and so hurriedly made the trip around the island of Oahu. Accompanied by Hon. Samuel Parker, Hon. J. A. Cummins, and others, we spent one night at the Kaneohe plantations, two nights at the residence of Mr. W. C. Lane, and passed only a little more time at Mr. Cecil Brown's.

HANALEI VALLEY ON THE ISLAND OF KAUAI

At all of these places the people who came to receive us were delighted to have the opportunity to show their loyalty and manifest their love. We stopped at Kahuku, at Laie, amongst the residents of the Mormon faith, and then rode on to Waialua, where I found that my husband had indeed executed a great surprise for me. A large wooden *lanai*, or outer room, had been built, capacious enough to accommodate some one hundred and fifty or more persons. He had thought what a pleasure it would be to have this cool and pleasant resort, where, after the heat of the day or a row up the stream of Anahulu, I might take my comfort in sitting under the grateful shade, with all the friends I might select and invite to meet and rest with me there. It proved to be all that his kindness foresaw and desired, and also served as a reception-room for pleasant dances and other festivities.

After staying at Waialua a few days, where Mrs. Halstead and her husband, a well-known planter of that locality, entertained us, and also visiting some other prominent people of the district, we turned our steps toward Ewa, where Mrs. Kahelelaukoa Brown gave a grand *luau* in our honor. From thence our party returned to the city, making, as we entered its streets, quite an imposing cavalcade. At Washington Place I found my husband delighted to meet me, but I noticed with solicitude that he seemed to be very feeble. He grew weaker and weaker from this time until the morning of his death.

I was not expecting the immediate event, but watching in the room, when he motioned to me to approach his bedside. I complied with the wish. Hon. Samuel Parker and Major W. T. Seaward entered about the same moment, and remained a few minutes with us. Out on the broad piazza at the farther end of the house were seated a few of my young lady friends, his faithful valet, Mainalulu, and the attendants, Mary Kamiki, Keamalu, and Kawelo. Dr. Trousseau, the physician in charge of the case, soon entered, and after a brief examination said that he thought the patient needed rest, and motioned to those who were present that they would be excused from the chamber. Accordingly they retired to the veranda, leaving me alone by my husband's bedside. This was at about one o'clock. I drew near to the foot of the bed, and stood where I could easily watch him while he was apparently sleeping. I had been thus standing but a few minutes when, noticing a slight quivering motion pass over his frame, I immediately went to his side, and then hastily called the friends in attendance and summoned the doctor. He examined the patient, and said that all was over. Just a few minutes before my husband passed away he made a peculiar motion of his hand which I have seen brethren of the Masonic fraternity use in the act of prayer. Was this the moment at which his spirit was taking its flight from earth, to enter that larger and grander brotherhood beyond the things which are seen?

The attending physician was quite affected by the death of Governor Dominis; for his friendship with my husband was one of many years standing, and they had the warmest esteem for each other. By this simple statement of fact, it will be noticed that I was entirely alone by the side of my husband when he died ; but there have been words of the cruelest import uttered by those who were not there, and could have known nothing of the facts.   May they be forgiven for the wrong done to me and to my husband's memory.

There was an immediate meeting of the ministers of my cabinet to decide what was to be done in regard to the obsequies of Governor Dominis.   That evening the remains were removed to Iolani Palace, and were laid in state.   This was on the twenty-seventh day of August, 1891.   It was the general wish, and the decision of the cabinet ministers, that the honors customarily granted to the deceased sovereigns should be accorded to my husband.   Consequently, the lying in state, the military guards, the watchers from the Masonic fraternity, the ladies in attendance bringing their *leis*, their garlands, their floral decorations, the *kahili* bearers with the plumes of office, all were employed in manner and detail as I have already described it in speaking of the funeral of my brother, His Majesty King Kalakaua.   The day appointed for the final ceremonies arrived ; and Governor Dominis was borne, with all the honors accorded to his brother the king, to his final resting-place, followed by many sincere mourners, who had, by the kind offices of which I have only made mention now, done all that could be done to soften my grief, and for whose sympathetic attentions I shall never cease to be grateful.

CHAPTER XXXVIII

HAWAIIANS PLEAD FOR A NEW CONSTITUTION

AFTER my husband's death, my retainers at Waikiki (to each of whom I had set apart a lot of land, so that each family might have its own home, and, further, that these might be handed down for the use of their children and children's children), proposed to come and stay with me in the city. So I accorded to each family one week, that all might have a share in this kindly office. This rule was laid down by me, and carefully observed from the date of my husband's death.

This will be, perhaps, the place to mention a matter which has been made use of in an evil way by certain of my enemies. On my accession to the throne my husband had been made prince consort, and after my brother's burial I had proposed to him that he should move to the palace; but in his feeble health he dreaded the long stairs there, which he would be obliged to climb, so I proposed to have the bungalow put in repair, and that the entire house should be placed at his service.

With this proposition he was much pleased, and hopefully looked forward to the time when, recovering from his illness, he would be able to take possession of his new home. He asked that there might be a small gate opened near the bungalow, so that he might easily come and go without being obliged to go through the form of offering to the sentry the password required for entrance by the front gate. His wish was immediately granted, and instructions given to the Minister of the Interior to that effect. The bungalow was handsomely fitted up, and all things were made ready for his occupation ; but owing to his continued and increasing ill-health he never moved into it.

Mr. C. B. Wilson and his wife (seeing that she was one of my beneficiaries, and in her younger days one for whom my husband and I had great consideration) asked if they might come and be near me. In response, I told them that they might take the room that had been occupied by the Princess Poomaikalani in the bungalow. That was all that passed between us about the matter. Mrs. Wilson and Mrs. Clark were in constant attendance upon me as ladies in waiting.

Mrs. Eveline Wilson from her childhood had professed a great fondness and love for me, and with two other young ladies, Lizzie Kapoli and Sophie Sheldon, had made my home theirs. Bright young girls, with happy hearts, and free from care and trouble, they made that part of my life a most delightful epoch to me. It was then that Mr. Wilson first sought the hand of pretty little Kittie Townsend. Thus we had known Mr. Wilson quite well as a young man when he was courting his wife. My husband and myself had warmly favored his suit ; and, with his wife, he naturally became a retainer of the household, and from time to time they took up their residence with us. But one cannot always tell what a young man of promise may be when he arrives at full manhood.

Mr. Samuel Parker called on me one day, and, after discussing some cabinet affairs, asked me directly, if there was any truth in the report that I had called in the advice or sought the assistance of Mr. C. B. Wilson in public affairs. To this I very naturally demanded the reason why he should ask such questions. He replied that Mr. Wilson had told persons down town that he knew of matters which were connected with the cabinet, and that it was through his advice that certain measures had been carried through. On the strength of these remarks, occasion had been taken by Mr. J. E. Bush and Mr. R. W. Wilcox to publish in their newspapers articles calculated to prove injurious to my reputation. I answered Mr. Parker that I consulted no one outside of my cabinet, and that no measures had ever been consummated excepting such as had been advised by the ministers. He recognized the truth of this statement, and communicated the substance of our conversation to his colleagues.

Mr. Bush and Mr. Wilcox at the very commencement of my regency had openly asked for billets of office ; a favor I had scarcely the power, and certainly not the intention, to grant, because all the offices were then filled by men whom I thought were good, loyal, and true to the crown. Mr. Bush had further published articles in his paper which did not meet with my approval, for they were attacks upon my brother, the king. Was he at work with the opposition party at the time he solicited office ? Whether this was so or not,

his subsequent actions showed at least the deepest ingratitude towards myself, who had showered favors on
him and on his family, educated his children, and kept
them all from poverty.   Mr. R. W. Wilcox I have spoken
of elsewhere.   It will be seen that he had also become
one of my enemies.

I was recently told that Mr. Wilson, at the time of
Mr. Wilcox's attempt in 1889, would enter the meetings which were held at the king's barracks, and then,
leaving the assembly, would stealthily go around to the
house of Mr. A. F. Judd, and report all that had transpired.   I have had no experiences more painful than
the evidences of ingratitude among those I have had
reason to think my friends; and I sincerely hope that
in this case I have been misinformed.

One evening, shortly after Mr. and Mrs. Wilson had
moved into the bungalow, he presented himself at the
Blue Room of the palace, and then first mentioned the
idea that a new constitution should be promulgated.
About two days after this suggestion I received a call
from Mr. Samuel Nowlein, who alluded to the same matter.   A few days after Mr. Joseph Nawahi, with Mr.
William White, had an interview with me by their request, and called my attention to the same public need.
Until these conversations, it had not occurred to me
as possible to take such a step in the interest of the native people; but after these parties had spoken to me,
I began to give the subject my careful consideration.
Twice Mr. White spoke to me on the matter before
I told him that I would like to have a conference with
all, to listen to an expression of their views.

Accordingly a meeting was called to be held at Mu-
olaulani Palace, at which there was to be an opportunity for them to compare their opinions and discuss them
in my presence.   I heard what the opinions of the gentlemen were, but gave them no intimation of my own
ideas or intentions, for I had really come to no definite
conclusion.   When the assembly was opened, I noticed
that Mr. Wilson was not present, nor did he attend any
of the meetings which were held for the consideration
of the matter of constitutional reform, but came singly
and alone to speak to me on the subject.   But it seems
that all this time, while I was simply reflecting on the
situation, each of them was going forward and engaging in the preparation or draft of a new constitution.

When completed, I was handed by one party a copy
of that it proposed, and by Mr. Wilson I was given a
copy of the one on which he had been engaged.   After
reading both over, I employed a young man, simply because he was a very neat penman, to make copies ; his
name was W. F. Kaae, but he was usually called Kaiu.
This is worthy of mention, because I subsequently discovered that, while upon this work for me, he took
copies to Mr. A. F. Judd for the examination of that
gentleman.   It can readily be seen by what kind of
persons I was surrounded ; it must be remembered that
I now write with a knowledge of recent events, but that
then I had the fullest confidence in the loyalty of those
who professed to be my friends.

The election of 1892 arrived, and with it the usual
excitement of such occasions.   Petitions poured in from
every part of the Islands for a new constitution ; these

were addressed to myself as the reigning sovereign.
They were supported by petitions addressed to the Hui
Kalaaina, who in turn indorsed and forwarded them to
me.   It was estimated by those in position to know,
that out of a possible nine thousand five hundred registered voters, six thousand five hundred, or two-thirds,
had signed these petitions.   To have ignored or disre-
garded so general a request I must have been deaf to
the voice of the people, which tradition tells us is the
voice of God.   No true Hawaiian chief would have done
other than to promise a consideration.of their wishes.

My first movement was to inquire of the parties active
in the matter what they had to propose.   I asked the
Hui Kalaaina if they had any draft of a constitution
prepared for my examination.   The committee replied
that they had not.   After leaving my presence, they
applied to Mr. W. R. Castle, and requested him to draw
one out for them.   Soon after the committee again entered my presence, this time bearing a neatly written
document ; but whether it had been drawn by Mr. Castle
or by others, it is difficult for me to say.   This I handed
back to the committee, telling them to keep it until
some future day, when I would ask them for it ; because
I did not intend at that moment to make any announce-
ment of my purposes.

September 1st, 1892, witnessed the opening of the
legislative assembly.   There was nothing lacking of that
pomp and display which had been first inaugurated in
the days of Kanikeaouli, the third of the Kamehamehas.
These forms and ceremonies were suggested and taught
to the Hawaiian people by Dr. G. P. Judd, Mr. W.

Richards, and Mr. R. Armstrong, men who originally came to Hawaii with no other avowed object than that of teaching the religion of Jesus Christ; but they soon resigned their meagre salaries from the American Board of Commissioners for Foreign Missions, and found positions in the councils or cabinets of the Kamehamehas more lucrative and presumably more satisfactory to them.

Lunalilo had an official staff, and many of his aids-de-camp were white men, as also happened with Kamehameha V., Kalakaua, and all the recent Hawaiian sovereigns. Dr. E. Hoffman, Mr. W. F. Allen, Mr. M. T. Monserrat, Mr. Prendergast, and many others whose names I might mention, have been perfectly willing to wear the uniform of the crown, to display their gilt lace and brass buttons on state occasions, and to ride richly caparisoned horses with shining accoutrements through our streets; and as long as the missionary party chose the men that were to be thus decked out, honored, and exhibited, it was never alleged that the Hawaiian kings loved display, and sought pomp and fuss and feathers. Yet what had our earlier monarchs ever done for the public good? Individually, nothing. They had acquiesced in the course laid down for them by the missionaries. The government established by these pious adventurers was the government of the day.

Those of their number who were able to get into government service drew their salaries faithfully, and spent or saved as they saw fit, but observed a truly "religious" silence as to the folly of spending money on public displays. This is the more remarkable, because there were other ways, even then, of securing treas-

KING STREET, WITH GOVERNMENT BUILDING AND OPERA HOUSE

ury deficiencies. I remember that when G. P. Judd, W. Richards, and R. Armstrong were cabinet ministers, a deficiency so inexplicable occurred that the cabinet was required to resign immediately, and to one of the retiring members the popular appellation " *kauka-kope-kala* " subsequently adhered pretty tenaciously. I refrain from translating, as the title is not one of honor ; but it still clings to the family as an heirloom.

It is more to the point that Kalakaua's reign was, in a material sense, the golden age of Hawaiian history. The wealth and importance of the Islands enormously increased, and always as a direct consequence of the king's acts. It has been currently supposed that the policy and foresight of the " missionary party " is to be credited with all that he accomplished, since they succeded in abrogating so many of his prerogatives, and absorbing the lion's share of the benefits derived from it. It should, however, be only necessary to remember that the measures which brought about our accession of wealth were not at all in line with a policy of annexation to the United States, which was the very essence of the dominant " missionary " idea. In fact, his progressive foreign policy was well calculated to discourage it.

And for this reason, probably, they could not be satisfied even with the splendid results which our continued nationality offered them. They were not grateful for a prosperity which must sooner or later, while enriching them, also elevate the masses of the Hawaiian people into a self-governing class, and depose them from that primacy in our political affairs which they chiefly valued.

They became fiercely jealous of every measure which promised to benefit the native people, or to stimulate their national pride. Every possible embarrassment and humiliation were heaped upon my brother. And because I was suspected of having the welfare of the whole people also at heart (and what sovereign with a grain of wisdom could be otherwise minded?), I must be made to feel yet more severely that my kingdom was but the assured prey of these " conquistadores."

As I have said, the legislature was opened, and began its daily sessions. The usual measures were brought in, one after another, for consideration by the representatives of the people. But all other matters were persistently thrust aside in order to give time for the repeated dismissals of cabinets. By the account given by me of the revolution of 1887, it will be noticed that the constitution forced upon my brother at that date made the sovereign inferior to the cabinet. The ministry must be appointed by the monarch, but once appointed had absolute control over every measure, nor could the monarch dismiss them, and only a vote of the legislature could deprive them of their portfolios. That provision made the cabinet, as I have shown in previous pages, a perpetual foot-ball in the hands of political parties.

Therefore, this session of the legislature, instead of giving attention to measures required for the good of the country, devoted its energies to the making and unmaking of cabinets. I think there were four rapidly commissioned by me and voted out. But at this point I call attention to the statement which I made to Hon.

James H. Blount, the commissioner charged with the work of investigating the circumstances of the overthrow of the constitutional government of the Hawaiian Islands. In that statement will be found the matter which properly supplements this chapter, and need not be again detailed in this memoir. It naturally, together with some review of events already related, forms the connecting link between the opening ceremonies of the legislature and the enforced abdication of my authority.

Selected by reason of his perfect impartiality and long acquaintance with foreign affairs, this gentleman was sent out by His Excellency Grover Cleveland, President of the United States, and arrived in Honolulu on the twenty-ninth day of March, 1893. In July Mr. Blount made his final report, to which I need only allude to say that, as is well known, after digesting a mass of testimony on both sides, he decided that I was the constitutional ruler of the Hawaiian Islands. It was at this time that I made to him the statement which will be found in the closing pages of this volume.[1]

Of the manner in which Hon. J. H. Blount conducted the investigation, I must speak in the terms of the highest praise. He first met the parties opposed to my government, and took down their statements, which were freely given, because they had imagined that he could be easily turned in their favor. So they gave him the truth, and some important facts in admission of their revolutionary intentions, dating from several years back. Mr. Blount afterwards took the statements of the government, or royalist side. These were simply

[1] See Appendix B.

given, straightforward, and easily understood. Compare
the two statements, and it is not difficult to explain the
final report of Mr. Blount. All the evidence can be
reviewed by any person who may wish to do so, and a
judgment formed of the men who caused this revolution, as it has been bound in volumes, and can be seen
at the Library of Congress in the Capitol at Washington.

CHAPTER XXXIX

THE "CRIMES I AM CHARGED WITHAL"

THE three "intolerable" measures with which my government stands charged by those who succeeded in enlisting the aid of so powerful an ally as the United States in this revolution are as follows: —

First, — That I proposed to promulgate a new constitution. I have already shown that two-thirds of my people declared their dissatisfaction with the old one; as well they might, for it was a document originally designed for a republic, hastily altered when the conspirators found that they had not the courage to assassinate the king. It is alleged that my proposed constitution was to make such changes as to give to the sovereign more power, and to the cabinet or legislature less, and that only subjects, in distinction from temporary residents, could exercise suffrage. In other words, that I was to restore some of the ancient rights of my people. I had listened to whatever had been advised, had examined whatever drafts of constitutions others had brought me, and promised but little.

But, supposing I had thought it wise to limit the exercise of suffrage to those who owed allegiance to no other country; is that different from the usage in all other civilized nations on earth? Is there another country where a man would be allowed to vote, to seek for office, to hold the most responsible of positions, without becoming naturalized, and reserving to himself the privilege of protection under the guns of a foreign man-of-war at any moment when he should quarrel with the government under which he lived? Yet this is exactly what the quasi Americans, who call themselves Hawaiians now and Americans when it suits them, claimed the right to do at Honolulu.

The right to grant a constitution to the nation has been, since the very first one was granted, a prerogative of the Hawaiian sovereigns. The constitution of 1840 was drawn at Lahaina by a council aided by missionary graduates, but promulgated by the king without any appeal to other authority. That of 1852 was drawn by Dr. Judd, John II., and Chief Justice Lee. It was submitted to the legislature, not to the people, and, as amended by the members, became the law of the land. In 1864 there was an attempt to hold a constitutional convention : but, as I have shown in this history, Prince Lot, or, as he then was, Kamehameha V., dissolved the convention, because dissatisfied with its inaction, and in a week's time declared the former constitution abrogated ; and, without asking a vote from anybody, gave the land a new and ably drawn constitution, under which the country was prosperously ruled for twenty-three years, or until it was overthrown by aliens determined to coerce my brother. Then followed their own draft of 1887, which also was never ratified by any deliberative assembly.

Such, in brief, is the history of constitution making

in Hawaii; and from this mere statement of the facts it will be seen that of all the rulers of the Hawaiian Islands for the last half-century, I was the only one who assented to a modification of the existing constitution on the expressed wishes, not only of my own advisers, but of two-thirds of the popular vote, and, I may say it without fear of contradiction, of the entire population of native or half-native birth.   Yet, with the above historical record before them in a book written and printed by one of their own number, the missionary party have had the impudence to announce to the world that I was unworthy longer to rule, because on my sole will and wish I had proposed to overthrow "the constitution."

Second, — I am charged by my opposers with signing a lottery bill.   I have already shown, in the communication of the cabinet to my brother, and the ruling of the Supreme Court supporting their view, that, according to the "bayonet" constitution, made and enforced by the missionary party, the sovereign *shall* and *must* sign such measures as the cabinet presents for signature. This is, in another form, an absolute denial of the power of the veto.   But even had I held veto power, it may be noted here that on many accounts the bill was popular.   No one would have been more benefited than my accusers.   The government of Hawaii was to take no part in the lottery, but was to receive a fixed and openly stated sum of money for its charter.   Among the advantages guaranteed was that the projectors should build a railroad around the large island of Hawaii, thus employing the people and benefiting land-holders.

We were petitioned and besought to grant it by

most of the mercantile class of the city, — shopkeepers, mechanics, manufacturers, — in fact, all the middle class of the people.   Nor is the reason at all difficult to state by any one who knows our community.   When the people of native and part native birth prosper, business is good and the community is prosperous.   The prosperity brought by the reciprocity treaty and the sugar plantations had disappointed our expectations. The money went into the hands of the few, who safely invested in foreign interests and enterprises every dollar of it, save the amount of wages paid to foreign and Mongolian labor.   But the advantages to be received from the charter of this, which in some American localities is called a "gift enterprise," would be immediately put in circulation among our own people, because spent on much-needed public works, and thus would bring some little prosperity to them parallel to that enjoyed by foreigners.

I am not defending lotteries.   They are not native productions of my country, but introduced into our "heathen" land by so-called Christians, from a Christian nation, who have erected monuments, universities, and legislative halls by that method.   I am simply explaining what this bill intended, because, by the reports sent to their correspondents in the United States, the missionary party represented me as a grand vender of lottery tickets, by which I was to become rich and powerful; whereas the scheme, be it good or bad, would not have been to my individual profit, but to that of my native people.

Third, — I proposed to issue licenses for the importation and sale of opium. I did think it would be wise to adopt measures for restricting and controlling a trade which it is impossible to suppress. With a Chinese population of over twenty thousand persons, it is absolutely impossible to prevent smuggling, unlawful trade, bribery, corruption, and every abuse. There were more scandals connected with the opium traffic than I have the time to notice here. Some of the most prominent citizens have been connected with these affairs, and frauds have been unearthed even in the custom-house itself. The names of Mr. Parks, of Mr. W. F. Allen, and more recently of Mr. Henry Waterhouse, have been associated with some very questionable dealings in this drug; and it may be doubted whether the practice of hushing up such matters is favorable to good morals in any community. The Provisional Government seems to have had no scruples in the matter; for the sons of the missionaries exported a large quantity of confiscated opium, and sold it for fifty thousand dollars in British Columbia.

The British government has long since adopted license instead of prohibition, and the statute proposed among the final acts of my government was drawn from one in use in the British colonies; yet I have still to learn that there has been any proposition on the part of the pious people of London to dethrone Her Majesty Queen Victoria for issuing such licenses.

I have thus, for the first and only time, reviewed the position of my opponents in regard to the only public charges which they made against my administration of government; and the reader can judge if all or any of them are of a nature to justify revolt against authority, and the summoning of aid of a foreign vessel of war, as they outrageously stated at the time, — "to protect American life and property!"

My appointments of cabinet officers were never given the test of experience; because the ministry was invariably voted out by the legislature "for want of confidence" without just cause, and in one notable instance within an hour or so from the time when I sent in the names. It is a matter of great satisfaction to me when I look back at the actions of that legislature, to reflect that none of the ministers of my selection have ever been voted out for any crime, for any defalcation in their accounts, or for failure in the exercise of their duties in public office. But it is a source of sincere regret to me that the members of that legislative assembly should have so forgotten themselves, the dignity of their position, and the responsibility with which the people had intrusted them as representatives, as to permit themselves to behave in such an unpatriotic manner.

The Macfarlane cabinet was one of the greatest popularity amongst the Hawaiian people on account of the stand Mr. Macfarlane took in the House, and his courage in replying to the false and uncalled-for speeches of J. L. Stevens, the American Minister resident.

CHAPTER XL

OVERTHROW OF THE MONARCHY

AFTER the so-called Provisional Government had been recognized by Minister Stevens, and I had referred in writing my case to the United States, there was no more for me to do but retire in peace to my private residence, there to await the decision of the United States government. This I did, and cautioned the leaders of my people to avoid riot or resistance, and to await tranquilly, as I was doing, the result of my appeal to the power to whom alone I had yielded my authority. While in Washington in 1897, I had prepared for me as brief a statement as possible from official documents there of the reference of my case to the decision of the United States government as arbitrator in the matter.[1]

It has been my endeavor, in these recollections, to avoid speaking evil of any person, unless absolutely demanded by the exigencies of my case before the public. I simply state facts, and let others form their own judgment of the individuals. But of Minister John L. Stevens it must be said that he was either mentally incapable of recognizing what is to be expected of a gentleman, to say nothing of a diplomatist, or he was decidedly in league with those persons who had con-

[1] A copy will be found in Appendix C.

spired against the peace of Hawaii from the date of the
"Queen's Jubilee" in 1887. Several times in my presence, to which he had access by virtue of his official
position, he conducted himself with such a disregard of
good manners as to excite the comment of my friends.

His official despatches to his own government, from
the very first days of his landing, abound in statements
to prove (according to his view) the great advantage
of an overthrow of the monarchy, and a cession of my
domains to the rule of the United States. His own
daughter went as a messenger to the largest one of the
islands of my kingdom to secure names for a petition
for the annexation of the Hawaiian Islands to the
American Union, and by an accident lost her life, with
the roll containing the few names she had secured. All
this took place while he was presumed to be a friendly
minister to a friendly power, and when my minister was
under the same relation to his government. Of his remarks regarding myself personally I will take no notice,
further than to say that, by his invitation, I attended a
very delightful lunch party at his house a few months
before the United States troops were landed.

Mr. Albert F. Willis arrived in Honolulu on Saturday, the fourth day of November, 1893. He came from
San Francisco on the same steamer with Rev. Dr.
C. M. Hyde, the local representative or agent of the
American Board of Missions. By this gentleman Mr.
Willis was approached and informed, until he became
imbued with Dr. Hyde's own prejudices against the
native people of the Hawaiian Islands and against their
queen. That clergyman's propensity to speak evil of

his neighbor may be recalled by those who read his remarks about the late lamented Father Damien. One of
the first acts of Mr. Willis was to send for me to come
to his residence, which I did, accompanied by my chamberlain, Mr. Robertson. Was it the place of the lady
to go to the house of the gentleman, or for the latter
to call on the lady? I leave it for others to decide. As
for myself, I simply felt that I would undertake anything for the benefit of my people.

At this time men were going about town with firearms; shots were at times flying about the city, whis-
tling through the air, or penetrating houses to the great
danger of the occupants; and no one was responsible
for the local disorder. Words of harm towards my person had been openly spoken by the revolutionists; spies
were in my household, and surrounded my house by day
and by night; spies were also stationed at the steps of
the Congregational church opposite my residence, to take
note of those who entered my gates, how long they remained, and when they went out. My respect for true
religion prevents my stating the active part one of the
preachers of God's Word took in this espionage. It was
under these circumstances that I prepared to visit Mr.
Willis in accordance with his request.

On entering the house of Mr. Willis, Mr. Mills directed me into the parlor, while he and Mr. Robertson
entered the opposite room. A Japanese screen divided
the apartments. I was seated on the sofa when Mr.
Willis, entering, took a chair, and sat down just in front
of me, near the screen. He informed me that he was
the bearer of the kindest greetings from President Cleve-

land, and that the President would do all in his power
to undo the wrong which had been done. He then
asked if I would consent to sign a proclamation of general amnesty, stating that I would grant complete protection and pardon to those who had overthrown my
government. I told him that I would consult my ministers on the matter. The suggestion did not seem to
meet with his approval.

I well knew, and it has been conclusively shown in
this history, that my actions could not be binding or
in any way recognized unless supported by the ministers in cabinet meeting. This was according to law,
and according to the constitution these very persons
had forced upon the nation. Perhaps Mr. Willis thought
that all he had to do was to propose, and then that my
place was to acquiesce. But he asked again for my
judgment of the matter as it stood, and seemed determined to obtain an expression of opinion from me. I
told him that, as to granting amnesty, it was beyond my
powers as a constitutional sovereign. That it was a
matter for the privy council and for the cabinet. That
our laws read that those who are guilty of treason should
suffer the penalty of death.

He then wished to know if I would carry out that
law. I said that I would be more inclined personally
to punish them by banishment, and confiscation of their
property to the government. He inquired again if such
was my decision. I regarded the interview as an informal conversation between two persons as to the best
thing for the future of my country, but I repeated to
him my wish to consult my ministers before deciding on

any definite action. This terminated the consultation, excepting that Mr. Willis specially requested me not to mention anything concerning the matter to any person whomsoever, and assured me he would write home to the government he represented.

He did so. It was a long month before he could receive any reply; but when it came he communicated the fact to me, and asked for another interview at his house. This time he also inquired if there was any other person I would like to have with me. I suggested the name of Mr. J. O. Carter, at which the American minister seemed to be highly pleased. So at the stated hour we all met. This time Mr. Willis had present as his stenographer Mr. Ellis C. Mills, afterwards American consul-general at Honolulu. He first read to me what he said were some notes of our former interview. From whence did these come? By Mr. Willis's own proposition we were to be entirely alone during that interview, and to all appearance we were so. Was there a stenographer behind that Japanese screen? Whatever the paper was, Mr. Willis finished the reading of it, and asked me if it was correct. I replied, "Yes."

Doubtless, had I held the document in my hand, and had I been permitted to read and examine it, for the eye perceives words that fall unheeded on the ear, I should then have noticed that there was a clause which declared that I was to have my opponents beheaded. That is a form of punishment which has never been used in the Hawaiian Islands, either before or since the coming of foreigners. Mr. Willis then asked me if my views were the same as when we met the first time;

and I again said "Yes," or words to that effect. Mr. Carter inquired if I rescinded so much of Mr. Willis's report as related to the execution of the death penalty upon those in revolt. To this I replied, "I do in that respect."

Yet, notwithstanding the fact was officially reported in the despatches of Mr. Willis, that I especially declared that my enemies should not suffer the death penalty, I found to my horror, when the newspapers came to Honolulu from the United States, that the President and the American people had been told that I was about to behead them all! There is an old proverb which says that "a lie can travel around the world while the truth is putting on its boots." That offensive charge was repeated to my hurt as often as possible; although I immediately sent my protest that I had not used the words attributed to me by Mr. Willis in our informal conversation, and that at my first official interview with him I had modified (so far as my influence would go) the law of all countries regarding treason.

At the interview held Saturday, Dec. 16, I did decline to promise executive clemency, and gave as my reason that, this being the second offence of these individuals, they were regarded as dangerous to the community. That their very residence would be a constant menace; that there never would be peace in my country, or harmony amongst the people of different nations residing with us, as long as such a disturbing element remained, especially after they had once been successful in seizing the reins of government. But on Monday, Dec. 18, Mr. Willis came to Washington Place;

and again acting under the advice of Hon. J. O. Carter, I gave to him a document recognizing the high sense of justice which had prompted the action of Mr. Cleveland, and agreeing that, in view of his wishes, the individuals setting up or supporting the Provisional Government should have full amnesty in their persons and their property, if they would work together with me in trying to restore peace and prosperity to our beautiful and once happy islands.

It was most unfortunate that the American minister should have so misrepresented me, or that I should have so misunderstood him, or that his stenographer (if there was one concealed at that interview) should have blundered, or that I should have been so overburdened by the many aspects of the painful situation as to be ignorant or unconscious of the importance of the precise words read in my presence. The only *official* communication made by me was to the effect that there should be perfect amnesty, and this was made in recognition of President Cleveland's courtesy and justice.

Events proved that it would not have made the least difference what I had said or what I had not said; for these people, having once gained the power, were determined never to relinquish it. Mr. Dole wrote to the American minister charging him with being in correspondence with me, and demanded of Mr. Willis if he was acting in any way hostile to his, that is, the Provisional Government. The very next day Mr. Willis sent word to Mr. Dole that he had a communication to make to him. So, Dec. 20, Mr. Willis went to President Dole, and delivered his message from President

Cleveland, in which Mr. Dole was asked to resign that power which he had only obtained through the acts of Minister Stevens and the United States troops. Mr. Willis's speech is a full and explicit confession of the ground taken by my government, that it was overthrown by a conspiracy to which the United States, through its minister, was a party; and after assuring Mr. Dole that I had granted full amnesty to all parties, asked him to resign and restore the old order of things. Mr. Willis says in his latest utterance on the subject: —

"It becomes my duty to advise you of the President's determination of the question which your action and that of the queen devolved upon him, and that you are expected to relinquish to her her constitutional authority. In the name of and by the authority of the United States of America, I submit to you the question, 'Are you willing to abide by the decision of the President?'"

Could there be any plainer recognition than this that I was the constitutional ruler of my people?

And yet I cannot help calling attention to the difference in the treatment accorded to the two parties, and their reference to the United States. Three days were given to Mr. Dole to consider Mr. Cleveland's decision, as announced to him by Mr. Willis. The documents were placed in his hands to study over; and were he so disposed he could call together his associates, compare their opinions, and then return a carefully written and diplomatic answer. This he did, under date of the 23d of December, at midnight, when he himself delivered his response to Mr. Willis. In contrast, I, a lone woman, was sent an order to go to the residence of a gentleman until that moment a stranger to me. Without the least warning of the nature of the communication to be made to me, and without a moment's deliberation or consultation with friendly counsellors, I was urged to give my opinion as to matters which in any government should be decided only after careful consideration ; and then my first immature impressions of the claims of my people and of justice were telegraphed broadcast, while my official and subsequent proclamation of entire amnesty was hardly noticed. *And yet, all this time, by Mr. Willis's own words, I was recognized by the United States as the constitutional sovereign of the Hawaiian Islands.*

The Hawaiian people almost worship the name of President Cleveland ; for he has tried to do what was right, and it was only because he was not supported by Congress that his efforts were not successful. Mr. Dole's answer, as could have been predicted by any who know the men composing the missionary party, was a refusal to comply with the request of President Cleveland. But, none the less, my grateful people will always remember that, in his message to Congress and in his official acts, Mr. Cleveland showed the greatest anxiety to do that which was just, and that which was for the honor of the nation over which he had been elected chief ruler: He has always had from me the utmost respect and esteem.

CHAPTER XLI

THE first annexation commission was sent to Washington by the parties who had been prominent in the overthrow of the monarchy during the closing days of the administration of President Harrison. When Mr. Carter and his fellow-commissioners, Messrs. Thurston, Wilder, Castle, and Marsden, arrived in Washington, President Harrison and Secretary Foster had received my letter of protest, so that they had ample time to consider the situation before the so-called commissioners were presented at the executive mansion. Yet, after having been fully warned by the statements in my letter, these men were received diplomatically.

I was the constitutional ruler the last time the Department of State had heard from the Islands.

The minister bearing my commission and seal was at that moment residing at the national capital.

I had informed President Harrison and his Secretary of State of the unjust and fraudulent actions of the revolutionists, of the well-known aid and counsel they had received from Mr. John L. Stevens, the American minister, and the substantial assistance given by the forces of the United States ship Boston, under command of Captain Wiltse, through which agencies, and those alone, my government had been overthrown.

PALACE SQUARE IN FRONT OF IOLANI PALACE

ADMIRAL SKERRETT REVIEWING THE MEN OF THE U.S.S. "BOSTON"

I had asked that justice should be done, and that the rights of my people should be restored.

President Harrison chose to set aside my statement and petition, and give audience to these irresponsible commissioners, sending to the Senate a treaty which, without the least authority, they offered to him.

These commissioners were self-chosen; but even allowing that they had been selected by the missionary party, with whom they were in sympathy, yet that was a mere petty minority, — only 637 voters against 9,500 of Hawaiian birth and nationality. Yet their proposition was certainly sent to the Senate, while no action whatever was ever taken upon mine, although in this I did not represent myself individually, but the constitutional government and the real people of Hawaii. I have been informed, since I visited Washington in 1897, that the Senate decided that these acts of President Harrison amounted to a recognition of the Provisional Government. Why should this be so, when it was a mere proposal placed before the President, and by him transmitted as such to the Senate? It was there simply for their consideration. No vote was taken on the question up to the day when it was withdrawn by his successor, President Cleveland. The pretence of recognition to these irresponsible commissioners was unjust to me, as well as a wrong to the Hawaiian people.

In contrast to this, the wise step taken by President Cleveland in sending a commissioner to investigate the situation was fair to both sides, and carried out by the man of his choice in a thoroughly impartial manner. When Mr. Cleveland was finally forced into some kind

of recognition of the missionary party, he used these
words, that he recognized "the right of the Hawaiian
people to choose their own form of government." My
people have had no choice since the Provisional Government came into power.

Nothing of importance seems to have transpired during the early part of the year 1894. All this time, however, the Hawaiian people were waiting with patience
to hear from the American continent that justice was
to be done, and their constitutional rights restored by
the great power to which they had trusted.

No messages or communications of any kind were
made to me all this time by the American minister, and
none were sent to me from Washington by the Department of State. Why was this? By Mr. Cleveland's decision, by Mr. Gresham's despatches to Mr. Willis, by
the declarations of that gentleman publicly made to
Mr. Dole, I, Liliuokalani, was the constitutional sovereign of the Hawaiian Islands; why should I have been
kept in complete ignorance of all that was taking place
at Washington, while the petty minority of alien residents, who had been summoned by the American minister "in the name of the United States of America
to resign power and authority," should receive official
despatches which ought to have been delivered to me?

Just before he left the Islands, Mr. Blount impressed
upon me with great solemnity the importance of the
continuance of the peaceful attitude of the Hawaiian
people, assuring me that if any disturbance should take
place on our part it would prompt the United States to
send vessels of war to the port, men would again be

landed, and the result would be the loss of the independence of our country. Believing that he spoke by authority, and that the day of release from the oppression of the stranger was near, I continued from the day of my retirement at Washington Place to impress upon all the necessity for abstaining from riot or disturbance.

The people listened to my voice, and obeyed my will with a submission that kept the community free from disorder far more than any law or restraint of that which has called itself a government. Many a time have I heard that the Hawaiians would no longer submit to their oppressors, that they were about to appeal to fire and the sword; but I have always dissuaded them from commencing any such measures. This discontent was not confined to the people of native or even part native birth. Those of foreign ancestry not in sympathy with the revolutionists, those whose daily comfort had been disturbed or whose business had been made unprofitable or ruined by the rich and powerful missionary party, appealed to me and my friends to restore the old order of things, that prosperity might again smile on the majority, instead of being locked up in the bank accounts of a very few.

It subsequently became known to me through other sources, although not until long after the date about which I now write, that the Senate had taken matters out of the hands of President Cleveland, and had conducted an independent investigation in the city of Washington, at which O. P. Emerson, Peter C. Jones, Z. S. Spalding, W. D. Alexander, Lieutenant Lucien Young,

Mr. E. K. Moore, L. G. Hobbs, W. T. Swinburne, Lieu-
tenant Laird, Mr. A. F. Judd, W. C. Wilder, J. H. Soper,
A. S. Wilcox, C. Bolte, Geo. N. Wilcox, John Emmeluth,
C. L. Carter, F. W. McChesney, W. B. Oleson, J. A.
McCandless, Minister John L. Stevens, James F. Morgan,
William R. Castle, L. A. Thurston, Dewitt Coffman, M.
Stelker, William S. Bowen, P. W. Reeder, Charles L.
Macarthur, Admiral George Belknap, N. B. Delameter,
Francis R. Day, Rev. R. R. Hoes, W. E. Simpson, N.
Ludlow, and S. N. Castle, gave either by affidavit or in
person their testimony against me.

So far as the above individuals knew anything whatever about the affairs of Hawaii, they were conspirators
against my government ; the obscurely known amongst
the number were from those who had been, as one of
them stated, simply rusticating at the Islands a while,
and had been poisoned against the native people by my
enemies.　Not a single witness on the side of constitutional government was examined by the committee, if
I except Hon. James H. Blount, who was called, and
courageously repeated all the statements of his report
to Mr. Cleveland.

Yet on such *ex parte* testimony as this, the Senate
made a lengthy and partisan report, which I never had
an opportunity to examine until my residence in Washington during the winter of 1897.　It is altogether too
long to find admittance here, but its meaning can be
expressed in a very few words.　It says that, rightfully
or wrongfully, the native monarchy had been overthrown, the parties who succeeded in this fraud and
imposition had been acknowledged as a government by

the administration of Mr. Harrison, and therefore the question would not be reopened nor the facts reviewed by the United States!

Where was proper consideration given to my own statement to President Harrison, made through my commissioner, Mr. Paul Neumann? Why were not the petitions of the patriotic leagues of my people put into the inquiry? Why was not the fact that there was such an inquiry going on communicated to me? Why were my enemies informed of that which was in progress, so that they could hurry to Washington, or send their testimony, while not one of my friends was given the opportunity to raise a voice in behalf of the disfranchised Hawaiian people or their persecuted queen? Whatever may be the answers to these questions, it is true that no message ever reached me. No further communication was ever made to me by the American minister, nor did I even hear, except through the most vague kind of rumor, that probably no more would be done in the cause of justice. Even the fact of the decision of the Senate was not communicated to me; yet it seems that it was all settled the last week in February, 1894, on the testimony of the above aliens.

Since the bold admissions of members of the missionary party made to Minister Blount of their own guilt, since the confession, by those who had established themselves at the head of a provisional government, of the intended crime of which my brother was to be the victim, all of which appears in black and white on the pages of their own testimony, the scornful title of "P. G." has clung to them, to their children, and will

be passed down to their children's children.   After the
truth was made public they became ashamed to hear
themselves called " P. G.'s," and, repudiating the name,
called themselves instead " Annexationists."

The so-called Provisional Government began in the
spring of 1894 to consider again a change of name.   So
they allowed a few of their chosen tools to vote for
what was called a constitutional convention, of which the
original conspirators, to the number of nineteen, who
had no warrant for their position save their own self-
given nominations, and eighteen others in sympathy
with them, enacted what they called a constitution ; and
in order to have some guns fired at its adoption, and
to curry favor with the United States, they announced
the so-called Republic on the fourth day of July, 1894,
and it was declared from the steps of Iolani Palace,
while the vessels of war in the harbor were saluting
for a totally different occasion.

During that same month Mr. Samuel Parker had
mentioned to me the necessity, in his opinion, of sending a Hawaiian commissioner to the United States to
see what could be done for our people.   Mr. Cornwell
also consulted me upon the same matter.   By conference with these gentlemen, it was decided that, instead
of sending five commissioners, as we had at first designed to do, that Hon. Samuel Parker, Mr. John A.
Cummins, Judge H. A. Widemann, with Major W. T.
Seaward as secretary, should visit the capital of the
United States, and represent those in Hawaii, whether
native or foreign, opposed to the missionary party, that
so the government of the majority might get a hearing

in the councils of that great nation to which alone I yielded my authority.

What was the result of this commission? That is impossible for me to say. They went and they returned. They brought me no papers giving an official account of their proceedings or actions while on the mission. Each had some bit of information to communicate verbally. About the only definite remark which recurs to me now is, that Secretary Gresham had informed them that Mr. Cleveland was suffering from a slight illness, and would be unable to see them for three or four days, at which intelligence they became discouraged, and left Washington. They had absolutely nothing to show to me for their time and the expenditure of my money.

A month after word was sent to me that the merchants of Honolulu, who were in sympathy with the monarchy, had decided to send Judge Widemann on a foreign mission in our interests, at which I was pleased, and acquiesced in the choice. He was gone about three months, and again returned with only a verbal statement to the effect, that, while on his way to England, he had heard that that nation was sending a message of recognition to the Republic of Hawaii. He continued on his journey as far as Germany, where he reported that the minister to whom he meant to present the statement of our side of the case was absent from the country on a tour of business or pleasure. So Judge Widemann returned without any favorable results.

All the expenses of these commissions from the very commencement, when I sent Mr. Paul Neumann to fol-

low the original commissioners of the first supporters of
the rebellion, were paid by me from my private purse.
And from the seventeenth day of January to the present hour, that remains true of every effort which has
been made to induce the government of the United
States to act under the righteous decision of its President, Grover Cleveland, supported by the impartial
report of Hon. James H. Blount.　No one, outside or
inside the Hawaiian Islands, has contributed a cent to
the repeated outlays I have made for the good of the
Hawaiian people.

Further, from the date of the overthrow of the constitutional monarchy to the present day, I have never
received from the Provisional Government, nor from
its successor, the "Republic of Hawaii," a single cent
of income from any source whatever.　Even those revenues of the crown lands which had been collected
prior to the seizure of the public treasury by the insur-
gents, and which remained in the hands of the commissioner at the time of my retirement from public life,
were never paid to me.　What became of these moneys
I do not say, but not a dollar of it was ever handed to
me.

For four years and more, now, these people have
confiscated and collected the revenues reserved from all
time in order that the chief highest in rank, that is, the
reigning sovereign, might care for his poorer people.
*Never were the revenues of these lands included in gov-
ernment accounts.*　They comprise 915,000 acres out of
a total extent of four millions, or about one-quarter, and
yield an income of about $50,000 a year.　They are by

legislative act and the rulings of the Supreme Court my own property at this day. But notwithstanding this, the doctrine that might makes right seems to prevail; and not content with depriving me of my income, and employing it to forward their own schemes, the present government is now striving to cede these lands, which they do not own and never can own, to the United States.

CHAPTER XLII

ATTEMPT TO RESTORE THE MONARCHY

At the time of the return of Mr. Widemann from abroad, the intensity of the feeling was at its height amongst the Hawaiian people that something should be done to save their country. Of their own accord they bought rifles, pistols, and other arms, stealthily keeping these for future use. During this time, too, they were privately informed where arms belonging to the men in power were kept; for although it is generally conceded all over the world, and common sense would seem to show how one should act toward one's enemies, yet there was the strangest intermingling of those of the two parties, which were called the " Royalists" and the "P. G.'s." Instead of recognizing each other as enemies, and keeping apart as such, they associated as in former days.

Visiting went on just the same, exchanges of thought and opinion were the same. The Royalists, open hearted and free of speech, socially ignored the fact that the P. G.'s were, in every material sense, their enemies. These latter kept the situation in view, and with soft words studied to worm out of the unsuspecting all that they could in the way of information as to Royalist hopes and plans, that the particulars might be communicated to the P. G. government.

Moreover, many who swore allegiance to the " Republic of Hawaii" began to regret bitterly that they ever permitted themselves to support the revolutionary party. They had been in comfortable circumstances, had even laid aside for a rainy day, and felt that the savings of their years of prosperity would find them independent in life's decline. But since the overthrow of honest government they had lost, or been forced to spend, all they had accumulated, and the little business left to them would scarcely sustain their families.

Weary with waiting, impatient under the wrongs they were suffering, preparations were undoubtedly made amongst some in sympathy with the monarchy to overthrow the oligarchy. How and where these were carried on, I will not say. I have no right to disclose any secrets given in trust to me. To the time of which I now write their actions had been peaceful, out of respect and obedience to their queen. If, goaded by their wrongs, I could no longer hold them in check with reason ; if they were now, by one accord, determined to break away, and endeavor, by a bold stroke, to win back their nationality, why should I prohibit the outburst of patriotism ? I told them that if the mass of the native people chose to rise, and try to throw off the yoke, I would say nothing against it, but I could not approve of mere rioting.

On Jan. 6, 1895, came the beginning of a revolt. For three months prior to that date my physician, Dr. Donald McLelan, had been in attendance on me, and, as I was suffering very severely from nervous prostration, prescribed electricity. For two years I had borne the long agony of suspense, a terrible strain, which at last made great inroads on my strength.

The knowledge of the secreting of arms on my premises, the distribution of munitions of war amongst the people who were guarding my house and grounds, has been imputed to me. Whether any arms were brought there, where they were, or what they were, I never took occasion to inquire. I never saw a single pistol or rifle by day or by night. I remember that I had occasion to scold my gardener for the disturbed condition in which I often found my plants. It seemed as though some persons had been digging up the ground, and replacing the disturbed soil. But no arms were secreted by me or by my orders about the place, from the roof to the cellar, or from one end to the other of the garden, nor were any kept there to my knowledge, save parlor rifles and harmless old-fashioned muskets.

My husband had a passion for collecting ancient specimens of firearms, and for this purpose he set apart in the yard a small cottage which had once been a favorite retreat of his bachelor days. He had everything arranged prettily, and on its walls was a formidable show of antiquated instruments of war. I recall the appearance of one very old Arabian musket, which he took special pride in exhibiting to his friends. There was also an old-fashioned flute, and a sword which, so it was said, had formerly belonged to General Washington.

There were many other relics of antiquity in this line, which had been contributed by his friends, — large pistols and small pistols, loading with ramrods from the muzzle, clubs and spears from the South Sea Islands ;

and, in fact, it was quite a cabinet of curiosities of obsolete warfare.

He had, during his lifetime, rifles and shotguns of modern style of manufacture, which he took with him on his visits to the estates of Hon. Samuel Parker, or when we went to our country residence at Waialua. But these latter, after his death, were appropriated by his personal friends ; and there was therefore nothing on the place by which the least harm to any one could be done. Yet it was on the opening of this curiosity shop, as harmless as any gallery of family portraits, that the word was passed around town that a large quantity of firearms of different styles had been found secreted in a small house on the grounds of the queen.

I slept quietly at home the night of the outbreak. The evening before Captain Samuel Nowlein came in, and told me that his party was in readiness. This must have been about eight o'clock in the evening, as the meeting in the Congregational church had just begun as Captain Nowlein bade me farewell. He had not been gone very long when there seemed to be quite a commotion amongst the church members. They appeared to be hastening from the building. By this time it was quite dark. I retired, and heard nothing more about the uprising until the morning following. When Captain Nowlein went, he had left the premises under guard of one Charles H. Clark. The men who were usually on duty about my estate were still at their stations, without any firearms, without the least appearance of anticipated disturbance.

Now, as to the disturbance itself. At six o'clock in

the afternoon of the sixth day of January, it was tele-
phoned from Diamond Head that there was a conspiracy developed into action, and that the parties engaged
therein would be found at the house of Mr. Henry
Bertelmann. Captain Robert Waipa Parker took some
half dozen native policemen with him, and started for
the locality. On their way they stopped at the house
of Mr. Charles L. Carter, son of the Hon. H. A. P.
Carter, whom they informed of the nature of their
errand. Upon hearing it, Mr. Carter immediately said
that he would like to go with them, and "have a little
fun too," and suited the action to the word by clapping
two pistols into his belt. When they arrived at the
Bertelmann place there was some resistance, and shots
were exchanged between the police and the persons
assembled there. In the course of the fray Mr. Carter
was shot. It was reported that the wound was not in
a locality where it would be likely to be at all dangerous, yet he soon expired. A policeman received a shot
through the lungs at the same time, but he is alive and
well to-day. These, I believe, were all the serious cas-
ualties of the day.

CHAPTER XLIII

I AM PLACED UNDER ARREST

On the sixteenth day of January, 1895, Deputy Marshal Arthur Brown and Captain Robert Waipa Parker were seen coming up the walk which leads from Beretania Street to my residence. Mrs. Wilson told me that they were approaching. I directed her to show them into the parlor, where I soon joined them. Mr. Brown informed me that he had come to serve a warrant for my arrest; he would not permit me to take the paper which he held, nor to examine its contents.

It was evident they expected me to accompany them; so I made preparations to comply, supposing that I was to be taken at once to the station-house to undergo some kind of a trial. I was informed that I could bring· Mrs. Clark with me if I wished, so she went for my hand-bag; and followed by her, I entered the carriage of the deputy marshal, and was driven through the crowd that by this time had accumulated at the gates of my residence at Washington Place. As I turned the corner of the block on which is built the Central Congregational church, I noticed the approach from another direction of Chief Justice Albert F. Judd; he was on the sidewalk, and was going toward my house, which he entered. In the mean time the marshal's carriage continued on its way, and we arrived at the gates of Iolani Palace, the residence of the Hawaiian sovereigns.

We drove up to the front steps, and I remember noticing that troops of soldiers were scattered all over the yard. The men looked as though they had been on the watch all night. They were resting on the green grass, as though wearied by their vigils; and their arms were stacked near their tents, these latter having been pitched at intervals all over the palace grounds. Staring directly at us were the muzzles of two brass field-pieces, which looked warlike and formidable as they pointed out toward the gate from their positions on the lower veranda. Colonel J. H. Fisher came down the steps to receive me; I dismounted, and he led the way up the staircase to a large room in the corner of the palace. Here Mr. Brown made a formal delivery of my person into the custody of Colonel Fisher, and having done this, withdrew.

Then I had an opportunity to take a survey of my apartments. There was a large, airy, uncarpeted room with a single bed in one corner. The other furniture consisted of one sofa, a small square table, one single common chair, an iron safe, a bureau, a chiffonier, and a cupboard, intended for eatables, made of wood with wire screening to allow the circulation of the air through the food. Some of these articles may have been added during the days of my imprisonment. I have portrayed the room as it appears to me in memory. There was, adjoining the principal apartment, a bath-room, and also a corner room and a little boudoir, the windows of which were large, and gave access to the veranda.

THE QUEEN'S GUARDS AND THE BARRACKS

Colonel Fisher spoke very kindly as he left me there, telling me that he supposed this was to be my future abode ; and if there was anything I wanted I had only to mention it to the officer, and that it should be provided. In reply, I informed him that there were one or two of my attendants whom I would like to have near me, and that I preferred to have my meals sent from my own house. As a result of this expression of my wishes, permission was granted to my steward to bring me my meals three times each day.

That first night of my imprisonment was the longest night I have ever passed in my life ; it seemed as though the dawn of day would never come. I found in my bag a small Book of Common Prayer according to the ritual of the Episcopal Church. It was a great comfort to me, and before retiring to rest Mrs. Clark and I spent a few minutes in the devotions appropriate to the evening.

Here, perhaps, I may say, that although I had been a regular attendant on the Presbyterian worship since my childhood, a constant contributor to all the missionary societies, and had helped to build their churches and ornament the walls, giving my time and my musical ability freely to make their meetings attractive to my people, yet none of these pious church members or clergymen remembered me in my prison. To this (Christian ?) conduct I contrast that of the Anglican bishop, Rt. Rev. Alfred Willis, who visited me from time to time in my house, and in whose church I have since been confirmed as a communicant. But he was not allowed to see me at the palace.

Outside of the rooms occupied by myself and my

companion there were guards stationed by day and by
night, whose duty it was to pace backward and forward
through the hall, before my door, and up and down the
front veranda.   The sound of their never-ceasing footsteps as they tramped on their beat fell incessantly on
my ears.   One officer was in charge, and two soldiers
were always detailed to watch our rooms.   I could not
but be reminded every instant that I was a prisoner,
and did not fail to realize my position.   My companion
could not have slept at all that night : her sighs were
audible to me without cessation ; so I told her the morning following that, as her husband was in prison, it was
her duty to return to her children.   Mr. Wilson came in
after I had breakfasted, accompanied by the Attorney-
general, Mr. W. O. Smith ; and in conference it was
agreed between us that Mrs. Clark could return home,
and that Mrs. Wilson should remain as my attendant;
that Mr. Wilson would be the person to inform the government of any request to be made by me, and that any
business transactions might be made through him.

On the morning after my arrest all my retainers residing on my estates were arrested, and to the number
of about forty persons were taken to the station-house,
and then committed to jail.   Amongst these was the
agent and manager of my property, Mr. Joseph Heleluhe.
As Mr. Charles B. Wilson had been at one time in a
similar position, and was well acquainted with all my
surroundings, and knew the people about me, it was but
natural that he should be chosen by me for this office.

Mr. Heleluhe was taken by the government officers,
stripped of all clothing, placed in a dark cell without

light, food, air, or water, and was kept there for hours in hopes that the discomfort of his position would induce him to disclose something of my affairs. After this was found to be fruitless, he was imprisoned for about six weeks; when, finding their efforts in vain, his tormentors released him. No charge was ever brought against him in any way, which is true of about two hundred persons who were similarly confined.

On the very day I left the house, so I was informed by Mr. Wilson, Mr. A. F. Judd had gone to my private residence without search-warrant; and that all the papers in my desk, or in my safe, my diaries, the petitions I had received from my people, — all things of that nature which could be found were swept into a bag, and carried off by the chief justice in person. My husband's private papers were also included in those taken from me.

To this day, the only document which has been returned to me is my will. Never since have I been able to find the private papers of my husband nor those of mine that had been kept by me for use or reference, and which had no relation to political events. The most important historical note lost was in my diary. This was the record made by me at the time of my conversations with Minister Willis, and would be especially valuable now as confirming what I have stated of our first interview.

After Mr. Judd had left my house, it was turned over to the Portuguese military company under the command of Captain Good. These militiamen ransacked it again from garret to cellar. Not an article was left

undisturbed. Before Mr. Judd had finished they had
begun their work, and there was no trifle left unturned
to see what might be hidden beneath. Every drawer
of desk, table, or bureau was wrenched out, turned up-
side down, the contents pulled over on the floors, and
left in confusion there. Some of my husband's jewelry
was taken ; but this, on my application *and offer to pay
expenses*, was afterwards restored to me.

Having overhauled the rooms without other result
than the abstraction of many memorandums of no use
to any person besides myself, the men turned their attention to the cellar, in hopes possibly of unearthing an
arsenal of firearms and munitions of war. Here they
undermined the foundations to such a degree as to en-
danger the whole structure, but nothing rewarded their
search. The place was then seized, and the government
assumed possession ; guards were placed on the premises, and no one was allowed to enter.

CHAPTER XLIV

IMPRISONMENT — FORCED ABDICATION

For the first few days nothing occurred to disturb the quiet of my apartments save the tread of the sentry. On the fourth day I received a visit from Mr. Paul Neumann, who asked me if, in the event that it should be decided that all the principal parties to the revolt must pay for it with their lives, I was prepared to die? I replied to this in the affirmative, telling him I had no anxiety for myself, and felt no dread of death. He then told me that six others besides myself had been selected to be shot for treason, but that he would call again, and let me know further about our fate. I was in a state of nervous prostration, as I have said, at the time of the outbreak, and naturally the strain upon my mind had much aggravated my physical troubles; yet it was with much difficulty that I obtained permission to have visits from my own medical attendant.

About the 22d of January a paper was handed to me by Mr. Wilson, which, on examination, proved to be a purported act of abdication for me to sign. It had been drawn out for the men in power by their own lawyer, Mr. A. S. Hartwell, whom I had not seen until he came with others to see me sign it. The idea of abdicating never originated with me. I knew nothing at all about such a transaction until they sent to me, by the hands of Mr. Wilson, the insulting proposition written in abject terms. For myself, I would have chosen death rather than to have signed it ; but it was represented to me that by my signing this paper all the persons who had been arrested, all my people now in trouble by reason of their love and loyalty towards me, would be immediately released. Think of my position, — sick, a lone woman in prison, scarcely knowing who was my friend, or who listened to my words only to betray me, without legal advice or friendly counsel, and the stream of blood ready to flow unless it was stayed by my pen.

My persecutors have stated, and at that time compelled me to state, that this paper was signed and acknowledged by me after consultation with my friends whose names appear at the foot of it as witnesses. Not the least opportunity was given to me to confer with any one; but for the purpose of making it appear to the outside world that I was under the guidance of others, friends who had known me well in better days were brought into the place of my imprisonment, and stood around to see a signature affixed by me.

When it was sent to me to read, it was only a rough draft. After I had examined it, Mr. Wilson called, and asked me if I were willing to sign it. I simply answered that I would see when the formal or official copy was shown me. On the morning of the 24th of January the official document was handed to me, Mr. Wilson making the remark, as he gave it, that he hoped I would not retract, that is, he hoped that I would sign the official copy.

Then the following individuals witnessed my subscription of the signature which was demanded of me : William G. Irwin, H. A. Widemann, Samuel Parker, S. Kalua Kookano, Charles B. Wilson, and Paul Neumann. The form of acknowledgment was taken by W. L. Stanley, Notary Public.

So far from the presence of these persons being evidence of a voluntary act on my part, was it not an assurance to me that they, too, knew that, unless I did the will of my jailers, what Mr. Neumann had threatened would be performed, and six prominent citizens immediately put to death. I so regarded it then, and I still believe that murder was the alternative. Be this as it may, it is certainly happier for me to reflect to-day that there is not a drop of the blood of my subjects, friends or foes, upon my soul.

When it came to the act of writing, I asked what would be the form of signature ; to which I was told to sign, " Liliuokalani Dominis." This sounding strange to me, I repeated the question, and was given the same reply. At this I wrote what they dictated without further demur, the more readily for the following reasons.

Before ascending the throne, for fourteen years, or since the date of my proclamation as heir apparent, my official title had been simply Liliuokalani. Thus I was proclaimed both Princess Royal and Queen. Thus it is recorded in the archives of the government to this day. The Provisional Government nor any other had enacted any change in my name. All my official acts, as well as my private letters, were issued over the signature of Liliuokalani. But when my jailers required me to sign

" Liliuokalani Dominis," I did as they commanded.
Their motive in this as in other actions was plainly to
humiliate me before my people and before the world.
I saw in a moment, what they did not, that, even were
I not complying under the most severe and exacting
duress, by this demand they had overreached themselves.   There is not, and never was, within the range
of my knowledge, any such a person as Liliuokalani
Dominis.

It is a rule of common law that the acts of any person deprived of civil rights have no force nor weight,
either at law or in equity ; and that was my situation.
Although it was written in the document that it was my
free act and deed, circumstances prove that it was not ;
it had been impressed upon me that only by its execution could the lives of those dear to me, those beloved
by the people of Hawaii, be saved, and the shedding of
blood be averted.   I have never expected the revolutionists of 1887 and 1893 to willingly restore the rights no-
toriously taken by force or intimidation ; but this act,
obtained under duress, should have no weight with the
authorities of the United States, to whom I appealed.
But it may be asked, why did I not make some protest
at the time, or at least shortly thereafter, when I found
my friends sentenced to death and imprisonment ?   I
did.   There are those now living who have seen my
written statement of all that I have recalled here.   It
was made in my own handwriting, on such paper as I
could get, and sent outside of the prison walls and into
the hands of those to whom I wished to state the circumstances under which that fraudulent act of abdica-

tion was procured from me.   This I did for my own satisfaction at the time.

After those in my place of imprisonment had all affixed their signatures, they left, with the single exception of Mr. A. S. Hartwell.   As he prepared to go, he came forward, shook me by the hand, and the tears streamed down his cheeks.   This was a matter of great surprise to me.   After this he left the room.   If he had been engaged in a righteous and honorable action, why should he be affected?   Was it the consciousness of a mean act which overcame him so?   Mrs. Wilson, who stood behind my chair throughout the ceremony, made the remark that those were crocodile's tears.   I leave it to the reader to say what were his actual feelings in the case.

CHAPTER XLV

BROUGHT TO TRIAL

So far was my submission from modifying in any way the course of the government, that the principal prisoners were, after all, condemned to death. Their sentences were passed the same as though my signature had not been obtained. That they were not executed is due solely to a consideration which has been officially stated : " Word came from the United States that the execution of captive rebels would militate against annexation. That about settled it."

Proceedings against me, personally, were not modified. Every day thereafter papers were brought to me from the office of President Dole, a legal service, I suppose it is called, being made on me by Major George C. Potter, an aid-de-camp of the president's staff. In the first of these I found myself charged with the crime of "treason." After about a week had gone by, the accusation was changed to "misprision of treason." The substance of my crime was that I knew my people were conspiring to re-establish the constitutional government, to throw off the yoke of the stranger and oppressor ; and I had not conveyed this knowledge to the persons I had never recognized except as unlawful usurpers of authority, and had not informed against my own nation and against their friends who were also my long-time friends.

The names of those who had informed, and by whose testimony I was to be convicted, were Captain Samuel Nowlein, Charles H. Clark, W. W. Kaae, Charles Warren, Keahikaauwai, George H. Townsend, and Captain Davies of the steamer Waimanalo.

February 5th was to be the day of my trial. After the summons had been served, Mr. Paul Neumann, in consultation with Mr. Wilson, called to consult with me, as it had been a question whether or not I should personally appear in court, as it would be undignified and humiliating. Humiliation! What had I left? It was the intention of the officers of the government to humiliate me by imprisoning me, but my spirit rose above that. I was a martyr to the cause of my people, and was proud of it. So I told them that I would attend; and on the morning of the 8th, at the hour appointed, Sergeant Kenake appeared, and conducted me, attended by Mrs. Wilson, to the court-room.

It was the former throne room of the palace, and was crowded with curious spectators. The diplomatic corps, Mr. Albert F. Willis, Minister of the United States, A. G. S. Hawes, British Commissioner, Monsieur De Verlet, French Commissioner, Senior Canavarro, Portuguese Commissioner, and Mr. F. Schmibu, the Japanese Consul, were all present. There were also ministers of the gospel, and a liberal representation from all classes, including many ladies of Honolulu society. In the centre of the room was the table before which the Military Commission (as it was called) was

convened.   It was before such an audience and by such
a tribunal that I was to be tried for treason.

At one end of the table sat Mr. W. A. Whiting, as
president of the court.   He had once, early in my
reign, been Attorney-general, and a member of my cabinet.   Opposite to him was Mr. W. A. Kinney, the
Judge Advocate.   Besides these there were some half-
dozen young men, — Colonel Fisher, Messrs. Zeigler,
Camara, Pratt, Wilder, W. C. and J. W. Jones, — none
of them names of any prominence or responsibility in
the community.

The trial proceeded, Mr. A. F. Judd being the first
to give his testimony against me.   I cannot recall all
that was said or done, nor is it necessary ; but I know
that, to make complete the work of saving the lives of
my friends, I was compelled to testify as in the statement, and to affirm that it was through the advice of
other friends I abdicated.

The only charge against me really was that of being
a queen ; and my case was judged by these, my adversaries, before I came into court.   I remember with
clearness, however, the attack upon me by the Judge
Advocate, the words that issued from his mouth about
"the prisoner," "that woman," etc., uttered with such
affectation of contempt and disgust.   The object of it
was evidently to humiliate me, to make me break down
in the presence of the staring crowd.   But in this they
were disappointed.   My equanimity was never disturbed ;
and their own report relates that I throughout preserved
"that haughty carriage" which marked me as an "unusual woman."

I said nothing to their taunts and innuendoes, and showed no emotion; but when the proper time came, I denied that I had been guilty of any treasonable action, and asked my counsel to submit the following statement: —

"In the year 1893, on the fifteenth day of January, at the request of a large majority of the Hawaiian people, and by and with the consent of my cabinet, I proposed to make certain changes in the constitution of the Hawaiian kingdom, which were suggested to me as being for the advantage and benefit of the kingdom, and subjects and residents thereof. These proposed changes did not deprive foreigners of any rights or privileges enjoyed by them under the constitution of 1887, promulgated by King Kalakaua and his cabinet, without the consent of the people or ratified by their votes.

"My ministers at the last moment changed their views, and requested me to defer all action in connection with the constitution; and I yielded to their advice as bound to do by the existing constitution and laws.

"A minority of the foreign population made my action the pretext for overthrowing the monarchy, and, aided by the United States naval forces and representative, established a new government.

"I owed no allegiance to the Provisional Government so established, nor to any power or to any one save the will of my people and the welfare of my country.

"The wishes of my people were not consulted as to this change of government, and only those who were in practical rebellion against the constitutional government were allowed to vote upon the question whether the monarchy should exist or not.

"To prevent the shedding of the blood of my people, natives and foreigners alike, I opposed armed interference, and quietly yielded to the armed forces brought against my throne, and submitted to the arbitrament of the government of the United States the decision of my rights and those of the Hawaiian people. Since then, as is well known to all, I have pursued the path of peace and diplomatic discussion, and not that of internal strife.

"The United States having first interfered in the interest of those founding the government of 1893 upon the basis of revolution, concluded to leave to the Hawaiian people the selection of their own form of government.

"This selection was anticipated and prevented by the Provisional Government, who, being possessed of the military and police power of the kingdom, so cramped the electoral privileges that no free expression of their will was permitted to the people who were opposed to them.

"By my command and advice the native people and those in sympathy with them were restrained from rising against the government in power.

"The movement undertaken by the Hawaiians last month was absolutely commenced without my knowledge, sanction, consent, or assistance, directly or indirectly ; and this fact is in truth well known to those who took part in it.

"I received no information from any one in regard

to arms which were, or which were to be, procured, nor
of any men who were induced, or to be induced, to join
in any such uprising.

"I do not know why this information should have
been withheld from me, unless it was with a view to my
personal safety, or as a precautionary measure. It would
not have received my sanction; and I can assure the
gentlemen of this commission that, had I known of any
such intention, I would have dissuaded the promoters
from such a venture. But I will add that, had I known,
their secrets would have been mine, and inviolately
preserved.

"That I intended to change my cabinet, and to appoint certain officers of the kingdom, in the event of
my restoration, I will admit; but that I, or any one
known to me, had, in part or in whole, established a
new government, is not true. Before the 24th of January, 1895, the day upon which I formally abdicated,
and called upon my people to recognize the Republic
of Hawaii as the only lawful government of these
Islands, and to support that government, I claim that
I had the right to select a cabinet in anticipation of
a possibility; and history of other governments supports
this right. I was not intimidated into abdicating, but
followed the counsel of able and generous friends and
well-wishers, who advised me that such an act would
restore peace and good-will among my people, vitalize
the progress and prosperity of the Islands, and induce
the actual government to deal leniently, mercifully, char-
itably, and impassionately with those who resorted to
arms for the purpose of displacing a government in the

formation of which they had no voice or control, and
which they themselves had seen established by force
of arms.

"I acted of my own free will, and wish the world to
know that I have asked no immunity or favor myself,
nor plead my abdication as a petition for mercy. My
actions were dictated by the sole aim of doing good to
my beloved country, and of alleviating the positions
and pains of those who unhappily and unwisely resorted
to arms to regain an independence which they thought
had been unjustly wrested from them.

"As you deal with them, so I pray that the Almighty
God may deal with you in your hours of trial.

"To my regret much has been said about the danger
which threatened foreign women and children, and about
the bloodthirstiness of the Hawaiians, and the outrages
which would have been perpetrated by them if they had
succeeded in their attempt to overthrow the Republic
government.

"They who know the Hawaiian temper and disposition understand that there was no foundation for any
such fears. The behavior of the rebels to those foreigners whom they captured and held shows that there
was no malignancy in the hearts of the Hawaiians at
all. It would have been sad indeed if the doctrine of
the Christian missionary fathers, taught to my people
by them and those who succeeded them, should
have fallen like the seed in the parable, upon barren
ground.

"I must deny your right to try me in the manner
and by the court which you have called together for this

purpose. In your actions you violate your own constitution and laws, which are now the constitution and laws of the land.

" There may be in your consciences a warrant for your action, in what you may deem a necessity of the times ; but you cannot find any such warrant for any such action in any settled, civilized, or Christian land. All who uphold you in this unlawful proceeding may scorn and despise my word ; but the offence of breaking and setting aside for a specific purpose the laws of your own nation, and disregarding all justice and fairness, may be to them and to you the source of an unhappy and much to be regretted legacy.

" I would ask you to consider that your government is on trial before the whole civilized world, and that in accordance with your actions and decisions will you yourselves be judged. The happiness and prosperity of Hawaii are henceforth in your hands as its rulers. You are commencing a new era in its history. May the divine Providence grant you the wisdom to lead the nation into the paths of forbearance, forgiveness, and peace, and to create and consolidate a united people ever anxious to advance in the way of civilization outlined by the American fathers of liberty and religion.

" In concluding my statement I thank you for the courtesy you have shown to me, not as your former queen, but as an humble citizen of this land and as a woman. I assure you, who believe you are faithfully fulfilling a public duty, that I shall never harbor any resentment or cherish any ill feeling towards you, whatever may be your decision."

What follows is a partial report of the court's proceedings regarding my statement.

" After deliberation the court requested that the following portions of the statement be withdrawn : —

" A minority of the foreign population made my action the pretext for overthrowing the monarchy, and, aided by the United States naval forces and representative, established a new government."

" I owed no allegiance to the Provisional Government so established, nor to any power or to any one save the will of my people and the welfare of my country."

" The wishes of my people were not consulted as to this change of government, and only those who were in practical rebellion against the Government were allowed to vote upon the question whether the Monarchy should exist or not."

" This selection was anticipated and prevented by the Provisional Government, who, being possessed of the military and police power of the kingdom, so cramped the electoral privileges that no free expression of their will was permitted to the people who were opposed to them."

" All who uphold you in this unlawful proceeding may scorn and despise my word, but the offence of breaking or setting aside for a specific purpose the laws of your own nation, and disregarding all justice, may be to them and to you the source of an unhappy and much to be regretted legacy."

" Mr. Neumann replied, that the paragraph, relating to the establishment of the Provisional Government was made as a statement from the accused, was claimed as an actual fact, reflected upon no one. It set forth her views, and he must decline to ask his client to withdraw it. The words, ' and only those who were in practical rebellion against the constitution of the state,' etc., Mr.

THE THRONE ROOM, IOLANI PALACE

Neumann agreed should be stricken out. As to the passage setting forth that the accused owed no allegiance to the Provisional Government, counsel made the same answer as to the first item.

"The court retired, and returned with the decision that the objectionable passages should be stricken out. Colonel Whiting read them, and ordered that they be stricken from the record."

During the course of my trial, I noticed, in one of the seats behind those occupied by the foreign ministers a peculiar-looking man, who wore top-boots, and had long, flowing hair. I was afterwards told that this was Joaquin Miller, the "poet of the Sierras," and was shown specimens of his poetry, especially that which he had written on my deposition, and in which he had alluded to me in the most favorable terms. I have been told that he was sent out as a press correspondent, with the expectation that he would take the opposite view, and that when the "government" found out his real sentiments he was forced to leave Honolulu.

There was also one lady frequently present, who seemed to take a great interest in the proceedings of the court-martial. I recognized in her the wife of Lieutenant Werlich of the United States ship Philadelphia.

A few days after these events there was a parade of the men of the steamship on shore. After drilling out on the plains, they marched into the city, and made use of the walls of the Kawaiahao church, directly opposite my place of imprisonment, to show their agility and skill in scaling ramparts. In the yard about this great edifice lie buried the remains of many members of the old missionary families.   But entirely without consideration for the sacredness of the spot, the troops were practised and cheered on at these walls ; they clambered back and forth, came tumbling down one over the other, and showed their superior strength or quickness, while an officer was taking the time required for the drill. From thence they were called to order by the bugle, then marched in front of my windows with their guns pointing towards the building itself.

But while all this was going on, I saw a lady approach the palace until she stood beneath my window ; there she stopped, and, looking up, kissed her hands to me.   She remained, making no motion to leave, for perhaps ten minutes.   Just as she was turning to depart, she raised her veil, and I at once recognized the countenance of the same lady who had been so faithful an attendant at my trial.   As I stood watching her friendly attitude, kindly tears of sympathy rolled down her cheeks.   I had known Mrs. Werlich as a welcome visitor at my own house in the days of my freedom, and it was a consolation for me to think that she had remembered me at the hour when I was a prisoner.

CHAPTER XLVI

SENTENCED — MY PRISON LIFE

AT two o'clock on the afternoon of the 27th of February I was again called into court, and sentence passed upon me. It was the extreme penalty for "misprision of treason," — a fine of $5,000, and imprisonment at hard labor for five years. I need not add that it was never executed, and that it was probably no part of the intention of the government to execute it, except, perhaps, in some future contingency. Its sole present purpose was to terrorize the native people and to humiliate me. After Major Potter had read to me my sentence, and carefully pocketed the paper on which it was written, together with the other papers in the case (I might have valued them, perhaps, as souvenirs), I was conducted back to my place of confinement.

No especial change was perceptible in my treatment or mode of life by reason of my trial and sentence. Though I was still not allowed to have newspapers or general literature to read, writing-paper and lead-pencils were not denied; and I was thereby able to write music, after drawing for myself the lines of the staff. At first I had no instrument, and had to transcribe the notes by voice alone; but I found, notwithstanding disadvantages, great consolation in composing, and transcribed a

number of songs.   Three found their way from my prison
to the city of Chicago, where they were printed, among
them the "Aloha Oe," or "Farewell to Thee," which
became a very popular song.

I was notified that I might be permitted to walk the
veranda for my relaxation after the business hours of
the day.   My friends were allowed to send me tokens
of sympathy, so bouquets of flowers and baskets of fruit
of all varieties came in almost every day.   I had also, at
pleasure, the flowers of my own gardens at Uluhaimalama.   In good things for my table I did not suffer.
Rich cakes, clear jellies, and many other delicacies
arrived every day of my imprisonment.   Where so many
were attentive, it seems hardly possible to mention individuals; yet the names of Mrs. S. C. Allen, Mrs.
Mary Carter, Mrs. Samuel Parker, Mrs. Haalelea, Mrs.
Coney, Mrs. James Campbell, Mrs. Minerva Fernandez,
Mrs. Victoria Ward, and Mr. and Mrs. Mana recur to
me at this moment, and, besides, many other ladies, to
whom I am sure I have never ceased to be grateful for
their kind remembrance.

It was the duty of the guards to search whatever
was sent to me before it was delivered into my hands;
so the baskets, whether of food, flowers, clothes, or
papers, went to them first, and at least at the start
were closely examined; yet there were some kindly
disposed towards me and not over-critical.   Every newspaper, however, had to come through the hands of Mr.
Wilson; and if he detected in it anything whatever relating to the government, he would take it away, not
permitting me to see it.   I used to find great comfort

in the bits of newspaper that were wrapped around my bouquets which were brought to me from my own garden at Uluhaimalama.

These were generally wrapped in the newspapers, foreign and local, obtained from Mr. Whiting's house, near my own ; and I cannot resist adding that even in my imprisonment the humor of the thought occurred to me, that, if any person ever literally fulfilled the ancient proverb about "living in glass houses," it was this so-called judge who had been called to pass sentence upon me. Some of the very wealthy under the monarchy had retreats in the suburbs of the town, somewhat answering to what Americans call "summer residences ;" and these were called "glass houses," because so open, or largely composed of glass. Under the oligarchy several in the government are not content with less than two such pleasure houses.

Flowers from home I unwrapped myself, so as to be sure to save these bits of news which I sought opportunity at intervals to read. There were times when I saw something of such interest that I could not resist the temptation to mention it to my companion, Mrs. Wilson. Then it seems she would faithfully report all that I said to her husband, whose custom it was to call every other day, sometimes at longer periods, for the purpose of ascertaining if there was anything required. At such times he would withdraw with his wife to the boudoir, where she would repeat to him what had been said by me, telling him also what had been received in the prison through her. By some things she occasionally mentioned he thought that newspapers had been secretly sent in ; but when finally he discovered that they had come as wrapping-paper, it made him very angry, and his poor little wife had to suffer for it, even bursting into tears at his sharp reproaches. For this reason I became quite guarded in what I said to her.

Our first duty in the morning after the regular devotions of the day was to arrange our flowers and decorate our apartments. At half-past seven the military companies would return from their parade ; and at eight precisely Captain Good, attended by one of the officers, would knock at my door, which was always opened by Mrs. Wilson, unless Mrs. Milaina Ahia were with me. (Mrs. Wilson usually went out on Saturday evening, and returned to me on Monday morning. During this absence her place was taken by Mrs. Ahia.) On opening the door Captain Good inquired what there was he could do for us, and if the prisoner was within and safe. On being answered in the affirmative, he would touch his cap, and return to report to his superior officer, Colonel McLean, and then rejoin his company. After their departure I occupied my time in crochet-work, in attending to my ferns or pots of flowers, or in reading the books allowed me. I also found much pleasure in the society of my canary-birds, and in practising on my autoharp and guitar. These luxuries had, after the first severity, been permitted to me.

I received letters ; but they were always opened, and, I presume, read, before being delivered. Rt. Rev. Alfred Willis, the Anglican Bishop of Honolulu, sent me a Book of Common Prayer. Sisters Beatrice and Alpertina offered little acts of tenderness and kindness which brought anew to my mind that passage in Scripture, "I was in prison and ye visited me." Although my Christian (?) jailers denied to me their sacred ministration and actual presence, yet none the less were these good and true Christians there in the loving tokens of kind remembrance, and in the spirit of the Divine Lord, during my bondage.

In June of 1895 there was a rumor that I was to be released; but day after day went by, July came and went, and I was still a prisoner. My health was not strong, and my regular medical attendant had gone to San Francisco. It was proposed by Dr. Cooper and Colonel McLean, that I should take a drive somewhere or somehow every day; but I did not feel inclined to go about town under guard of soldiers, and preferred to take long walks on the veranda by night, always, of course, under the inspection of the guard or sentry on duty there.

In August an epidemic broke out, to which Mrs. Wilson was one of the first to succumb. She had to leave me for a few days, but returned on her recovery. While she was away, I was stricken with the disorder; but I used such remedies as I happened to have with me, and recovered without serious consequences. After this we heard that the whole city was suffering. It was said to be a form of Asiatic cholera. Many deaths occurred, and it was some three months before normal conditions were restored. It was at this time that the ladies of Honolulu, both native and foreign, organized a society for the relief of the poor, who, under the circumstances, were unable to support themselves. There were relief stations in the outskirts all around the city,

where ladies who had been assigned to each district
assembled to supply necessary provision to those who
were in need. It was a most praiseworthy mission ; and
although I could not be present personally, I provided
a house and lot on my place at Waikiki for carrying on
the benevolent enterprise under the care of Mrs. James
Campbell and Mrs. Douglass, who had charge of that
district.

CHAPTER XLVII

RELEASED ON PAROLE

ON the 6th of September, about eight months after my arrest, I was notified by Colonel McLean that he was no longer responsible for my custody, and that at three o'clock that afternoon I might leave the palace. So a carriage was called, and I was driven from the doors of the beautiful edifice which they now style Executive Building, and was assured that I was under no further restraint. My pardon, as it was called, arrived at a later day. All the intervening time I was supposed to be under parole, and could have been arrested and recommitted at any moment.

As, in company with Mr. and Mrs. Wilson, I was driven from my prison — once my palace — to the gateway at Washington Place, my earlier home, it seemed as though Nature, our kind mother, smiled on my return. The flowers, the shrubs, the trees, had never to me looked so charming. How I enjoyed their welcome! Surely they could not have been so beautiful when I saw them daily in previous year ! The orchids, the violets, the chrysanthemums, the geraniums, were still in bloom, and seemed to greet me with joy, expressive as silent. Bunches of red bananas hung from their stalks, clusters of yellow Loquot plums danced in the sunshine, and the bright red berries of the coffee-tree drooped down gracefully, waiting to be gathered. But my welcome was not altogether from the silent, waving leaves. Those of my people who had been released from imprisonment were here to greet me also with their fond *Aloha*.

On the morning following Mr. Wilson informed me that I had been released only on parole, and had been placed in his charge by President Dole. My custodian further notified me that but sixteen servants were allowed to me, and that my retainers (accustomed to maintain a system of watches for my protection ever since the death of my husband) were not to be permitted to come near me again. I was also prohibited from going where there was any concourse of the people, nor could I have any gathering at my own house. In consequence of these regulations I never went to church or to any public place. But I was not forgotten by his lordship, the bishop, who with Mrs. Willis was one of the first to call on me. Other friends expressed their sympathy in person ; amongst these Mrs. J. S. Walker, who had lost her husband by the treatment he received from the hands of the revolutionists. He was one of many who from persecution had succumbed to death.

It was at this time that Bishop Willis invited me to be confirmed as a member of his church ; to which proposal I very gladly assented, and I find much comfort in its fellowship.

The duties of Mr. Charles B. Wilson could not have been very irksome. I do not remember requiring him to do anything, or asking a favor at his hands. He took good care to keep my gates under lock and key, that no visitors might enter without his knowledge, because he was obliged — he said — to give to Mr. Dole a faithful report of all my visitors and doings each day. Some of my friends who prayed to be allowed to visit me were denied. I was very conveniently spared, however, the calls of strangers, who would have encroached upon my retired life simply from motives of curiosity.

Two events of some interest to me should be mentioned as related to these days. While the Philadelphia was the flag-ship of the squadron of the Pacific, the time of Admiral Irwin expired, and he was daily expecting his successor. Before he left, he very courteously called on me at Washington Place. He was accompanied by a member of his personal staff. I appreciated this mark of his attention, and it has never been forgotten by me ; for it showed a kindly spirit on his part towards one who had received many officers of the navy in other days and under different circumstances.

On another occasion Admiral Walker visited the Islands. Exactly on what mission I have never been informed. If, as I have sometimes heard, and if one is to judge from the long report he made to the Department of the Navy on his return, it was for investigating the political situation, he certainly did not adopt the method of fairness and equal treatment to both sides pursued by Hon. James H. Blount. He was scarcely in position to have any but the most prejudiced ideas ; for he was an old friend and guest of one of my enemies, and immediately on his arrival the missionary party took possession of him, and scarcely allowed him to move unless some one of their number was at his elbow.

On the 6th of February, 1896, while at dinner with Mrs. Wilson and Mr. Kamakau, we were informed that a messenger from the office of Mr. Dole was waiting to enter my presence in order to deliver a document; but Mrs. Wilson went for the paper, and took it from the young man, Mr. Alexander St. Maur McIntosh. I did not see him; but the document proved to be my release from parole as prisoner, although I was still forbidden to leave the island of Oahu. Mrs. Wilson said that this could not possibly be genuine; because her husband had not been made aware of it, and that everything like this had to come to me through him. I re-read the document to be assured there was no mistake. Mrs. Wilson immediately started to notify her husband, who sent her back for the paper, which I allowed her to take. It convinced, but much astonished, Mr. Wilson, for he made the comment that he ought to have been notified first; but it would appear that the president thought otherwise, and, without advising the custodian, had released the prisoner from his unwelcome custody.

Some days later, in company with Mr. and Mrs. Joseph Heleluhe, I took a drive out to my residence at Waialua, where we spent two very delightful weeks with the Rev. Mr. Timoteo and his agreeable wife. We had a quiet little celebration all to ourselves, fishing and riding, and the time sped by so pleasantly that we forgot to count the hours. While there we received a visit from Hon. Samuel Parker; Mr. Boyd,

Secretary of American Legation ; Mr. Lanse (who has since married Miss Widemann) ; Mr. J. S. Walker, the younger ; and others, — who spent a pleasant day with us on the beach. We caught fish, and placed them immediately on hot coals, supplementing our picnic with bread and butter, and our native *poi*. Then, a week or so later, I went to my residence at Waikiki ; and in this, my ocean retreat, I lived until my recent visit to the United States, only now and then, for a change, making a trip to my estates at Kahala. My life at the seashore was a tranquil and uneventful one, although while I was there a circumstance transpired of grave importance to my people.

CHAPTER XLVIII

MR. JOSEPH KAHOOLUHI NAWAHI

ONE morning, in the month of October, 1896, I heard of the death of Mr. Joseph Kahooluhi Nawahi o Kalaniopuu; and I shared the common sorrow, for this was a great blow to the people. He had always been a man who fearlessly advocated the independence of Hawaii Nei. He was for twenty years a legislator, and was one of the most active members of the legislative session of 1892–1893; with Mr. William White he had maintained a strict fidelity to the wishes of the people by whom he had been elected. The behavior of these two patriots during the trying scenes of this session, in such marked contrast to that of many others, won them profound respect. They could never be induced to compromise principles, nor did they for one moment falter or hesitate in advocating boldly a new constitution which should accord equal rights to the Hawaiians, as well as protect the interests of the foreigners. The true patriotism and love of country of these men had been recognized by me, and I had decorated them with the order of Knight Commander of Kalakaua.

When the vessel drew near on which were the remains of the dead patriot, the people turned out *en masse* to draw the carriage, on which the casket was placed, to his late home.   No private individual in our land had ever received such a demonstration of love and respect as was now shown to the lamented member of the House.   High honors were accorded to him.   The services were read by the Rev. E. S. Timoteo, after which there was a long procession in line.   The casket was accompanied by all the members of the Hui Kala-aina, and also of the Hui Aloha Aina, which last society was of his own establishment.   Then followed the chief mourners and the ladies of the Patriotic League.   The long, sorrowful escort conducted the body on board the steamer Keauhou ; and after some last impressive services, the crowd watched the little steamer bearing off all that was mortal of the Hon. J. K. Nawahi towards Hilo, where on arrival another grand demonstration was made.   He was laid in state at the Haili church in obedience to the expressed wish of the people.

He was a member of the legislature when I appointed him as a cabinet minister, and was voted out with the ministry on the motion of " lack of confidence." He then consulted me as to his future, and stated that if he should run for the district of Hilo he felt confident of his election.   Acting upon my advice, he left at the first opportunity for Hilo, arriving just in time to appear as a candidate in opposition to the candidate of the missionary party.   He was returned by a large majority. Then it became necessary for him to leave on this same evening for the port of Honolulu, and the only vessel or means of reaching there was at Hamakua ; but he was falsely informed by those in sympathy with his enemies that there was no way by which he could go.

Nevertheless he fitted out two whaleboats with sails, compass, provisions, and water, and sailed immediately for the island of Mauai. At two o'clock next morning, as they were passing off Hamakaua, they saw the red light of the steamer Iwalani, and recognized that they had been purposely deceived so as to prevent the people's delegate from taking part in the deliberations at the legislature. All next day they were crossing the channel of Alenuihaha, but by evening the two boats reached Hana in safety. They awaited at the hospitable home of Judge Kaai the first vessel for Oahu, which landed them duly at Honolulu. Thus, by the One who rules the winds and the waves, Mr. Nawahi had been favored with a most prosperous voyage ; and, much to the surprise of his enemies, arrived in time to take his seat in the legislature amongst those of his party and his personal friends, by whom he was warmly congratulated on his election and his prompt appearance.

At his death the Provisional Government, whose agents control all the despatches sent to the United States, caused it there to be promulgated that the liberal party had, since the loss of Mr. Nawahi, become discouraged, and were ready to vote for annexation. This was expressly to deceive the people of the United States. The cause of Hawaiian independence is larger and dearer than the life of any man connected with it. Love of country is deep-seated in the breast of every Hawaiian, whatever his station. Yet the above fact is worthy of notice as the testimony of our enemies to the sturdy patriotism of Mr. Joseph Kahooluhi Nawahi.

After the obsequies were over, and the remains of the deceased legislator were borne to Hilo, notice was given by the members for a new election of president to the two patriotic societies at whose head he had stood. This action was a great astonishment to the Provisional Government and all the friends of the missionary party, for it was hoped that the loss of such a leader would cause these organizations to dissolve. The Hui Aloha Aina and the Hui Kalaaina, with the sister organization of the Women's Patriotic League, are societies much dreaded by the oligarchy now ruling Hawaii. Sufficient time was given to reach the members in the most distant parts of the Islands, who were notified to meet in convention, which they did. Perfect harmony prevailed; and James Keauiluna Kaulia was elected president of the Hui Aloha Aina, while David Kalauokalani was chosen as the head of the Hui Kalaaina; and both these societies are still intent on their patriotic work.

One day in the month of October, 1896, while with trowel in hand I was separating and transplanting my ferns at my Waikiki residence, Major George C. Potter entered, bearing a document, which on examination I found purported to be an entire release of all restrictions, an absolute pardon, and a *restoration of my civil rights.* This, to be sure, places me in the same position as before my arrest and trial; but let me ask, if I was deprived of my civil rights at the moment of my imprisonment, of what value was the signature procured to my supposed or alleged act of abdication? Was it legal, of binding force, or effective? This question I will leave for decision to all those learned in the law;

they can draw their own conclusions as to the probable worth of an acknowledgment of that document as my free act and deed, or of the proper value of the form of signature not my own which at the request of others was attached thereto.

CHAPTER XLIX

A CHANGE OF SCENE TO FORGET SORROW

On receiving my full release I felt greatly inclined to go abroad, it made no difference where, as long as it would be a change. Calling to mind my many acquaintances in San Francisco, and remembering the relatives of my husband living there, and across the bay in Oakland, I decided to sail for that city, and at once quietly began my preparations.

On the fifth day of December, 1896, shortly after breakfast, with my companion, Mrs. Kia Nahaolelua, I drove up to the residence of President Dole. As I entered, he rose from his seat, approached me at once, and extended his hand, which I took. Asking us to be seated, he inquired of me to what he was indebted for the honor of this early visit. I informed him of my intention to take a trip to San Francisco. He inquired if I intended to go farther on, to which I replied I would probably visit my relations in the city of Boston, and perhaps might cross the Atlantic to call on my niece, the Princess Kaiulani, in England. At this Mr. Dole rose and called his wife, who entered immediately, and greeted me with a pleasant smile. In the course of an agreeable conversation they expressed their great anxiety and solicitude for me, in that I was undertaking such a journey in the depth of winter.

The climate of Boston, they said, was one of great severity; especially was this true in its effect upon strangers, and they warned me to prepare myself most carefully against the dangers of a winter there. Thanking them for their kind interest, I bade them good-by; but the president very gallantly escorted me to my carriage, and of his own accord proposed to send from the foreign office passports for myself and for those of my party. He then politely bowed an adieu as the carriage was driven out of his yard, and thus we parted.

Taking leave of my cousin, the Prince Kalanianaole, on the way, I returned to my own residence. Intending to make but a hasty stop there, I found awaiting me Mr. D. Kalauokalani, the president of the Hui Kalaaina, and Mr. William White, also Mrs. Joseph Nawahi, the chairman of the central committee of the Women's Patriotic League. They expressed much surprise at learning that I was about to leave so soon; but my trunks and other baggage awaiting transportation spoke silently in support of my intentions. A few words of explanation and direction were exchanged, the farewells to all of my household were said, and my party started for the wharf.

There I found Hon. J. O. Carter, with Mrs. Carter and their family, waiting to see me off. There were a few other friends, and only a few, for I had purposely kept my intention to depart to myself. I shook hands with Mr. F. J. Testa, the proprietor of the *Independent*, who seemed very much surprised to see me, and then mounted the gangway that led up the side of the vessel, accompanied by Mr. Carter. Having taken a glance at

H.M. QUEEN LILIUOKALANI
WITH HER LADY-IN-WAITING AND HAWAIIAN SECRETARY

the rooms which were assigned to me, I returned to the deck, where Major George C. Potter, aid to Mr. Dole, had already arrived, and presented to me my passport.

It was signed by Mr. W. O. Smith as Minister of Foreign Affairs, granting to *Liliuokalani of Hawaii* permission to come and go in distant parts under the protection of the Hawaiian government, and charging all representatives of that government to afford me protection.

But I could not help noticing that in making out this document the name of the family of my husband, Governor Dominis, — the name they had compelled me to affix to the document, and which, as there combined, had never been mine, or my legal signature, — was not mentioned, and perhaps they had failed to think of it. What had become of that signature they had required to my act of alleged abdication? Passports were also given for my suite, Mr. Joseph Heleluhe and Mrs. Kia Nahaolelua.

Hon. Samuel Parker came on board the steamship, and asked in astonishment where I was going. I gave him a like answer to that given to President and Mrs. Dole, and then the steamer proceeded on her way out of the harbor. The usual farewells of waving handkerchiefs and hats signalized our departure, and then for the first time in years I drew a long breath of freedom. (For what was there worthy of that sacred name under the circumstances in which I had lived on shore?) Not knowing but what every word, every look, every act, of mine was being noted down by spies to be reported somewhere to my hurt.

The captain of the China was very kind, the officers and every one on board most attentive, and a short and pleasant run of five days brought us to the coast of California. When the steamer was fast to the wharf at San Francisco, we were met by Colonel George W. Macfarlane, who awaited us; and, conducting us to our carriage, we were driven at once to the California Hotel, where apartments had been engaged for me and my suite. I telegraphed at once to my friends in Boston, notifying them of my arrival on American soil, and in reply received a despatch kindly inviting me to join them in the celebration of their Christmas holidays. I remained in San Francisco ten days, and had every reason to be content with my welcome.

Many friends had hastened to call upon me; amongst these were Mr. and Mrs. Claus Spreckels, Mrs. J. D. Spreckels and her lovely daughter, Miss Emma Spreckels, Mr. and Mrs. C. A. Spreckels, Mr. Charles R. Bishop, Mr. and Mrs. Shrader of San Rafael, Mrs. Annie Barton of Berkeley, Mrs. Toler of Oakland, Mrs. Hitchings, and many other persons of prominence whose names have escaped my memory. Colonel and Mrs. Macfarlane, with their niece, Miss Gardie Macfarlane, had their apartments at the hotel where I stopped; and this made me feel at home at once, for they were most kind and attentive throughout my stay.

And it seems, too, that I was not to be without a delightful travelling companion, for Mrs. Kaikilani Graham, formerly of Honolulu, was in California, and was on the point of directing her course eastward with her children. So preparations were made for crossing the continent,

and we took the Sunset Limited *via* New Orleans.
Colonel Macfarlane had decided that to be our best
route, so that I and my suite might get accustomed gradually to the change of climate, and pass by degrees into
the cold weather of the East.   It was a kind thought
on his part, and one to which perhaps I owe more than
can now be estimated.   Taking this beautiful curve to
the southward, we passed through the charming open
country in and about Los Angeles, where we saw miles
of orange-groves, the trees all laden with their golden
fruit.

Miles after miles of rich country went by as we
gazed from the windows of the moving train, and all
this vast extent of territory which we traversed belonged
to the United States ; and there were many other routes
from the Pacific to the Atlantic with an equally bound-
less panorama.   Here were thousands of acres of uncul-
tivated, uninhabited, but rich and fertile lands, soil
capable of producing anything which grows, plenty of
water, floods of it running to waste, everything needed
for pleasant towns and quiet homesteads, except population.   The view and the thoughts awakened brought
forcibly to my mind that humanity was the one element
needed to open to usefulness and enjoyment these rich
tracts of land.   Colonies and colonies could be established here, and never interfere with each other in the
least, the vast extent of unoccupied land is so enormous.
I thought what splendid sugar plantations might here
be established, how easily and profitably rice might be
grown, and in some other spots with what good returns
coffee could be planted.   There was nothing lacking in

this great, rich country save the people to settle upon it, and develop its wealth.

And yet this great and powerful nation must go across two thousand miles of sea, and take from the poor Hawaiians their little spots in the broad Pacific, must covet our islands of Hawaii Nei, and extinguish the nationality of my poor people, many of whom have now not a foot of land which can be called their own. And for what? In order that another race-problem shall be injected into the social and political perplexities with which the United States in the great experiment of popular government is already struggling? in order that a novel and inconsistent foreign and colonial policy shall be grafted upon its hitherto impregnable diplomacy? or in order that a friendly and generous, yet proud-spirited and sensitive race, a race admittedly capable and worthy of receiving the best opportunities for material and moral progress, shall be crushed under the weight of a social order and prejudice with which even another century of preparation would hardly fit it to cope?

As we passed eastward on our journey, the people crowded to the railway stations, eager, no matter how brief our stop, to get a glimpse of the Queen of Hawaii. At times this curiosity became so troublesome that the train officials were obliged to lock the car-doors, or close up our section, to prevent intrusion. At such times as these Mrs. Graham proved herself not only a pleasant companion, but of great service; she was always a skilful and ready defence against importunities. She was tall, handsome, very commanding in her presence, and very ladylike and polite in her manner. She was always courteous to the news-gatherers; and they retired quite pleased with such statements as she was able to give concerning me and my journey, and not a little charmed with the strategist who had communicated the information. At Washington we parted, she going to New York, and I to Boston.

We reached the national capital in six days, and were much interested in observing the snow, which lay on the ground, covered the tops of the houses and the roofs of our cars. It was a new sight to my suite, because in our country it only appears as a white mantle resting on the summits of our highest mountains. We made no stay in the city of Washington, for my friends in the Puritan city were expecting me. Having telegraphed my approach, in response to my wish Captain Julius A. Palmer met me on the arrival of the train at the Park-square Station at about nine o'clock on the evening of Christmas Day. The train, having been detained a few hours, was behind its schedule time of arrival. Captain Palmer conducted me to the Parker House, where my cousin, Mr. William Lee, with his wife, Mrs. Sara White Lee, and their daughter, Miss Alice Lee, were awaiting me.

I was at once amongst my friends, or rather, with my own family; for kisses, embraces, and congratulations followed each other very rapidly. I was received also with greetings of *leis*, made after the pattern of those in my own land; and thus my husband's relatives had made me feel I was not a stranger in a strange land, and contrived almost to make us forget the distance from our own beautiful Hawaii. It is indeed pleasant to receive such greetings from faithful hearts and loving hands in a foreign land. In order to be near my cousins, after a few days' rest at the Parker House, I moved to the Stirlingworth Cottage, just off Beacon Street, in Brookline.

CHAPTER L

A NEW ENGLAND WINTER

At Stirlingworth Cottage I passed a most delightful month, although the frost often covered the window panes, the snow whirled around the house, and the icicles formed on the trees ; the kindly greetings of my Boston friends and the warmth of their hearts deprived a Northern winter of all its gloom. The health of my party was excellent, and it seemed to be a matter of surprise to those who met us that we suffered so little by the change from the mild air of our beautiful islands to the rigors of a New England winter.

The first Sunday of my stay in Boston I accepted the kind invitation of Mr. and Mrs. George W. Armstrong to test the pleasures of a sleighride with them in their carriage-sleigh. In an open sleigh were seated Miss Alice Lee and the members of my suite, Mrs. Kia Nahaolelua, Mr. Joseph Heleluhe, and Captain Julius A. Palmer. The last-named gentleman visited me every day during my residence in his native city, attending to my correspondence or other business simply from motives of love to my people and of interest in me ; and as long as I remained in Boston he declined other compensation than the approval of his own conscience.

It was a bright and beautiful day when the jingling

bells and prancing horses acquainted me with the much-praised experience of sleigh-riding; and my kind host had determined that I at least should suffer no inconvenience from the cold, for our sleigh was abundantly provided with robes, and was warmed by a recently invented apparatus. My two Hawaiian attendants, however, in the open sleigh, felt the cold most severely. In truth, I must say that I failed to see the delight and exhilaration of the sport, although I enjoyed the afternoon very much indeed; but if I had had the same charming companions on a good road with an easy-riding carriage, it seems to me the pleasure of the ride would have been greater. It reminded me of the play of the Hawaiian children, where they draw each other along with smooth logs for runners. But it was extremely thoughtful in Mr. and Mrs. Armstrong to suggest this for my entertainment, and was only one of the many ways in which these friends showed their goodness of heart towards me. When I returned from a little trip to Niagara, Mr. Armstrong met me at the station, and cordially placed his private carriage and driver at my disposal to convey me to my Brookline apartments, which were not far from his elegant residence on Beacon Street.

During my sojourn in Brookline I attended All Saints' Church. The rector was the Rev. Mr. Addison, and I was pleased to notice the close attention given to his sermons by the congregation. He seemed to be a very popular man with his parishioners; and well they might appreciate such a pastor, for he showed himself to be a man whose heart and soul were in the great and glorious work of teaching the truths of Christianity, and leading others in the worship of God.

One morning Cousin Sara (Mrs. Lee) brought a letter from a lady who was collecting dolls for an International Doll-Show, to be exhibited at fairs for the benefit of charities for children. Having always been interested in the welfare of the young, I was happy to grant the request to have a Hawaiian doll for the charitable object. It much amused my cousin to see me sewing; and it was a pastime to me to make the clothing for the very pretty doll, that resembled somewhat some of my people who had intermarried with the foreigners.

The doll, for some reason, did not make its public *début* until quite recently; and I take the opportunity to insert here a clipping from the *Boston Globe*, Dec. 4, 1897, of the occasion, which is noteworthy, as that paper, I am informed, has been strongly for annexation, and heretofore has had but few kindly comments for the other side.

"Mrs. William Lee of Brookline gave an interesting talk last evening to a goodly gathering of women, and a slight sprinkling of men, at the doll-show opened in Hotel Thorndike, for two days, yesterday, for the benefit of the New England Home for Crippled Children.

This doll-show, which for variety and size exceeds any previous one in Boston, is notable for one thing, — in having among the exhibits three genuine royal dolls, that is to say, three dolls contributed by royalty. Two of them, miniature representations of Eskimo babies, made by the Eskimos themselves, and dressed in full Arctic costume of sealskin, were sent here by Queen Victoria from her own private collection, which is said to be the largest and finest in the world.

The third one was given by ex-Queen Liliuokalani of Hawaii, who dressed it and decorated it herself in the mother-hubbard-like gown characteristic of Hawaiian women, and the head wreath and neck garland of flowers to which they are so partial on gala occasions. The ex-queen named the doll Kaiulani, for her niece and heir.

Mrs. Lee talked about her friend Liliuokalani, whose name, she said, signifies the preservation of the heavens, and gave an interesting description of Hawaii's history and the peculiar customs of the people.

She asserted that the native Hawaiians are more intelligent and better educated than they are generally credited with being; most of them being able to read and write their own language, and many of them being equally accomplished in English.

Their constancy and their trustful nature, she claimed, have been their misfortune. At one period, she said, Hawaii was governed by no laws save the Ten Commandments.

Mrs. Lee expressed the opinion that in view of the power wielded by the whites, and the little influence possessed by the natives at the time of the late revolution, it was no wonder the queen wished to promulgate a new constitution to restore to her people some of the rights of which they had been deprived.

She said further: ' I tell you from the bottom of my heart, I have never found a more devout and perfect Christian under all circumstances than Liliuokalani. I have never yet heard her utter an unkind word against those who persecute her.

I am American by ancestry from the earliest days of the Massachusetts Bay Colony, and I love the American flag, and would be the last to see it hauled down if rightly raised; but (here Mrs. Lee spoke with visible emotion) if a Captain Kidd or any other pirate should raise the American flag simply as a decoy in order to destroy, we should be the first to resent it.

I do not oppose annexation as such, but it grieves me to see the way our countrymen have gone to work to bring it about.

I believe the Hawaiians should have their independent government, and that the natives should have something to say as to what that government shall be.' "

On New Year's Day, 1897, a brilliant reception was given by Mrs. William Lee at her residence, where I found myself the guest of honor. It might be noticed here, that, in regard to such occasions as this, the feelings of one who has been imprisoned, politically or otherwise, can only be understood by a person who has passed through the ordeal. With Mrs. Lee's numerous friends and high social position, she would most gladly have given to me an opportunity to receive attentions from the clubs and societies of which she is a distinguished member, and I would thereby have met many very delightful people. But although, since my earliest remembrance, I have been accustomed to ceremonies and receptions, yet, even after a winter's experience in Washington, it is not easy for me to get over that shrinking from the gaze of strangers acquired by recent years of retirement, eight months of experience as a prisoner, and the humiliations of the time when I was under the supervision of government spies or custodians.

Therefore, while I was grateful to Mrs. Lee for the wish, I told her that save in her own house and to meet her personal friends, I would be obliged to decline public receptions. But the number of gallant gentlemen, beautiful ladies, and fair young girls (two of whom served as ushers) that honored this occasion, caused me to be happy that I had made an exception. Music was furnished by some of the younger visitors, one of whom, Miss Sara MacDonald, a sister of the two charming ushers, played most sweetly and skilfully on the harp; and Mrs. Frank M. Goss, Mrs. Farwell, and the Misses Morse and Foster, assisted at the beautifully decorated refreshment table. Although the invitations had only been received on the morning of the reception, the attendance was very large. It comprised many of the most prominent people of Boston and Brookline, as well as those of surrounding towns.

The lovely January day was terminated by a light fall of snow, through which we found our way back to our home, with much gratitude in our hearts towards the kind entertainers and their many pleasant friends who had wished the Hawaiian party a happy New Year.

Mr. J. T. Trowbridge and Mr. W. T. Adams, the latter better known as Oliver Optic, two very interesting literary gentlemen, I met by the introduction of Mr. and Mrs. Lee. Although of advanced years, Mr. Adams was a bright and genial man, and his conversation was adorned with flashes of quiet wit and abounded in good humor, just as he shows himself in his fascinating books. He has since died; and these, his life-long friends, will long mourn his loss to them and to literature.

While at Stirlingworth Cottage Mr. and Mrs. Yeaton, whom I had met at Mrs. Lee's reception, very kindly presented me with a token which I shall always prize, — a paper-cutter, made by the gentleman himself from the original wood of the old ship-of-war, the Constitution. I have an indistinct recollection that the frigate visited the Islands years ago, when I was quite young, and that I was then told that she was one of the most famous of American vessels.

During my stay in Boston, I made a winter excursion to Niagara Falls. The trip was accomplished in three or four days, without the least inconvenience, although we were all strangers to the route, and to the hotel where rooms had been engaged by wire for myself and suite. All the tales I had ever heard of the grandeur of the great cataract fell far short of the truth; and I was impressed with an awe quite impossible to express in words when I came to look upon that everlasting volume of waters. As I stood at the edge of the precipice on Goat Island, my most constant thought and vivid impression was that of the insignificance of man when brought face to face with nature. While standing by this, one of the great wonders of the world, I felt as in the very presence of the Creator.

And yet man knows no fear, and his ingenuity has mastered here, as elsewhere, the strength of the elements; and by his inventive genius and skill he is now turning this fierce *Kühleborn* into an obedient servant. A company has been created, and its efforts to build a flume supplied from the cataract have been successful. The water-power is carried into a large shed, and there made to generate the electricity which furnishes the whole district about the Falls with light and power. The current for these and various other purposes, I am informed, is carried over more than twenty miles to the city of Buffalo.

We had a fine view from the American side of the Falls; there were wreaths of mist curling upward in the

air, blown into fantastic shapes by the breezes which
came forth from the Cave of the Winds.   Showers also
passed over the river, or followed its rapid flow.   After
lunch we took carriages and drove along the brink, then
crossed the great Suspension Bridge to the Canadian
side.   The bridge itself is a wonder, showing to rare
advantage the ingenuity of the brains which contrived
and the hands which built it.   At the Horseshoe Fall,
as well as while approaching it, we found abundant evidences of the wintry season ; there were icicles on the
fences and houses, the trees were covered with shining
crystal, and the trellis-work of wire on the banks at the
edge of the precipice was marvellously garnished with
pendent icicles of every size and shape.   We also visited
the boiling lake, had our photographs taken out-of-doors
on the snow, and, after a most instructive and delightful
visit, returned to our Brookline quarters with a picture
to be treasured in memory for life.

Before leaving Boston, as it was my intention to do
some time during the month of January, my cousin,
Mr. N. G. Snelling, gave a family party at his house, to
which my suite was invited, and I had the pleasure of
meeting as many of the family as could be brought together.   More than thirty relatives and a few of the
most intimate friends of the kind host were present.
An elegant table laden with refreshments and adorned
with flowers occupied the centre of one of the rooms,
and the event was made in all respects as delightful as
possible to us.

To meet these relatives, and receive from the lips of
each some cordial expression of welcome, was unusually

grateful after my long, sad experiences; and it vividly recalled to me the previous family gathering, when my dear husband greeted his family kin, and we, with Queen Kapiolani, were Boston's honored guests.

CHAPTER LI

WASHINGTON —PSEUDO–HAWAIIANS

On Friday, Jan. 22, 1897, I bade adieu to my cousins, Mr. and Mrs. William Lee, and the other friends who had rendered my four weeks' stay at Boston so interesting and agreeable that I had scarcely noticed the flight of time, and took the evening train for Washington. By my request, Captain Julius A. Palmer accompanied me as my private secretary, and remained as one of my suite from that date to the 7th of August, when he asked and most cheerfully received permission to take a vacation, for he had been most constant and devoted in every official duty. Captain Palmer had been presented to me at Honolulu just as I have met other visitors and correspondents; we had no personal acquaintance until my visit to Boston, but I knew those in my native city who were connected with his family by marriage. Besides which, his interest in the Hawaiian people, and his reputation as a man of unblemished honor and integrity, recommended him to me; and I needed the services of some person more familiar with matters and manners in the United States than could be expected of my Hawaiian secretary, Mr. Joseph Heleluhe, who was now on his first trip abroad.

I have found Captain Palmer to be well informed on

all matters relating to Hawaii, whether in those earlier days when he visited the Islands under the monarchy, or since 1893 under the rule of the Provisional Government. Like many others I might mention, he went there soon after the overthrow, and was petted and flattered by the party in power. But all the time he was quietly investigating the situation for himself. The result of his observations was a conclusion that the right of the Hawaiian people to choose their own form of government should be affirmed, and that they should be protected in this choice by the power of the United States, in which event he was fully assured that their queen would be overwhelmingly restored to her constitutional rights.

While in Boston I was constantly asked if there was any political significance in my visit to America, and if I expected to see the President. It seemed wise to say nothing about my purpose at that time, but frankness would now indicate an opposite course. By the first vessel that arrived from Honolulu after I had reached San Francisco, documents were sent to me by the patriotic leagues of the native Hawaiian people, those associations of which I have already spoken in full; and these representative bodies of my own nation prayed me to undertake certain measures for the general good of Hawaii. Further messages of similar purport reached me while I was visiting my Boston friends.

All the communications received, whether personally or in form, from individuals or from the above-mentioned organizations, were in advocacy of one desired end. This was to ask President Cleveland that the former

form of government unjustly taken from us by the
persons who in 1892 and 1893 represented the United
States should be restored, and that this restoration
should undo the wrong which had been done to the
Hawaiian people, and return to them the queen, to
whom constitutionally, and also by their own choice,
they had a perfect right.

This was further in the line of the only instructions
which to this day have ever been given by the United
States to the so-called Republic of Hawaii, and those
were that the President acknowledges *the right of the
Hawaiian people to choose their own form of government*.
Were that one sentence literally carried out in fact to-
day, and the Hawaiians sustained in the carrying out
of the same, it would be all that either my people or
myself could ask.

The second package of documents received by me
in Boston was addressed to President McKinley, and
was similar to the others I already had, only they were
addressed to Hon. Grover Cleveland while he was president. Accompanying these papers were other documents, showing that full power was accorded to me, not
only as their queen, but individually, to represent the
real people of Hawaii, and in so doing to act in any
way my judgment should dictate for the good of the
Hawaiians, to whom the Creator gave those beautiful
islands in the Pacific. Commissions were also issued
to Mr. Joseph Heleluhe, empowering him to act with
me ; he having been chosen by the Hawaiians as the
special envoy of those deprived by the Provisional Government, not only of the franchise, but also of any repre-

sentation at the capital of that American nation to which they have never ceased to look for the redress of national wrongs, brought upon them by the hasty action of United States officers.

When I speak at this time of the Hawaiian people, I refer to the children of the soil, — the native inhabitants of the Hawaiian Islands and their descendants. Two delegations claiming to represent Hawaii have visited Washington at intervals during the past four years in the cause of annexation, besides which other individuals have been sent on to assist in this attempt to defraud an aboriginal people of their birthrights, — rights dear to the patriotic hearts of even the weakest nation. Lately these aliens have called themselves Hawaiians.

They are not and never were Hawaiians. Although some have had positions under the monarchy which they solemnly swore by oath of office to uphold and sustain, they retained their American birthright. When they overthrew my government, and placed themselves under the protectorate established by John L. Stevens, — as he so states in writing, — they designated themselves as Americans; as such they called on him to raise their flag on the building of the Hawaiian Government. When it pleased the Provisional Government to give their control another name, they called it the Republic of Hawaii. To gain the sympathy of the American people, they made the national day of the Independence of the United States their own, and made speeches claiming to be American citizens. Such has been their custom at Honolulu, although in Washington they represent themselves as Hawaiians.

At Honolulu these annexationists made speeches abusing the Senate of the United States for the delay in annexing Hawaii; they further said the most grossly insulting things of President Cleveland because he frustrated their plans, and included Secretary Gresham in their condemnation because he failed to recognize them as Americans. Of these pseudo-Hawaiians, Mr. Hatch is a lawyer from New Hampshire. His first exploit in the ring of adventures was not a diplomatic success. He met some of his annexation associates at Canton, Ohio. Mr. McKinley sent word that the state of his health obliged him to decline to receive visitors, so the embassy returned to the national capital. "Minister" Cooper, another alien (less than a year in Hawaii in 1893, when he stood on the steps of Iolani Palace, and read the proclamation against me), has been given office, probably as a reward for the risk he ran. Mr. William A. Kinney has been better acquainted with life at Salt Lake City, as it was in the past, than with simple, amiable — but, alas, no longer happy — Hawaii. Without military experience, he was commissioned a captain, and afterward charged with the duty of Judge Advocate in attacking me, and those of my people who sought liberty from the foreign oppressor. So I could go on multiplying indefinitely recollections of these and other so-called Hawaiians. Those who are not recent arrivals are sons of the missionaries, or allied to the families connected with the American Mission, and claim foreign citizenship to this day. When a political question was under discussion, they would be very active in soliciting the native Hawaiian vote for the side of the missionary party.   The true Hawaiian, you see, has no representation in these several commissions.

The number of articles written or inspired by the Commissioners or their allies is enormous ; articles skilfully calculated to deceive the American people on most important topics ; also articles intended to place me in an awkward or utterly false position in the great and good land where I have been four times a visitor.   I can see the inspiration of it all, because I know the character of several of the men so engaged.   Allusion to episodes in the career as a monarchical official of one of these men has already been made.   Mr. Thurston's political methods need no mention.   His measures with the press are well known ; but, unfortunately for him, he rewarded newspaper enterprise once too often.   His position as at least a nominal member of the diplomatic corps gave him certain advantages, which he treacherously used to give official correspondence to the press. For this he was promptly rebuked by Secretary Gresham, and recalled to Honolulu as *persona non grata*.   The Dole government was too weak to defend its agent, and Mr. Thurston went home in disgrace.   He is again attempting to negotiate a treaty, bartering away his adopted country.

Another without gratitude, and false to the country to which he owes his life, whose letters to the press have frequently appeared, is Sereno E. Bishop of Honolulu, a man who owes his seventy years or more to the vigor given to his infancy from the breasts of Hawaiian women.   Broadcast have been his letters reviling my people, and repeating the vilest of falsehoods as to myself, since he failed to have Hawaii annexed by praising the country, its people, and his queen.   One has but to peruse Mr. Bishop's paper in the *Review of Reviews* for September, 1891, to see how false must be his later statements.   I trust those who read these pages will obtain that number of the *Review*, and read the article.

I cannot impress too strongly upon those who truly desire to know about my country and to do it justice, the importance of reading that "article" of September, 1891.   Although it was written not to serve Hawaii, but in the interest of the annexationists, the plea used was that the Hawaiians had shown themselves so capable of self-government, and were so proud of their autonomy in the Pacific, that they would be well qualified to be United States citizens.   How vastly opposite and false is the plea that is made by them now for annexation !

Early in their present mission the Annexationists secured the services of Mr. John W. Foster, who succeeded Mr. Blaine as Secretary of State under Mr. Harrison, and employed him to deliver in Washington a lecture on Hawaii.   Before this, I had received a letter from an American residing in that city, advising me to lose no time in retaining the services of Mr. Foster in presenting my case to the National government.   To this, as to several other offers of legal aid, I returned the reply that I thanked the friendly counsellors, but that I had already in my letters and protest placed my case before the Chief Executive (since my first communication more than one president has occupied that position), and that I would trust in their honor for redress.   But if I had not believed in the

integrity of the American nation, and its treaty-making
representatives, it would have been well to have awaited
the delivery of this lecture, before retaining the services
of Mr. Foster ; because had he shown such a lamentable
ignorance of my affairs as he did of those of Hawaii
when he tried to speak of that country, her rulers, her
people, even her situation geographically and socially,
my case as a client would have suffered from his ignorance.   Notwithstanding the historical truths, that although the gospel has been preached in Polynesia for a
century or more, and that there is no other nation which
has made such rapid progress in civilization and Christianity, yet Mr. Foster had the assurance to stand up
in Washington, and revile all the native Hawaiian sovereigns.   Not content with using bad language about my
brother, King Kalakaua, and myself, he had to take up
each one of the Kamehamehas, and refuse to them successively even one good quality, or to the Island people
one redeeming characteristic.

    This is only one of Mr. Foster's blunders, — truly a
serious one.   Another blunder savors of the ridiculous ;
I did not see it, but it was described to me by those
who did.   It seems that his remarks were to be illustrated by lantern slides ; and on opening this series of
illustrations, there first appeared on the screen a dark
form, which no one in the audience could recognize, yet
the lecturer nothing daunted, with pole in hand, began
to describe the situation of the Islands ; then it suddenly occurred to him that the dots on the Pacific as
shown by the slides were placed near enough over to
annex, if not to the United States, then to Mexico ; so

he paused in his remarks while the artist made a second attempt; but he had only fled from one extreme to another, for now the unfortunate group, so far as location was concerned, had every appearance of annexation to Japan.   This was going from Scylla to Charybdis. It was not until the third trial, when poor little Hawaii regained that position in the Pacific Ocean in which the hand of the Creator had left her, that the lecturer, after some hesitation in order to be sure that this time he was right, dared to proceed with his discourse.   There was not one original idea in his lengthy misrepresentation of my native land, its people, and its sovereigns.

Mr. Foster made one brief trip to Honolulu, in the interest, it is said, of the cable company projected by Mr. Z. S. Spaulding.   Whether this was a mere pretence or an original motive ending in failure, cannot be decided now.   But the present rulers took charge of him at once, as they do of all new-comers; and he was greeted, feasted, and generally entertained by the members of the government and by their friends.   A meeting was held where the cable scheme was discussed, annexation also receiving some notice.   A feeble opposition was developed under the leadership of Mr. W. G. Irwin.   Mr. Foster immediately replied that unless there was perfect agreement on the part of the planters, nothing could be done, there was no further use for his services; and if the cable scheme was so unpopular he might as well leave, which he did without even warning those friends who had been so attentive to him.   Soon after his arrival in Washington, he delivered his lecture, and then had it printed at the public expense, and sent to the Senate by the money of the people, all upon a subject about which he knew nothing save the absurd stories and intentional misrepresentations repeated to him by those who were writing them out continually for American newspapers.

Time would not admit of a particular criticism of each of the individuals who have been working so hard at Washington from the close of the last Republican administration to the present date, with the sole object of bettering a small minority of American ancestry at the cost of forty thousand Hawaiians (not to count those of other nationalities to the number of over sixty thousand), who have no voice in public affairs, either in Hawaii or in the representation of the present government at Washington. And to oppose this project, and represent this down-trodden people, there was in Washington simply the presence of one woman, without legal adviser, without a dollar to spend in subsidies, supported and encouraged in her mission only by three faithful adherents, and such friends as from time to time expressed to her their sympathy.

Amongst the last-named, even in the city of my husband's family, I could not count the representative of the Hawaiian Republic. Somewhere about the year 1848, possibly earlier, a young man from Boston landed on the shores of our Islands; he was about eighteen years of age, an entire stranger, coming out to those distant fields of labor to seek his fortune. My adopted father, the chief Paki, befriended him, gave him the first helping hand which welcomed him to his new country, and rendered him such assistance as was in fact the

means of showing to him the opportunity of making
his way in the world ; as years passed by he established
himself in business, and soon became one of the leading
merchants of Lahaina, at that time the port of call in
the Islands for the whaleships, ranking second only to
Honolulu.

It was then the base of supplies to this fleet of vessels, was a thoroughly thrifty place, and a business city
of growing commercial importance.   But the oil-wells of
the land have thrown into neglect the oil-ships of the
sea, and since this decline and decay Lahaina is little
more than a city of ruins.   Mr. Gilman probably saw
the approaching decline of the industry by which the
place was supported ; for he broke up his business connections there, sundered certain personal ties, and returned to the East with a very handsome fortune, it is
said, the result of the accumulation of years of mercantile
life on Hawaiian soil and under Hawaiian laws.   From
Honolulu he returned to Boston, where he has resided
ever since, save that once, since the overthrow of the
monarchy, he made a brief visit to his Honolulu friends.

In 1887, during my journey with Queen Kapiolani,
we met Mr. Gilman, who was at that time very kind and
attentive to me.   To be sure, he had a point to gain ; he
wanted a decoration from the king, and did not hesitate
to say so.   On the return of the queen's party to the
Islands, letters were received from Mr. Gilman, directly
applying for the honor to my brother.   Chiefly by means
of my personal influence his petition was granted, and
he was made a Knight Companion of the Order of Kalakaua, and the decoration forwarded to him.

The next thing I heard from Mr. Gilman was that he had espoused with alacrity and fidelity the cause of the revolutionists of the month of January, 1893, and that he avowed his implicit belief in all the absurd and wicked statements circulated by the missionary party against my own character and that of my people. Papers were sent to me where Mr. Gilman had repeated and vouched for the truth of these abominable political slanders ; and at first I could scarcely credit it, for this man was often at the house of my adoption, and showed great partiality for my society when I was a young girl and he a young man. He knew Paki and Konia, a couple of the strictest morality, whose household was organized on the basis of the most regular family habits and the most pious Christian customs ; and these had taken me from my very birth under their parental care.

He further knew me as the foster-sister and daily companion of Mrs. Bernice Pauahi Bishop, where I was ever under the kind care of her husband, Hon. Charles R. Bishop, a couple whose principles of exalted piety, whose love for all that is good, honorable, and pure, are too well known to need at this moment the least praise from me, and whose protection was ever and always surrounding my earlier life. From their house, when married, I went directly to that of my husband's mother, with whom I lived to the day of her death, not so very long ago.

Such were the lives of those with whom my own life has been passed ; such were the families with whom Mr. Gilman knew I had been in daily association, and where he met me. At the time when he hastened to avow his

allegiance to my enemies, and to ask them for the decoration of a consular station, in the year 1893, I was fifty-
six years of age.   Yet the past was reckoned by him
as naught; he permitted himself to be instantly prejudiced against his early friend, and to be led away by the
base slanders and political falsehoods of her adversaries.
He proceeded to vilify me in such articles as those sent
to me from his pen, and has been a zealous servant of
the men who placed him in office; he has rushed into
print not only his own misstatements, but has endeavored to nullify the influence of any article written in
my favor, or in defence of the rights of the Hawaiian
people.

Such has been the animosity, openly and secretly
expressed, toward me, not only as a queen, but as a
woman, by those whom all the claims of gratitude
should bind to me as friends, and who should rally to
my assistance, that, since leaving home and arriving in
America, I have constantly received communications
from Hawaii, often by special message, begging me to
be careful of my life, still regarded as "infinitely precious to the people of the Islands," reminding me that I
was surrounded by enemies, some of whom from home
were entirely unscrupulous, and assuring me that great
anxiety was felt by all classes, as it was a persistent
rumor that evil was intended me.

CHAPTER LII

ARRIVING in Washington on Saturday, my party took rooms at the Shoreham ; and amongst the very first callers to greet me was the Hon. Daniel Nash Morgan, the Treasurer of the United States. A Mason of the highest degree himself, Mr. Morgan noticed at once the jewel of the Mystic Shrine which I wore upon my breast, and asked for its history.

I told him that General Powell, a grand commander of the Mystic Shrine in the Western jurisdiction, visited the Hawaiian Islands about the time of my return from the Queen's Jubilee. When he met me he took the decoration of the order from the lapel of his own coat, and pinned it on the front of my dress. As he fastened it on my breast, wishing me God-speed, he said that, should I travel and find myself in need of any aid or protection, it would be of great assistance to me ; and I have worn it ever since. Mr. Morgan was much interested in this narration, and, with his charming wife and lovely daughter, as well as with others of his family, did much to render my stay in Washington pleasant to me.

My first call, after arriving at the Shoreham, was at the White House. The day of my departure from Boston, President Cleveland had gone on one of his hunting-excursions. This was immediately telegraphed over the land, and his going made out to be a consequence of my coming. As no person, excepting the three members of my suite, knew of my intention to visit Washington, of course this was impossible. However, it was as true as the long list of falsehoods written during my residence at Washington and elsewhere.

On Monday morning, Jan. 25, Mr. Cleveland set the gossips at rest by appearing at the executive office; and at eleven o'clock my secretaries delivered to Hon. Henry T. Thurber, the President's secretary, a brief note from me, advising him of my presence in the city, and offering to express to him my friendly feeling by a personal call, if it would be convenient to receive me. I had suggested no day nor hour; but they had scarcely reached the hotel on their return when a most courteous note was received from the President, conveying to me his sympathy, and welcoming me to call upon him at three o'clock that very afternoon, which I did with the three members of my suite.

The President received me in the little Red Reception-room. Every door opened as we passed in; and the crowd of reporters on the piazza were forced to be content with a mere glimpse of my party, and to draw on imagination for any account of the interview. Not a hint was given by me as to any intention to visit Mrs. Cleveland. The President very naturally spoke of his wife, who had shown me such consideration the last time I was in the executive mansion; and I expressed the hope that she continued in good health after so many trying duties and social responsibilities had been laid upon her.

To this Mr. Cleveland immediately said that he would like to have me see for myself, and that he hoped she was at home, but that he had come directly from his business office, and had had no opportunity to speak with her since hearing from me. He then added that he would ascertain, and went to the corridor to inquire of the usher, who told him that Mrs. Cleveland had gone out for her afternoon walk; so we resumed our conversation, during which I handed him the documents prepared for his inspection by the patriotic leagues of which I have already spoken.

These he took impressively, thanking me for them. It was a great pleasure to me to tell him personally how dear his name was to the Hawaiian people, and how grateful a place he held in my own heart because of his effort to do that which was right and just in restoring to us our lost independence. We always thought him to be sincere in his attempt to right the wrong; and since I have fully acquainted myself with the obstructions placed in his way by the supporters of Minister John L. Stevens, I understand far better than formerly that he failed through no fault of his own. It was a very pleasant interview; and when it was over, I returned with my party to my hotel.

Mrs. Cleveland's accidental absence was made use of by the press to cast a slur upon me. No one seemed to notice that had the first lady in the land been rude as reported — well, it would not have been Mrs. Cleveland, that is all. Two or three days later, a note arrived

unexpectedly from the executive mansion, which stated
that Mrs. Cleveland would be happy to see me, and
that as she was to give a private reception at five o'clock
in the afternoon, she thought that if I would call a
quarter of an hour or so previous to that hour, we could
have a pleasant chat together in her parlor.

The delicacy of thus arranging in advance that I
might have the opportunity for social enjoyment apart
from the visitors is indeed worthy of a lady whose grace
and beauty are in accord with the kindness and goodness of her heart. At the hour appointed, accompanied
by the three members of my suite, I again visited the
White House parlors, and was received by the lovely
mistress of those halls.

It is not my purpose to detail private conversation
with those who have made me their guest ; but it must
be testified here that I never have had the least cause
to retract my early assurance that in Grover Cleveland
I had met a statesman of splendid ability, rare judgment,
and lofty standards of right. And equally do I believe
that to few among the nations has it ever been granted
to have at the head a woman more worthy the name of
queen than that one who presided with so much grace
and dignity for eight years at the White House.

One day in February, the proprietor of the Shoreham notified me, that, as I had failed to engage my
apartments for inauguration week, he had rented them
to others, and that every room in the hotel would then
be occupied because of the crowd of visitors that occasion would summon to the city. Rather than await the
arrival of the future occupants of those rooms, and then

have to look out for my party when the throng should
be doing likewise, it seemed best to me to move at
once. So I sent my secretaries to consult Mrs. Mary
Longfellow Milmore, widow of Joseph Milmore, the celebrated sculptor, and sister-in-law of Martin Milmore.

Knowing me simply from history, and sympathizing
with me by reason of the kindness of her own heart,
Mrs. Milmore had written to me while I was in Boston,
and then had followed her cordial letters by calling on
me when I arrived in Washington. To any lady travelling or residing in a strange city, there are many little
attentions which cannot be so perfectly rendered as by
a person of her own sex, one who understands the customs of the community, and is familiar with the places
and people. Mrs. Milmore not only came when I needed
advice as a recent arrival, but she continued her kind
and sympathetic visits to the latest days of my stay, at
about which time she herself went abroad for a European trip.

There rarely passed a day when her cheerful face
and friendly voice did not appear at my door. Flowers,
fruits, cakes, and other tokens of her loving care, came
almost daily ; and to her hospitable dwelling I often
went to luncheon, meeting, besides herself, Sister An-
gelica, or other friends who seemed to be of the same
kindly spirit as the generous hostess. Wherever I may
be in the future, her many attentions during that winter
cannot be forgotten, and she will always have a warm
remembrance in my heart.

By her advice and selection, on or about the 14th of
February, I moved with my party to the large thirteen-

story building on Q Street, N.W., known as "The Cairo." Its newness and immaculate cleanliness impressed me favorably at once. My rooms were in the southwest corner, from which I had a glorious view over the country and down the Potomac; and although unused to being on the tenth story of any building, yet, when I became accustomed to the height, it ceased to worry me. Everything was done by the owner, Mr. Schneider, and his lovely wife, as well as by the manager, Mr. Sherman, and his amiable wife, to render the stay of our whole party agreeable to us. There we remained until about the 9th of July, at which time I removed to New York City, with no further intention of visiting Washington, although I did subsequently return, for reasons which will be stated in the proper place.

CHAPTER LIII

INAUGURATION OF PRESIDENT McKINLEY

TIME would fail me to speak of the countless new friends who vied in making my visit to Washington one of the most delightful seasons I ever passed. It was my custom to give a reception about every fortnight; to receive callers at eight to nine any evening, and often at other times. Both houses of Congress were well represented at my receptions, if not always by the gentlemen themselves, by their wives or daughters. Although all were presented through Captain Palmer by name and by card, yet it will be seen that, when there were seldom less than two hundred callers, and my largest reception numbered nearly five hundred persons, it was not possible for me to return all calls.

I therefore made it a rule to pay return visits only to those connected with the government, and even then it was scarcely possible to keep up with the number of my visitors. But there are two persons at least of whom I must make mention by name. These are Senator George C. Perkins, formerly governor of the State of California, and Representative Samuel G. Hilborn, also of that State. Both of these gentlemen have visited Honolulu.

I had had the pleasure of entertaining Governor Per-

kins when he was there, but was in retirement at the
time Mr. Hilborn went there accompanied by his wife
and daughter.   Like many other visitors, Mr. Hilborn
landed in Hawaii supposing that my government had
been a failure, and that the present rulers were the
choice of the people, and annexation desirable for both
nations.   And like any person who goes there and
examines the situation frankly and fairly, Mr. Hilborn
returned with his mind made up to the contrary.

While I was at the Shoreham, Mr. Hilborn called,
and introduced his wife and daughter; and the beautiful
voice of Miss Grace Hilborn, as she sang some of my
own Hawaiian songs, to our instrument, the ukulele,
gave to me that joy, so sadly sweet, of listening to the
sounds of home in foreign lands.   This charming family never relaxed their attentions to me while I resided
in Washington, and I am indebted to each of them in
more ways than I can speak of in these recollections.
Mr. Hilborn is a hard-working man in his public life,
yet he always found the time for any friendly chat with
me if I wished to speak with some gentleman on whose
good judgment I could rely.

Governor Perkins received me on my first visit to
the Senate Chamber, where I went with my party simply
to watch the deliberations; he provided us at once with
seats in the gallery reserved for the personal friends of
the senators, but subsequently he did a greater and more
conspicuous kindness than this.   On Friday noon, the
26th of February, I informed Captain Palmer that I had
great curiosity to see the inauguration of the President
of the United States, if it were possible to get seats.

He said that it was rather late to make the proper arrangements. I requested him to communicate my wish to Governor Perkins. So, at two o'clock of that day he went to the Capitol, was welcomed by Senator Perkins, introduced to the members of the committee, and leaving the matter in their hands, he returned to the hotel.

Almost immediately on his arrival there, Captain Palmer received a despatch saying that it had been agreed between Senator Sherman and Secretary Olney that two seats in the gallery reserved for the diplomatic corps should be assigned to me, and that it was much regretted that I had not applied earlier, when I could have had seats for three, in the place of one attendant. We said nothing about our intentions; and leaving Captain Palmer and Mrs. Nahaolelua in the carriage, I, attended by Mr. Joseph Heleluhe, witnessed the interesting ceremonies.

The storm which burst from the reporters' gallery when they saw me there will be remembered by those who read any of the newspapers on the day following. As it had been a very gallant act on the part of quite a number of gentlemen, and especially of Secretary Sherman and Secretary Olney, I permitted nothing to be said by my secretaries in answer to the misrepresentations made in the press. But they were not to go unrebuked; for Mr. Sherman's letter, bearing the date of the very afternoon when my secretary called at the Senate chamber, was given by Mr. Olney to the press without comment, and there was immediate silence on the subject, for with which administration were the critics to find fault?

After the inaugural ceremonies were over we visited the building of the Central National Bank, where I was most courteously received by the president of the board of directors; and after resting with my suite in his office, we were conducted to a room in the building from which I saw and intensely enjoyed the grand procession. The day was all that could be desired; my friends accused me of having imported it from our own perfect climate expressly for the new administration. Although too weary to attend the ball in the evening, I felt that I would not have missed for anything that which I had seen during the day.

But there was another pleasure in store for me that very night; for in the carriage with the President, and representing the United States Navy, was Admiral George Brown, who, with his wife, had already visited me at the Shoreham. In meeting with me under the changed circumstances which had befallen since he knew me as the Princess Royal at the date of his attentions to my brother, the gallant sailor could not restrain his emotions, and the tears flowed from his eyes. On the last days of the sessions of the Senate, a bill had passed by unanimous consent permitting sundry officers of the United States service to receive decorations which had been conferred by King Kalakaua, and also by myself while reigning sovereign; and amongst these was one bestowed upon Admiral Brown.

"There, I have waited over four years for the privilege of wearing that," he exclaimed, as he entered my parlor that night; "and now that it is mine, I am determined that you shall be the very first one to see it." I thanked him warmly, as I handed him back his coveted decoration, for, indeed, I fully appreciated his loyalty in bringing it to show me. Since that meeting he has been retired from active service, but it is to be hoped that so gallant a gentleman and efficient an officer may long be spared to his friends and his country. I can never forget his kindness to my brother during the king's last days on earth.

One object of my visit to Washington was to ask a favor of the Masonic fraternity; so, while at the Shoreham, I sent a letter to Mr. Frederic Webber, Secretary of the Supreme Council, thirty-third degree, asking him to call at my apartments, a request with which he very promptly complied. He remembered me perfectly from our meeting in 1887, when he had been one of the thirteen Masons of high degree to call on the party of Queen Kapiolani; of that committee of the Supreme Council, General Albert Pike, now gone to the great majority, was the head. Besides this, Mr. Webber was, during the lifetime of Governor Dominis, in correspondence with my husband on matters connected with the order.

I showed Mr. Webber my jewel of the Mystic Shrine, which I prize very highly, and asked if I might be permitted to wear my husband's Masonic jewels; to which he replied in the affirmative, and then added he would like also to present me with a medal which was ornamented on one side with certain emblems of the thirty-third degree of Masonry, and on the other with a bas-relief likeness of General Pike. To thus receive permission to use the decorations or insignia of Masonry belonging to my

husband, and further to be presented with a likeness of
the head of the fraternity, and a valued correspondent
of Governor Dominis, was certainly a happy welcome
from the brotherhood my husband loved.

Secretary Webber also sent me books containing the
accounts of the meetings of the council, and of proceedings in many of their branches, thus informing me in
regard to the extent of their works of charity and benevolence.   On one afternoon, by his invitation, I visited
the chambers of the council, attended by my suite ; and
quite a number of the brethren were presented to me,
much to my pleasure, which I sincerely trust was recip-
rocated.   I was shown a photograph of my husband,
which, with his correspondence, is preserved there in
the archives of the order.   In more ways than I can
mention, Mr. Webber and his daughter showed themselves to be true friends during my visit.

From several benevolent and literary associations of
Washington requests were received to set apart a day
to receive their members as a body ; but to all such suggestions I instructed my secretary to reply that a committee of the ladies or gentlemen might call upon me
at their own convenience, but that I must decline any
large public receptions.   The only exception I made to
this rule was in favor of the National Park School for
young ladies at Forest Glen, Md., who sent one of the
faculty to ask the favor of a general reception.   I have
so long been interested in the education of the young,
especially of young girls, that I could not refuse myself
the pleasure.

The affair took place at the Shoreham ; and it was

indeed refreshing to look into the pure, good, beautiful faces before me. Including the teachers who came with them, the company numbered over a hundred. Their music interested me very much ; they sang with great taste and sweetness. They presented me with their college colors ; and I gave them a copy, made with my own hands, of my most popular song, the "*Aloha Oe*," or "Farewell to Thee," with which they seemed to be much pleased. But they were not quite satisfied, I was told, because I had made no address.

I have already spoken of the shrinking from publicity felt by me ever since my imprisonment, and I had prepared nothing ; however, I decided to tell them of one thought which impressed me, so, by the published report in the newspapers, this is what I said : —

"I wish to extend to you my thanks for the honor you have shown me by this visit. It shall always be remembered as a bright spot in my memory of this stay in America. I am glad to see you all, and to know that each of you is desirous of attaining intellectual advancement. It shows the progress of the world. The world cannot stand still. We must either advance or recede. Since my arrival in this country I have been impressed with its grandeur, but nothing more favorably impresses me than the advantages you have for learning. Again I desire to thank you, and I wish you all a prosperous and happy future."

There were many delegations of patriotic or literary societies amongst my visitors at the Cairo, such as Daughters of the Revolution, and Veterans of the Southern Confederacy. At Arlington, on Decoration

Day, I was overwhelmed with pleasant attentions by the Grand Army of the Republic. Then the delegates to the International Postal Congress ; the Chinese Embassy ; a large political delegation from Missouri ; Governor Clough, with some twenty members of his staff in full uniform, from Minnesota ; many associations of teachers from distant States ; frequent calls from the young ladies of colleges, — one after the other seemed to find pleasure in visiting me to pay their respects.

From all denominations of the Christian church I have received representative visitors, and from the Sisters of the Holy Cross and from the Methodist Society of Rev. Lucien G. Clark accepted invitations to be present at their receptions. At the former I twice had the pleasure of meeting Monseigneur Martinelli, the papal delegate to the capital. Rev. J. H. Perry, the rector of St. Andrews, was very kind and attentive ; and as I am a communicant in the Episcopal Church, I generally attended the church of his parish in Fourteenth Street.

CHAPTER LIV

MY LITERARY OCCUPATION

In the early part of May it became necessary for my companion, Mrs. Kia Nahaolelua, to return to Honolulu. Three months was the length of time I had expected to be absent when I asked her to accompany me; but five months had passed away, and her husband and large family of children needed her. So I sent her to San Francisco under the charge of Captain Palmer, where he was to meet Mrs. Joseph Heleluhe, and conduct her to Washington.

During their absence I invited my cousin, Mrs. William Lee, whom, after leaving Boston, I had met in New York on the occasion of the dedication of the Grant mausoleum, to visit me at the Cairo. In her honor I issued cards for a special reception given in the elegant ballroom of that hotel. Manager Sherman spared neither pains nor money to make the occasion worthy of the guest; choice flowers and music, some of it from Hawaiian sources, made the celebration a charming one. Mrs. Lee is a very handsome woman, of commanding presence, brilliant in conversation, cultivated in mind, and of a high order of intellect. During her short stay, for the days sped quickly by, she attracted much attention by her social qualities, and won the hearts of many of those with whom she came in contact.

The synopsis of my social pleasures for the six months or so I was in Washington is necessarily incomplete, and to render it perfect would be to extend these leaves into too much of a volume. With such numberless callers as I have daily received from all parts of the United States, the frequent courtesies from the families of congressional members, and the occasionally accepted invitations to the theatre, the opera, or other public entertainments (many of which invitations, while appreciating the kindly spirit, I was obliged to decline), my leisure moments were much occupied. It was singular, and at times amusing, to notice the question in the public journals, asking, "What is the queen doing in Washington?" and in reply, to read the ingenuity shown in inventing all sorts of political falsehoods, and publishing these as facts.

Besides what has been stated, my time was much engrossed with correspondence and literary labors, in which latter might be included my music. For I have been engaged on two other works besides " Hawaii's Story." During my imprisonment I had nearly translated an ancient poem which has been handed down exclusively in our family from the earliest days. This I completed during my visit to the national capital ; and it is now issued from the press of Lee & Shepard, Boston. It is the chant which was sung to Captain Cook in one of the ancient temples of Hawaii, and chronicles the creation of the world and of living creatures, from the shell-fish to the human race, according to Hawaiian traditions. It is not designed for general circulation, but for my friends, and will be placed in the libraries of some scientific societies.

For years my name has been at the head of a list of members of the Polynesian Society, as patron. This organization, with headquarters in New Zealand, is devoted to the study of languages, literature, folk-lore, history, in short, all things connected with the inhabitants of that vast extent of archipelago in the Pacific Ocean known as Oceanica. When I accepted the position as patron, Mr. Alexander assured me that it was tendered to me, not only because of the fact that the Hawaiians were the most highly civilized of any of the ancient people of those seas, but further, because I had been known so long as the friend of education, of art, and of all those refining influences which exalt the nation, and elevate the character of the individual. Therefore it seemed fitting for me to send to this society some account of our earliest days.

I have had more calls for my music than I could possibly supply. An edition of " Aloha Oe," published by me in Washington this winter, simply for gifts to my friends, is nearly exhausted. No copies have ever been offered for sale; but in response to the very general wish, I have collected a number of my songs, chants, and pieces written or translated by me during the past twenty years or more, and hope soon to put them into the hands of the publisher, so that any stranger desiring to possess samples of Hawaiian music may have that opportunity. Two specially prepared volumes of such compositions were appropriately bound and inscribed in

Washington the past winter. One of these was placed in the new Congressional Library; the other was sent abroad as my contribution to the souvenirs of this Jubilee year of Her Majesty, the great and good Queen Victoria.

From this brief sketch of my life at the capital, it would appear that my mind was fully employed, had there been no political questions to interest me. Yet was it natural that I should forget my own people and their misfortunes? Let me, therefore, return to the annexationists and their plots. While I had been no more than an interested observer, quietly awaiting the course of justice, and conscious of the strength derived from truth and right on my side, their commissioners, with such influences as their indomitable assurance could command, had been working very hard to get the present rule in Hawaii out of its political and financial difficulties, by passing over to the United States a country whose hospitality they have betrayed, a land which they do not and never can own.

My friends in Honolulu had never forgotten me, and the arrival of every mail kept me informed of all that transpired throughout Hawaii. With the advantages which were mine of learning the attitude of men and parties in Washington, there was little that took place with which I was not thoroughly acquainted before it reached the columns of the newspapers. Thus, understanding perfectly the kind of men sent one after another by the so-called Republic of Hawaii to Washington, I was easily able to separate truth from falsehood in the accounts inspired by the missionary party, published by them or their agents in Honolulu, written from thence to the press in America, or invented by enterprising scribblers for the purpose of deceiving the American public.

Having tried in vain to excite the American people against Great Britain, and having wilfully violated treaty obligations with the friendly power of Japan, they then got the Senate into a hopeless quarrel over the reciprocity treaty and the sugar schedule; so that to allay all these disturbances, and yet do nothing decisive, on June 16, 1897, President McKinley sent their annexation treaty to the Senate. Congress had been in session ever since December, and had shown no interest whatever in the troubles of a few adventurers two thousand miles from California, claiming to be both Americans and Hawaiians.

Nothing was done by me in the matter until the treaty was officially made public in the Senate. These commissioners had often said that there would soon be a treaty signed, and had so often deceived the people that it was well to await knowledge from the proper authority. But just as quickly as I learned that action had been taken upon the proposed cession of Hawaii to the United States, I sent my secretaries, Mr. Joseph Heleluhe and Captain Julius A. Palmer, to the Department of State with the following protest.

CHAPTER LV

MY OFFICIAL PROTEST TO THE TREATY

" I, LILIUOKALANI of Hawaii, by the will of God named heir apparent on the tenth day of April, A.D. 1877, and by the grace of God Queen of the Hawaiian Islands on the seventeenth day of January, A.D. 1893, do hereby protest against the ratification of a certain treaty, which, so I am informed, has been signed at Washington by Messrs. Hatch, Thurston, and Kinney, purporting to cede those Islands to the territory and dominion of the United States. I declare such a treaty to be an act of wrong toward the native and part-native people of Hawaii, an invasion of the rights of the ruling chiefs, in violation of international rights both toward my people and toward friendly nations with whom they have made treaties, the perpetuation of the fraud whereby the constitutional government was overthrown, and, finally, an act of gross injustice to me.

" Because the official protests made by me on the seventeenth day of January, 1893, to the so-called Provisional Government was signed by me, and received by said government with the assurance that the case was referred to the United States of America for arbitration.

YIELDED TO AVOID BLOODSHED.

" Because that protest and my communications to the United States Government immediately thereafter expressly declare that I yielded my authority to the forces of the United States in order to avoid bloodshed, and because I recognized the futility of a conflict with so formidable a power.

" Because the President of the United States, the Secretary of State, and an envoy commissioned by them reported in official documents that my government was unlawfully coerced by the forces, diplomatic and naval, of the United States; that I was at the date of their investigations the constitutional ruler of my people.

" Because such decision of the recognized magistrates of the United States was officially communicated to me and to Sanford B. Dole, and said Dole's resignation requested by Albert S. Willis, the recognized agent and minister of the Government of the United States.

" Because neither the above-named commission nor the government which sends it has ever received any such authority from the registered voters of Hawaii, but derives its assumed powers from the so-called committee of public safety, organized on or about the seventeenth day of January, 1893, said committee being composed largely of persons claiming American citizenship, and not one single Hawaiian was a member thereof, or in any way participated in the demonstration leading to its existence.

" Because my people, about forty thousand in number, have in no way been consulted by those, three thousand in number, who claim the right to destroy the independence of Hawaii. My people constitute four-fifths of the legally qualified voters of Hawaii, and excluding those imported for the demands of labor, about the same proportion of the inhabitants.

CIVIC AND HEREDITARY RIGHTS.

" Because said treaty ignores, not only the civic rights of my people, but, further, the hereditary property of their chiefs. Of the 4,000,000 acres composing the territory said treaty offers to annex, 1,000,000 or 915,000 acres has in no way been heretofore recognized as other than the private property of the constitutional monarch, subject to a control in no way differing from other items of a private estate.

" Because it is proposed by said treaty to confiscate said property, technically called the crown lands, those legally entitled thereto, either now or in succession, receiving no consideration whatever for estates, their title to which has been always undisputed, and which is legitimately in my name at this date.

"Because said treaty ignores, not only all professions of perpetual amity and good faith made by the United States in former treaties with the sovereigns representing the Hawaiian people, but all treaties made by those sovereigns with other and friendly powers, and it is thereby in violation of international law.

"Because, by treating with the parties claiming at this time the right to cede said territory of Hawaii, the Government of the United States receives such territory from the hands of those whom its own magistrates (legally elected by the people of the United States, and in office in 1893) pronounced fraudulently in power and unconstitutionally ruling Hawaii.

APPEALS TO PRESIDENT AND SENATE.

"Therefore I, Liliuokalani of Hawaii, do hereby call upon the President of that nation, to whom alone I yielded my property and my authority, to withdraw said treaty (ceding said Islands) from further consideration. I ask the honorable Senate of the United States to decline to ratify said treaty, and I implore the people of this great and good nation, from whom my ancestors learned the Christian religion, to sustain their representatives in such acts of justice and equity as may be in accord with the principles of their fathers, and to the Almighty Ruler of the universe, to him who judgeth righteously, I commit my cause.

"Done at Washington, District of Columbia, United States of America, this seventeenth day of June, in the year eighteen hundred and ninety-seven.

"LILIUOKALANI.

"JOSEPH HELELUHE.)
"WOKEKI HELELUHE. } Witnesses to Signature."
"JULIUS A. PALMER.)

In the matter of providing me with seats in the diplomatic gallery at the ceremonies of the inauguration, I have already expressed my gratitude to Secretary John Sherman. It is but just that I should repeat here my appreciation of the kind, gallant, and courteous treatment again received at his official hands.   For although it was my directions that this document should be delivered to any person authorized to receive it, yet as soon as Secretary Sherman saw the cards of my commissioners, he at once accorded them a private audience.

My protest, and a like remonstrance made on behalf of the patriotic leagues of the Hawaiian people by Hon. Joseph Heleluhe as their authorized commissioner, were both placed in the secretary's hands by that gentleman; and Mr. Sherman read them both through.   He then turned to Captain Palmer, and had an agreeable conversation on the points at issue, after which my commissioners retired.   The accustomed tissue of falsehoods was woven about this interview; some stating that Secretary Sherman had refused to see my messengers, others again giving the names of some one or other of his subordinates with whom my commissioners had had an interview, and finally asserting that the protests went into the archives of the department without examination, and were pigeon-holed; all of which statements, it is needless to say, were untrue.   Secretary Sherman by his action showed that, a skilled diplomatist, he had not forgotten to remain a gallant gentleman.

I refer to Appendix D for text of the treaty.

CHAPTER LVI

THE TREATY ANALYZED

ANYTHING like an extended criticism of the proposed treaty will not be attempted here. The first articles convey nothing, and do not even profess to convey anything; would not any capitalist, anticipating an investment of four millions, and a contingent liability of as much more, demand an exact schedule of the property for which he is paying, and a warrant of the legitimacy of the title?

Suppose that the claims of foreign governments for indemnification for acts of outrage and imprisonment committed under the rule of the Republic, the Japanese indemnity, and the value of the crown lands, should raise the debt limit to eight millions, do the parties ceding this territory come under personal obligations to pay the overplus indebtedness?

In regard to the crown lands, even the best-informed citizens of the United States do not understand the difference between these and the lands of the Hawaiian government. Originally all territory belonged to the king, by whom it was apportioned for use only, not for sale, to the chiefs, who in turn assigned tracts, small or large, to their people; an excellent system for us, by which the poorest native had all the land he needed,

and yet it could not be taken from him by any design-
ing foreigner.

But about fifty years ago there came, in place of our
own method, the land system, delivered to us by the
missionaries. In effect this divided the territory of the
Islands into three parts, not necessarily equal, although
nearly so. One-third was devoted to the use or expenses
of government; one-third was apportioned to the people;
and the remainder continued, as from all ages, the private property of the chief highest in rank, — in other
words, the reigning sovereign.

That part of Hawaii given by the king to the people
has almost entirely left them, and now belongs to the
missionaries and their friends or successors. Of the
portion reserved to the government nothing need be
said. If the present rule may be called a government,
it probably has the right to the income of these lands.
But one of their commissioners, Mr. Kinney, made a
public statement through the press that it would be as
well for an ex-president to claim the White House as
for me to claim my income in the crown lands.

Mr. Kinney could scarcely have chosen a more effective method to prove his ignorance; and in response I
have had the following brief statement prepared by one
who thoroughly understands the matter: —

By Mr. Kinney. — "The fealty of the native Hawaiian to his
chief knows no limit. Such loyalty exacts corresponding devotion; it was to meet this necessity that the chief highest in rank
was never divested of the crown lands or private purse."

Reply. — "The White House and other official estate form
an investment made with the money of the American people for

the use of their chosen executive. The crown lands were never the property of the people, no, not even of any monarchical government. Not citing the testimony of ages, when all the lands belonged to the chiefs, in 1848 the ruling king reserved these very lands as 'his private estate,' and the legislature confirmed this act 'as the private lands of His Majesty, his heirs and assigns forever.' In 1864 the Supreme Court decided that 'each successor' could regulate and dispose of the same according to his will and pleasure as private property.

"In 1865 payment was made to Queen Emma in lieu of dower in these lands, although she had not been on the throne, but was the widow of a monarch deceased two years previously. In 1880 Mr. Spreckels paid the Princess Ruth $10,000 to release her claim to a small tract of these lands, although she had never ascended the throne. The act of the legislature by which these lands were made 'inalienable, to descend to the heirs and successors of the Hawaiian crown (N. B., not of any Kamehameha) forever,' has never been reversed, the constitution expressly confirming this by the words, the 'successor elected shall become a new stirps for a royal family, regulated by the same law as the present royal family.'

"Were Kalakaua, Liliuokalani, or Kaiulani, of another race (instead of having, as they most certainly have, the blood of Kamehamehas), it would still be true that no intelligent lawyer would invest the money of his client in a tract of hereditary crown land unless the living representatives were to join in the deed. It is just possible that the lawyers who have visited Washington know these facts, as the first two articles of their conveyance to us by treaty are only quit claim deeds; they expressly limit the grantors' warrant to that which at this date belongs to them. Any person could execute such a conveyance to the White House estate, and it would not convey anything, nor even pretend to put the grantee in possession of anything. Will American capitalists invest at their own risk in land which constitutes one-fourth of the whole proposed territory of Hawaii?"

But it is in the sixth article that the missionary

party show their determination to keep the same position under the flag of the United States that they have held at the Islands ever since the revolution of 1887. By this, *which is made part of the treaty, and so, if it should be ratified as it stands, it can never be changed, not even by Act of Congress,* the President is to appoint five commissioners, *two of whom shall be residents of the Hawaiian Islands;* by these all legislation in regard to that territory is to be recommended to Congress.

Which means that the missionary party shall continue to control all measures enacted in regard to Hawaii and the Hawaiians; that there shall be no essential change in their greedy and deceitful policy, that they shall still coin money through the manipulation of the sugar interest and the management of the plantations and the labor question. And what advantage or return will the United States Government ever receive from such a territorial administration as that? The President and Secretary of State having agreed to such enactment, it only remains for the needed two-thirds of the Senate to ratify it to make it the law of the land.

The voters of this great and good nation are too free from suspicion. They have no idea how they have been deceived, how much more they can be deceived. The poor Hawaiians, strangers on their native soil, excluded from their own halls of legislation, have had their experience; alas, a bitter one. The Japanese, urged and inveigled and bought to come to Hawaii while they were needed to increase the foreigners' gold, have had theirs; but the American people have theirs yet to get. The Hawaiian sugar planters are having theirs from the drain on their pockets to support Thurston and those he employs in this country.

Here I may state that seldom or never had the Hawaiian government, during the days of monarchy, been known to place itself in such a position as it has fallen into since in the hands of this missionary oligarchy. It has had to borrow money several times from the two banks in Honolulu, and to ask funds from the planters. When in prison in 1895, Mr. Wilson told me, in the presence of his wife, that that year's taxes had been mortgaged to the amount of $800,000 to Mr. C. B. Bishop. Under the monarchy there was always enough from its own revenues to pay all expenses until the time came when such enterprising people as wanted to make money for themselves came into office, and prevailed on the government to make *new improvements;* from that time the government became indebted.

There is one more bit of political history of which I will speak, and I shall then have said all that it is my intention to give to the public for the present. Soon after the inauguration of President McKinley, it was my hope to assure him in person of my kindest wishes for a happy and successful term of office, but more especially to present to him, as the representative of my people, certain documents and petitions which had been sent to me for the purpose; then my duty in the case would have been done.[1]

[1] After the overthrow of the monarchy, these people had no representation at home or abroad, and such is their condition to this day. Comprising four-fifths of the legally qualified voters, they are voiceless, save those few who, for the purpose of obtaining the necessaries of life, have sworn allegiance to the present government. In this connection, the following statement, which is sent

No attempts of any kind or nature were ever made in my behalf by any person whomsoever, to arrange an interview between the President and myself. No public man in Washington, whoever he may be, has ever declined to see me or any one of my party. The despatches which the press have published on that point have not a basis of truth. Events transpiring at the capital made it inexpedient for me to carry out the wishes and requests of my people.

The President was so overwhelmed with pressing business, so beset by office-seekers, his time so filled with matters requiring his direct attention, that he could not be expected to give consideration to any subject outside of the administration of the affairs of the United States government ; which, there being no annexation movement above board at that time (the first week in March), was certainly the case with the matter intrusted to me by my people.

On the 10th of July I bade adieu to the beautiful city of Washington, where I had spent such a delightful half-year. I had called at the Capitol two or three times, not with any petition or request, but simply to

to me from Honolulu, may be of interest as showing how few now assume to govern a nation of 109,000 persons. The registered voters in 1890, under the monarchy, numbered 13,593 persons.

The registered voters in 1894, under the Provisional Government, for delegates to the so-called Constitutional Convention, numbered 4,477.

The actual voters in 1896, under the so-called Republic, numbered, for Senators, 2,017, and for Representatives, 3,196. In other words, there were qualified to vote for Senators and Representatives 2,017 persons, and for Representatives only 1,179.

From figures already in, it is doubtful whether the total vote to be cast in September next will exceed 2,000.

thank those gentlemen who had kindly taken an interest in me and in the Hawaiian people.   I had also left
my card for those Senators whose families had been
represented among my callers, and made a few parting
visits to my friends in the city.

On Saturday afternoon I arrived in New York, and
remained at the Albemarle two weeks, visiting the
places of interest, attending the opera, and receiving the
visits of a few of my friends who lived in that city or
its immediate vicinity.

But while there, I received further information from
the patriotic leagues, the members of which organizations expressed much regret that I had not presented
the documents in my hands to President McKinley, and
urging me to do this at once.   Accordingly on Saturday,
the 24th of July, with my whole party, I returned to
Washington, this time taking rooms at the Ebbitt
House.   On Monday morning I sent the papers to President McKinley, by the hands of Mr. Joseph Heleluhe,
and Captain Palmer, who accompanied him.

Then, learning that it was the regular reception-day
of the President, and also the last one prior to his vacation, without consultation with any person, I told the
members of my suite that, before leaving Washington
again, we would call socially on the President.   Arriving
at the door of the White House, I requested Captain
Palmer to send up our cards, which he did before we
entered the East Room ; and in response an officer, who
had received his instructions, came to us, conducted us
to the farther end of the room, and provided us with
seats, which we were requested to retain when the Pres-

ident should enter to meet the hundred or so strangers who were standing at the opposite end of the large reception-room.

While we were waiting, one of the President's secretaries came down from his office with a special message from President McKinley to like effect. After the President had finished his official handshaking, he approached the place where I sat. Observing him, I arose and advanced to meet him. We had a most delightful conversation ; and I found him to be a most agreeable gentleman, both in manner and in words. He spoke very prettily of his wife's delicate health, alluding to the matter of his own accord, and voluntarily expressing his regret that he could not at once invite me in to visit her. I have been thus particular to describe the facts of my social relations to the White House, because upon no subject has the desire been more frequently shown to prejudice me and my cause in the eyes of the American people.

Strangers have remarked that in no part of the world visited by them have they found the rules of etiquette so exactly laid down and so persistently observed as in Honolulu, when the Islands were under the monarchy. It is to be expected, therefore, that I know what is due to me ; that further, as the wife of the governor of Oahu, as the princess royal, and as the reigning sovereign, it was not necessary for me to take lessons in the departments of social or diplomatic etiquette before residing in the national capital of the United States, or making and receiving visits of any nature.

CHAPTER LVII

HAWAIIAN AUTONOMY

IT has been suggested to me that the American general reader is not well informed regarding the social and political conditions which have come about in the Sandwich Islands, and that it would be well here to give some expression to my own observation of them. Space will only permit, however, a mere outline.

It has been said that the Hawaiian people under the rule of the chiefs were most degraded, that under the monarchy their condition greatly improved, but that the native government in any form had at last become intolerable to the more enlightened part of the community. This statement has been substantially repeated recently by certain New England and Hawaiian "statesmen" in speeches made at the Home Market Club in Boston. I shall not examine it in detail; but it may serve as a text for the few remarks I feel called upon to make from my own — and that is to say, the native Hawaiian — standpoint.

I shall not claim that in the days of Captain Cook our people were civilized. I shall not claim anything more for their progress in civilization and Christian morality than has been already attested by missionary writers. Perhaps I may safely claim even less, admit-

ting the criticism of some intelligent visitors who were
not missionaries, — that the habits and prejudices of
New England Puritanism were not well adapted to the
genius of a tropical people, nor capable of being thoroughly ingrafted upon them.

But Christianity in substance they have accepted ;
and I know of no people who have developed a tenderer
Christian conscience, or who have shown themselves
more ready to obey its behests. Nor has any people
known to history shown a greater reverence and love
for their Christian teachers, or filled the measure of a
grateful return more overflowingly. And where else
in the world's history is it written that a savage people,
pagan for ages, with fixed hereditary customs and be-
liefs, have made equal progress in civilization and Christianity in the same space of time ? And what people
has ever been subjected during such an evolution to
such a flood of external demoralizing influences ?

Does it make nothing for us that we have always
recognized our Christian teachers as worthy of authority in our councils, and repudiated those whose influence
or character was vicious or irreligious ? That while
four-fifths of the population of our Islands was swept
out of existence by the vices introduced by foreigners,
the ruling class clung to Christian morality, and gave its
unvarying support and service to the work of saving
and civilizing the masses ? Has not this class loyally
clung to the brotherly alliance made with the better
element of foreign settlers, giving freely of its authority
and its substance, its sons and its daughters, to cement
and to prosper it ?

But will it also be thought strange that education and knowledge of the world have enabled us to perceive that as a race we have some special mental and physical requirements not shared by the other races which have come among us? That certain habits and modes of living are better for our health and happiness than others? And that a separate nationality, and a particular form of government, as well as special laws, are, at least for the present, best for us? And these things remained to us, until the pitiless and tireless "annexation policy" was effectively backed by the naval power of the United States.

To other usurpations of authority on the part of those whose love for the institutions of their native land we could understand and forgive we had submitted. We had allowed them virtually to give us a constitution, and control the offices of state. Not without protest, indeed; for the usurpation was unrighteous, and cost us much humiliation and distress. But we did not resist it by force. It had not entered into our hearts to believe that these friends and allies from the United States, even with all their foreign affinities, would ever go so far as to absolutely overthrow our form of government, seize our nation by the throat, and pass it over to an alien power.

And while we sought by peaceful political means to maintain the dignity of the throne, and to advance national feeling among the native people, we never sought to rob any citizen, wherever born, of either property, franchise, or social standing.

Perhaps there is a kind of right, depending upon

the precedents of all ages, and known as the " Right of Conquest," under which robbers and marauders may establish themselves in possession of whatsoever they are strong enough to ravish from their fellows. I will not pretend to decide how far civilization and Christian enlightenment have outlawed it. But we have known for many years that our Island monarchy has relied upon the protection always extended to us by the policy and the assured friendship of the great American republic.

If we have nourished in our bosom those who have sought our ruin, it has been because they were of the people whom we believed to be our dearest friends and allies. If we did not by force resist their final outrage, it was because we could not do so without striking at the military force of the United States. Whatever constraint the executive of this great country may be under to recognize the present government at Honolulu has been forced upon it by no act of ours, but by the unlawful acts of its own agents. Attempts to repudiate those acts are vain.

The conspirators, having actually gained possession of the machinery of government, and the recognition of foreign ministers, refused to surrender their conquest. So it happens that, overawed by the power of the United States to the extent that they can neither themselves throw off the usurpers, nor obtain assistance from other friendly states, the people of the Islands have no voice in determining their future, but are virtually relegated to the condition of the aborigines of the American continent.

It is not for me to consider this matter from the

American point of view; although the pending question
of annexation involves nothing less than a departure
from the established policy of that country, and an ominous change in its foreign relations.   It is enough that
I am able to say, and with absolute authority, that the
native people of Hawaii are entirely faithful to their
own chiefs, and are deeply attached to their own customs and mode of government; that they either do not
understand, or bitterly oppose, the scheme of annexation.   As a native Hawaiian, reared and educated in
close intimacy with the present rulers of the Islands
and their families, with exceptional opportunities for
studying both native and foreign character, it is easy
for me to detect the purpose of each line and word in
the annexation treaty, and even to distinguish the man
originating each portion of it.

I had prepared biographical sketches and observations upon the mental structure and character of the
most interested advocates of this measure.   They have
not refrained from circulating most vile and baseless
slanders against me; and, as public men, they seemed
to me open to public discussion.   But my publishers
have flatly declined to print this matter, as possibly it
might be construed as libellous.

And just here let me say that I have felt much per-
plexity over the attitude of the American press, that
great vehicle of information for the people, in respect
of Hawaiian affairs.   Shakespeare has said it is excellent to have a giant's strength, but it is tyrannous to
use it like a giant.   It is not merely that, with few
exceptions, the press has seemed to favor the extinc-

tion of Hawaiian sovereignty, but that it has often treated me with coarse allusions and flippancy, and almost uniformly has commented upon me adversely, or has declined to publish letters from myself and friends conveying correct information upon matters which other correspondents had, either wilfully or through being deceived, misrepresented. Perhaps in many cases *libellous* matter was involved. Possibly the press was not conscious of how cruelly it was exerting its strength, and will try, I now trust, to repair the injury.

It has been shown that in Hawaii there is an alien element composed of men of energy and determination, well able to carry through what they undertake, but not scrupulous respecting their methods. They doubtless control all the resources and influence of the present ruling power in Honolulu, and will employ them tirelessly in the future, as they have in the past, to secure their ends. This annexationist party might prove to be a dangerous accession even to American politics, both on account of natural abilities, and because of the training of an autocratic life from earliest youth.

Many of these men are anything but ideal citizens for a democracy. That custom of freely serving each other without stipulation or reward which exists as a very nature among our people has been even exaggerated in our hospitality to our teachers and advisers. Their children, and the associates they have drawn to themselves, are accustomed to it. They have always been treated with distinction. They would hardly know how to submit to the contradictions, disappointments, and discourtesies of a purely emulative society.

It would remain necessary for them to rule in Hawaii, even if the American flag floated over them. And if they found they could be successfully opposed, would they seek no remedy? Where would men, already proved capable of outwitting the conservatism of the United States and defeating its strongest traditions, capable of changing its colonial and foreign policy at a single *coup*, stop in their schemes?

Perhaps I may even venture here upon a final word respecting the American advocates of this annexation of Hawaii. I observe that they have pretty successfully striven to make it a party matter. It is chiefly Republican statesmen and politicians who favor it. But is it really a matter of party interest? Is the American Republic of States to degenerate, and become a colonizer and a land-grabber?

And is this prospect satisfactory to a people who rely upon self-government for their liberties, and whose guaranty of liberty and autonomy to the whole western hemisphere, the grand Monroe doctrine, appealing to the respect and the sense of justice of the masses of every nation on earth, has made any attack upon it practically impossible to the statesmen and rulers of armed empires? There is little question but that the United States could become a successful rival of the European nations in the race for conquest, and could create a vast military and naval power, if such is its ambition. But is such an ambition laudable? Is such a departure from its established principles patriotic or politic?

.   .   .   .

Here, at least for the present, I rest my pen.   During my stay in the capital, I suppose I must have met, by name and by card, at least five thousand callers. From most of these, by word, by grasp of hand, or at least by expression of countenance, I have received a sympathy and encouragement of which I cannot write fully.   Let it be understood that I have not failed to notice it, and to be not only flattered by its universality, but further very grateful that I have had the opportunity to know the real American people, quite distinct from those who have assumed this honored name when it suited their selfish ends.

But for the Hawaiian people, for the forty thousand of my own race and blood, descendants of those who welcomed the devoted and pious missionaries of seventy years ago, — for them has this mission of mine accomplished anything ?

Oh, honest Americans, as Christians hear me for my down-trodden people !   Their form of government is as dear to them as yours is precious to you.   Quite as warmly as you love your country, so they love theirs. With all your goodly possessions, covering a territory so immense that there yet remain parts unexplored, possessing islands that, although near at hand, had to be neutral ground in time of war, do not covet the little vineyard of Naboth's, so far from your shores, lest the punishment of Ahab fall upon you, if not in your day, in that of your children, for "be not deceived, God is not mocked."   The people to whom your fathers told of the living God, and taught to call " Father," and whom the sons now seek to despoil and destroy, are crying aloud to Him in their time of trouble; and He will keep His promise, and will listen to the voices of His Hawaiian children lamenting for their homes.

It is for them that I would give the last drop of my blood; it is for them that I would spend, nay, am spending, everything belonging to me. Will it be in vain? It is for the American people and their representatives in Congress to answer these questions. As they deal with me and my people, kindly, generously, and justly, so may the Great Ruler of all nations deal with the grand and glorious nation of the United States of America.

APPENDIX A.

[From *San Francisco Chronicle*, Monday, Sept. 5, 1887.]

THE government of the Sandwich Islands appears to have passed from the hands of the king into the hands of a military oligarchy that is more domineering than Kalakaua ever was. Before the recent revolt of the Europeans in Honolulu the press of the city was very plain-spoken. It printed unadorned truths about the king, and the latter made no effort to suppress such unpleasant utterances. Now, under the new *régime*, the newspapers are kept in check with military thoroughness. It seems incredible, but it is an actual fact, that not one of the Honolulu journals dared to reprint the comments of the American press on the so-called revolution, although such comment would have been very interesting reading to all Hawaiians. Even the reports of court proceedings are dry and matter-of-fact records, very different from the ordinary accounts. In a word, the freedom of the press of Honolulu is a myth under the reform party, and the man who looks for the facts in the Honolulu journals will not find them.

APPENDIX B.

While retaining the essential facts, parts of this statement
have been omitted to avoid unnecessary repetition, as much of the
matter therein contained will be found substantially the same incorporated in "Hawaii's Story."

His Excellency James H. Blount:

Sir, — On the morning of the 26th of November, 1890, I went
to Iolani Palace, where I met His Majesty Kalakaua's ministers,
Messrs. J. A. Cummins, C. N. Spencer, G. Brown, and A. P. Peterson, awaiting the appearance of His Majesty.

We did not have to wait long, and were ushered into the
library, the king seating me in his chair, and formally introducing
his ministers to me.   After exchanging assurances of fidelity to
each other and faithfulness in the discharge of their official duties,
the ministers left, and the king and I were left to talk over matters.

He told me of things that had transpired a few months back.
That some of the ministers had thrown guns and ammunition into
the sea from the steamer Waimanalo.   It was done to prevent him
from having them, and had evidently been directed by the reform
party, with whom a portion of his ministers were in accord, instead
of keeping them for his protection and safety.   These ministers
were working with a party of conspirators, who are the very same
parties who have been the means of the overthrow of my government on the 17th of January, 1893.   They are called the missionary or reform party.   The king went on to say that his guards had
been reduced to twenty men, and they were barely sufficient to protect me if there should be any disturbance.   He had requested

Mr. Cummins, Minister of Foreign Affairs, to send back to the palace all the guns that were at the station-house, and that the carriages had been sent to the palace, but the guns themselves had been kept back. It was an insult by his cabinet; and he felt keenly his weakness, that he had no more power or influence since his cabinet was working against him. He explained all these things because he wanted me to study my situation so as to be able to cope with it.

The time of his departure on the United States ship Charleston drew near, and he bade the queen and myself farewell; and I felt in my own heart some misgivings that I should never see him again. I spent a few nights in the palace, and realized the insecurity of the situation. Every two or three nights there was an alarm of some kind. There was a fear that something was going to happen; what that something was no one could tell. Mr. Cummins had heard of some conspiracy, but could not prove anything.

During the session of 1890 the Honolulu Rifles were disbanded, but the members of that company were still allowed to carry arms in the streets and to wear the uniforms. I asked my husband, the Hon. John O. Dominis, how all this could be allowed. He referred me to the Minister of Foreign Affairs. On inquiring of the minister, he said that they were part of the Knights of Pythias, and were permitted to carry arms. This was very unsatisfactory, and my husband and I concluded that there must be some underhanded dealings somewhere. After that I preferred to remain at Washington Place, only going to the palace during office hours.

A few weeks passed, and during that time grand preparations were made to receive the king on his return; but the morning of the 29th of January, 1891, the city was startled with the news that the United States ship Charleston was in sight with the Hawaiian flag flying at half-mast.

On the 15th of February, 1891, the funeral took place; and on Monday, the 16th, at 9 A.M., Mr. Cummins and I had a private conference. He evidently wanted to know what my decision would be. I told him I thought they ought to resign, and I would give him another position.

At ten I met the following gentlemen in the cabinet council:

Mr. J. A. Cummins, Mr. C. N. Spencer, Mr. G. Brown, Mr. A. P. Peterson. I told them I had studied over the situation, and concluded that they could not remain as my cabinet; that they ought to resign. They said they had also considered the question, and concluded that I ought to give them new commissions, and asked me to give them more time to consider, and it was granted them. Two weeks elapsed, when the cabinet consulted the supreme bench, and were told that they could not hold their seats or positions without I gave them new commissions; so they resigned.

The reading of the king's will took place, and Admiral Brown was invited by the queen dowager to be present. I appointed my new cabinet. They were Mr. S. Parker, Minister of Foreign Affairs; Mr. C. N. Spencer, Minister of Interior; Mr. H. A. Widemann, Minister of Finance; Mr. W. A. Whiting, Attorney-General. I also appointed Mr. C. B. Wilson marshal. Before I appointed my ministers, Messrs. Bush and Wilcox called and offered their services; but as Mr. Bush had shown his ingratitude to the late king, and Mr. Wilcox a disposition of disobedience on the occasion of his revolution of 1889, I felt I could not have such men for ministers, and appointed others, which made them very angry.

In the month of August (1891) the reform party began their policy of dismissing the ministry. They made promises to Mr. Cummins of the national reform, and Bush, Wilcox, and Ashford of the liberal party, and P. P. Kanoa, of seats in the cabinet if they joined their party; and they did so, besides taking Kamauoha, Iosepa, and another member with them, which made the reform party very strong. On the 31st of August, for no good cause, the Parker ministry was voted out in accordance with a clause in the constitution of 1887, that any minister could be voted out by a majority of the members of the House for "want of confidence." It had been decided by myself and cabinet that our policy should be one of economy and retrenchment. This had been our course from the commencement of my reign.

The Parker ministry had no sooner gone out than twenty-five Hawaiians, members of the House, petitioned me to appoint Mr. Parker again. Next day Mr. Baldwin asked for audience, and came with a request that I would receive the Hons. Kanoa and Kauhane, and ask them to form a cabinet for me. I received those gentlemen; but they brought with them a petition with a list of names, principally of the reform party, that I would nominate from those names my cabinet. They called this (*sic*) "a constitutional principle." I knew if I yielded to their request, I should be yielding my own right under the constitution, which gave me the right to appoint, and the House to dismiss.

Two weeks passed, and I appointed Ministers Parker, Gulick, Macfarlane, and Neumann. The policy of this ministry was retrenchment in all directions; and Mr. Macfarlane, as Minister of Finance, immediately set to work with that purpose in view, and laid many satisfactory plans for them to pursue. In order to carry out the rigid economies prepared by Mr. Macfarlane, I consented to a reduction of $10,000 in the appropriation for my privy purse, and further reductions in "household expenses, state entertainments, and the military." They had, however, been in office only a few days when the American minister, J. L. Stevens, made a request through Minister Parker that he would like to call on me the next day, the 16th of October, and that he would bring his secretary with him.

The hour was set for eleven, and a cabinet council was called to sit at ten. When the hour arrived, the cabinet rose to depart. I asked them to remain; but Mr. Macfarlane begged to be excused, as he had once, while a noble in the House, brought in a resolution against Mr. J. L. Stevens on account of a speech he made on the 30th of May reflecting on the administration in Hawaii. Mr. Gulick and himself were excused, and Mr. Parker and Mr. Neumann remained. Mr. Parker went to the door and received Mr. Stevens, and at the same time asked what was the purpose of his visit, that he might apprise me. Mr. Stevens said he would mention it to me in person. They entered, followed by Mr. H. W. Severance. He seated himself in a manner which no gentleman would assume in the presence of a lady, and drew from under his arm a document which he read, stating that my government had grossly insulted him, the Ambassador of the United States and Minister Plenipotentiary for that nation, and holding them responsible for an article which appeared in the *Bulletin* reflecting upon his indifference in sending relief to the captain and crew of a shipwrecked American vessel.

He then read a clause in international laws relating to a minister's position in foreign lands. While he was reading he seemed to be laboring under great excitement and anger; and when he finished reading, I rose, and said my cabinet would give the matter their best consideration, whereupon Mr. Stevens and Mr. Severance took their leave. Was he seeking to make trouble? I remarked to Mr. Parker and Mr. Neumann that it appeared that way. Next day a lunch was given by the ladies of the Central Union Church; the occasion was to help pay for the new church on Beretania Street. Mr. Henry Severance took the occasion to say to me that he was entirely ignorant as to the intention of Minister Stevens before they arrived at the palace, as he had not told him of the object of the visit, and was surprised at Mr. Stevens's conduct. I did not answer. Some correspondence passed between Mr. Stevens and my ministers, which resulted in the cabinet entering a suit for libel against the *Bulletin*, which was afterwards withdrawn by Mr. Stevens.

It was during this month that a meeting was held at the residence of Mr. Alexander Young, and a discussion arose as to my obstinacy in not appointing one of their number. They called this "constitutional principle." At this meeting it was proposed to dethrone me. The question was asked how it was to be accomplished, when it was stated that Captain Wiltse of the Boston would assist.

Changes of ministry followed rapidly. The Cornwell cabinet lasted only one hour. Its members were W. H. Cornwell, J. Nawahi, C. T. Gulick, and C. Creighton. Without giving this cabinet any trial, they were immediately voted out.

Here I must mention that when the Macfarlane ministry was voted out, I wished to send them back to the House again; but Mr. Macfarlane and Mr. Neumann advised to the contrary. I felt loath to give up a cabinet composed of men in whom I had reason to know the community had confidence that their transactions would be straightforward and honest.

DISBANDMENT OF THE ROYAL HOUSEHOLD GUARD

The Wilcox (reform) cabinet came next. They were appointed by stratagem, as I found out afterwards. The policy of this cabinet was retrenchment, no changes in the monetary system of the country, and to make a commercial treaty which would bring us in closer relationship with the United States.

Their first policy they failed to carry out, as they went into all sorts of extravagant measures, such as $5,000 for sending a commission to Washington — and that commission was to consist of Thurston, Wilcox, and others — with the purpose of annexing these Islands; $12,000 to send the band to Chicago, and $50,000 for the Volcano road. All these measures were for Mr. Thurston's private benefit, but were passed in the House. It had always been customary for the ministry to consult the king or sovereign in cabinet council on any measure of importance; but in this instance, and on all occasions, the cabinet had already decided on those measures, and simply presented them to me for my signature. I had no resource but to acquiesce.

Whenever I expostulated their answer was generally, "We have consulted the chief justice, and are of one opinion." I found that I was simply a nonentity, a figurehead, but was content to wait patiently until the next session, when probably they would be voted out.

It required diplomacy to overthrow the Wilcox cabinet, and the liberals used it. The cabinet felt secure because those who worked amongst the members as wire-pullers were so sanguine about their success; but where corruption is practised there is no stability, and such it proved in this instance. A short time before the overthrow of the Wilcox cabinet, Cummins, Bush, R. W. Wilcox, Ashford, and their followers, finding that their hopes of being in the cabinet would never be realized, left, and turned to help the liberals once more, and with the aid of some of the nationals they were successful. These members had been deceived by the Thurston party, and they now combined to help the liberals.

Mr. White was the introducer of the bill providing for a constitutional convention; also the opium and lottery bills. He watched his opportunity, and railroaded the last two bills through the House; but he failed in regard to the first bill. A vote of want of confidence was then brought in.   The liberals won; and the cabinet was voted out, partly because they were so sure of their success and on account of their own corrupt practices.

The next day Messrs. Parker, Cornwell, Colburn, and Peterson were appointed.   These gentlemen were accepted by the majority of the people in the House, who applauded them on their entrance, because they were men of liberal views, although they were not considered representative men, because they were not backed by moneyed men.   The same day of their appointment they advised me to sign the opium and lottery bills.   I first declined, as I wanted to please my lady friends; but they said there should be no hesitation on my part, as the House had passed those bills by a large majority, and they had been signed by the president and committee.   I had no option but to sign.   It took place on the 13th of January, 1893.

During the month of November, 1892, a private note was sent me informing me of the intentions of the American minister, J. L. Stevens, with the aid of some of our residents, to perfect a scheme of annexation, and that the cabinet had knowledge of the fact; but I gave little heed to it at the time.   On the 17th of December, 1892, another note was received, of which the following is a copy:

HER MAJESTY QUEEN LILIUOKALANI.

May it please Your Majesty :

Madam, — Referring to the confidential communication I took the liberty of addressing Your Majesty a few weeks ago, about the attitude and utterances of the American representatives here, the perfect correctness of which have been confirmed by subsequent information, I now beg to be allowed to state, that through the same trustworthy source I have been informed that in a very late moment of effusion, some American official gave to understand that he had instructions to press and hurry up an annexation scheme, which he confidently expected to carry through at no distant date, with the help and assistance of the present cabinet.

If Your Majesty will kindly weigh this information by the side of the bold open declarations and annexation campaign made at the present time in the *Bulletin* by the Rev. Sereno Bishop, the well-known mouthpiece of the annexation party, I think that Your Majesty will be able to draw conclusions for yourself, and realize that there is not only danger ahead, but that the enemy is in the household, and that the strictest watch ought to be kept on the members of the present cabinet.

This again in strictest confidence from

Your Majesty's humble and faithful servant,

———

This was written by a gentleman in whose word I have great confidence as a man who had the best interest of Hawaii at heart. It was on the receipt of this note that I sent for the British commissioner, James H. Wodehouse, and asked his advice on the matter. I asked whether he thought it would be wise for me to invite all the foreign representatives of the diplomatic and consular corps, fearing that a disturbance might arise over the political situation. He said that he should not interfere with our local matters, and he dissuaded me from the idea, as he said it was like acknowledging that there was actual danger; and asked, "Did I think there was any danger?" I answered, "There might be."

The morning of the 14th of January, 1893, arrived with all preparations for the closing of the legislature. At 10 A.M. I called a cabinet meeting for the purpose of apprising them of their positions in the House, and other preliminary instructions. I told them it was my intention to promulgate a new constitution. The cabinet had to meet the legislature, and we adjourned. At 12 M. I prorogued the legislature. I noticed that the hall was not filled as at the opening. There were many ladies present in the audience, and I also noticed that several members of the legislature belonging to the reform party were not there. This looked ominous of some coming trouble.

On entering the palace I saw Mr. Wilson at the entrance of the Blue Room. I went up to him, and asked if it was all ready. He replied, "Yes." Then I said, "You will have to be brave to-day;" and I passed into the Blue Room, and sat awaiting my ministers. A half-hour passed, and they did not come. After a little longer delay they arrived. I immediately judged from their countenances that something was wrong. I had a few days before planned that I would sign the constitution in the throne-room and in the presence of the members of the legislature, the majority of whom had been elected by the people for the purpose of working for a new constitution.

At the commencement of my reign petitions were sent from all parts of the kingdom asking for a new constitution. Mr. Iosepa of Hani, Kauhi of Ewa, Nahinu of Molokai, Kanealii of Waihee, Kamauoha of Kohala, and other members came to me repeatedly, and asked for a new constitution. Mr. Parker, from the commencement of his ministry, advocated a new constitution, as well as most of my friends, but I was cautious in my answers to them; but to Mr. Parker I had always said it would be a good thing, and he said he would sustain me when the proper opportunity arrived.

A month later I met two members of the legislature, and started to make up a new constitution from Kamehameha V.'s and that of 1887. After completing it, I kept it until the month of October, when I placed it in the hands of Mr. A. P. Peterson, and asked him to correct it, and if he found any defects to strike them out, and to put in such clauses as he thought would be good for the people and for the country. He took it, and kept it a whole month. To my knowledge he consulted many lawyers and others in regard to many points of interest in the document. When it was returned I looked it over and found no changes had been made, so I concluded that it was all right. A week before the closing of the legislature I asked Mr. Peterson to make a preamble for my new constitution, but up to the day of prorogation he had not made one.

Early in January I mentioned to Captain Nowlein of the Household Guards, and Mr. Wilson the marshal, my intention to promulgate a new constitution, and to prepare themselves to quell any riot or outbreak from the opposition. They assured me they would be ready; and I gave strict injunctions of secrecy, and showed Mr. Wilson a plan of the throne-room on the day of the signing. Mr. Parker and Mr. Cornwell had given me assurances of their support before their appointment as ministers, while Mr. Peterson understood that such was my intention, and although I had not mentioned it to Mr. Colburn, he had heard of it already from Mr. Peterson. It appears that immediately on their learning of my intentions, Mr. Colburn, on the morning of the 14th of January, immediately acted the part of a traitor, by going to Mr. Hartwell, a lawyer, and informing him of my intentions, and of course received instructions from him to strongly advise me to abandon the idea.

This, then, was the cause of the delay and my long waiting in the Blue Room. The members of the diplomatic corps had been invited, also the members of the supreme bench and members of the legislature, besides a committee of the Hui Kalaiaina. The latter were invited to be present because it was through them that many petitions had been sent to me. When the ministers arrived I told them everything in the throne-room was ready, and the guests were awaiting our presence; that we must not keep them waiting. I was surprised when the cabinet informed me that they did not think it advisable for me to take such a step, that there was danger of an uprising, etc. I told them I would not have taken such a step if they had not encouraged me. They had led me out to the edge of a precipice, and now were leaving me to take the step alone. It was humiliating. I said, " Why not give the people the constitution, and I will bear the brunt of all the blame afterwards." Mr. Peterson said, " We have not read the constitution." I told him *he had had it in his possession a whole month.*

The three ministers left Mr. Parker to try to dissuade me from my purpose; and in the meantime they all (Peterson, Cornwell, and Colburn) went to the government building to inform Thurston and his party of the stand I took. Of course they were instructed not to yield. When they went over everything was peaceful and quiet, and the guests waiting patiently in the throne-room. The ministers returned, and I asked them to read the constitution over. At the end I asked them what they saw injurious in the document. Mr. Peterson said there were some points which he thought were not exactly suited. I told him the legislature could make the amendments. He begged that I should wait for two weeks; in the meantime they would be ready to present it to me. With these assurances I yielded, and we adjourned to the throne-room.

I stated to the guests present my reasons for inviting their

presence. It was to promulgate a new constitution at the request
of my people; that the constitution of 1887 was imperfect and
full of defects. Turning to the chief justice, I asked, "Is it not
so, Mr. Judd?" and he answered in the affirmative, in the presence of all the members assembled.

I then informed the people assembled that under the advice
of my ministers I had yielded, as they had promised that on
some future day I could give them a new constitution. I then
asked them to return to their homes and keep the peace. Everything seemed quiet until Monday morning. Even if any great
commotion had been going on I would have remained indifferent;
the reaction was a great strain, and all that took place after that
I accepted as a matter of course. It was the disappointment in
my ministry.

At about ten A.M., Monday, the 16th of January, notice was
issued by my ministers, stating "that the position I took and the
attempt I made to promulgate a new constitution was at the earnest solicitation of my people — of my native subjects." They
gave assurances that any changes desired in fundamental law of
the land would be sought only by methods provided in the constitution itself, and signed by myself and ministers. It was intended
to reassure the people that they might continue to maintain order
and peace.

At about five P.M., however, the troops from the United States
ship Boston were landed, by the order of the United States minister, J. L. Stevens, in secret understanding with the revolutionary party, whose names are L. A. Thurston, Henry Waterhouse,
W. R. Castle, W. O. Smith, A. F. Judd, P. C. Jones, W. C. Wilder,
S. B. Dole, Cecil Brown, S. M. Damon, C. Bolte, John Emmeluth,
J. H. Soper, C. L. Carter. Why had they landed when everything
was at peace? I was told that it was for the safety of American
citizens and the protection of their interests. Then, why had they
not gone to the residences, instead of drawing in line in front of
the palace gates, with guns pointed at us, and when I was living
with my people in the palace?

Tuesday morning, at nine o'clock, Mr. S. M. Damon called at
the palace. He told me that he had been asked to join a revolu-

tionary council, but that he had declined. He asked me what he should do, and whether he should join the advisory or executive council, suggesting that perhaps he could be of service to me; so I told him to join the advisory council. I had no idea that they intended to establish a new government.

At about two-thirty P.M., Tuesday, the establishment of the Provisional Government was proclaimed; and nearly fifteen minutes later Mr. J. S. Walker came and told me "that he had come on a painful duty, that the opposition party had requested that I should abdicate." I told him that I had no idea of doing so, but that I would like to see Mr. Neumann. Half an hour later he returned with that gentleman, and I explained to him my position, and he advised that I should consult my friends. I immediately sent for Messrs. J. O. Carter, Damon, Widemann, Cleghorn, my ministers; Messrs. Neumann, Walker, and Macfarlane also being present. The situation being taken into consideration, it was found that, since the troops of the United States had been landed to support the revolutionists, by the order of the American minister, it would be impossible for us to make any resistance.

Mr. Damon had previously intimated to Mr. Parker that it was useless to resist, their party was supported by the American minister. Mr. Damon also said at the meeting that it was to be understood that I should remain at the palace, and continue to fly the royal standard. At six P.M. I signed the following protest : —

I, Liliuokalani, by the grace of God and under the constitution of the Hawaiian kingdom Queen, do hereby solemnly protest against any and all acts done against myself and the constitutional government of the Hawaiian kingdom by certain persons claiming to have established a Provisional Government of and for this kingdom.

That I yield to the superior force of the United States of America, whose Minister Plenipotentiary, His Excellency John L. Stevens, has caused United States troops to be landed at Honolulu, and declared that he would support the said Provisional Government.

Now, to avoid any collision of armed forces, and perhaps the loss of life, I do, under this protest and impelled by said forces, yield my authority until such time as the Government of the United States shall, upon the facts being presented to it, undo (?) the action of its representative, and reinstate me in the authority which I claim as the constitutional sovereign of the Hawaiian Islands.

Done at Honolulu this seventeenth day of January, A.D. 1893.

(Signed)   LILIUOKALANI R.

(Signed)   SAMUEL PARKER,
Minister of Foreign Affairs.

(Signed)   WM. H. CORNWELL,
Minister of Finance.

(Signed)   JOHN F. COLBURN,
Minister of Interior.

(Signed)   A. P. PETERSON,
Attorney-General.

(Addressed)

To S. B. DOLE, Esq., and others composing the Provisional Government of the Hawaiian Islands.

A letter was sent to the marshal of the kingdom requesting him to deliver everything to the Provisional Government.

All that night and next day everything remained quiet.

At ten A.M., the 18th, I moved to Washington Place of my own accord, preferring to live in retirement.

On the 19th of January, I wrote a letter to President Harrison, making an appeal that justice should be done.

HIS EXCELLENCY BENJAMIN HARRISON,
President of the United States :

My great and good Friend, — It is with deep regret that I address you on this occasion. Some of my subjects, aided by aliens, have renounced their loyalty, and revolted against the constitutional government of my kingdom. They have attempted to depose me, and establish a Provisional Government in direct conflict with the organic law of this kingdom. Upon receiving incontestable proofs that His Excellency the Minister Plenipotentiary of the United States had caused troops to be landed for that purpose, I submitted to force, believing that he would not have acted in that manner unless by authority of the government which he represents.

This action on my part was prompted by three reasons, the futility of a conflict with the United States, the desire to avoid violence and bloodshed and the destruction of life and property, and the certainty which I feel that you and your government will right whatever wrongs may have been inflicted upon us in the premises. In due time a statement of the true facts relating to this matter will be laid before you, and I live in the hope that you will judge uprightly and justly between myself and my enemies.

This appeal is not made for myself personally, but for my people, who have hitherto always enjoyed the friendship and protection of the United States.

My opponents have taken the only vessel which could be obtained here for the purpose; and hearing of their intention to send a delegation of their number to present their side of the conflict before you, I requested the favor of sending by the same vessel an envoy to you to lay before you my statement as the facts appear to myself and my loyal subjects.

This request has been refused; and I now ask you, in justice to myself and to my people, that no steps be taken by the Government of the United States until my cause can be heard by you. I shall be able to despatch an envoy about the second day of February, as that will be the first available opportunity hence; and he will reach you with every possible haste, that there may be no delay in the settlement of this matter.

I pray you, therefore, my good friend, that you will not allow any conclusions to be reached by you until my envoy arrives.

I beg to assure you of the continuation of my highest consideration.

(Signed)   LILIUOKALANI R.

It appears that President Harrison could not have taken notice of my appeal; for the 16th of February I find he sent a message to the Senate transmitting the treaty, with a view to its ratification, without having first investigated or inquired into all the conditions or points of our situation, or that of the United States itself. I will not attempt to write the President's message, as you are already aware of its text.

I also wrote a letter to Mr. Cleveland.

GROVER CLEVELAND,
      President-elect of the United States.

My great and good Friend, — In the vicissitudes which happened in the Hawaiian Islands, and which affect my people, myself, and my house so seriously, I feel comforted the more that, besides the friendly relation of the United States, I have the boon of your personal friendship and good will.

The changes which occurred here need not be stated in this letter. You will have, at the time at which it reaches you, the official information;

but I have instructed the Hon. Paul Neumann, whom I have appointed
my representative at Washington, to submit to you a *précis* of the facts
and circumstances relating to the revolution in Honolulu, and to supple-
ment it by such statements as you may please to elicit.

I beg that you will consider this matter, in which there is so much
involved for my people, and that you will give us your friendly assistance
in granting redress for a wrong which we claim has been done to us, under
color of the assistance of the naval forces, of the United States, in a friendly
port.   Believe me that I do not veil under this request to you anything
the fulfilment of which could in the slightest degree be contrary to your
position; and I leave our grievance in your hands, confident that, in so far
as you deem it proper, we shall have your sympathy and your aid.

I am, your good friend,

LILIUOKALANI R.

On the 31st of January the Hon. Paul Neumann received his
appointment as envoy extraordinary and minister plenipotentiary
to the United States of America.   On the 1st of February he
departed for Washington, with Prince David Kawanauakoa to accompany him on his commission, to negotiate for a withdrawal of
the treaty, and to restore to us what had been taken away by the
actions of the revolutionists.   At my request Mr. E. C. Macfarlane kindly consented to accompany the commission.

Happily Providence ordered otherwise than as was expected
by the revolutionists.   Man proposes and God disposes.   My
commissioners arrived in time to stay the progress of the treaty.
The members of the Senate became doubtful as to the correctness
of the actions of the commissioners of the Provisional Government.

President Harrison's term expired.   President Cleveland's first
act has been to withdraw that annexation treaty; the second, to
send a commissioner to investigate the situation in Hawaii Nei.

Your arrival in this country has brought relief to our people
and your presence safety.   There is no doubt but that the Provisional Government would have carried out extreme measures
toward myself and my people, as you may have already seen ere
this, by their unjust actions.   If the President had been indifferent to my petitions, I am certain it would have brought serious
results to myself and tyranny to my subjects.   In this I recognize

the high sense of justice and honor in the person who is ruler of the American nation.

In making out this lengthy statement I will present the main points : —

(1) That it has been a project of many years on the part of the missionary element that their children might some day be rulers over these Islands, and have the control and power in their own hands, as was the case after the revolution of 1887. Mr. W. W. Hall openly stated that they had planned for this for twelve years. It was a long-thought-of project, a dream of many years. So also said Mr. F. S. Lyman of Hilo, in his speech to the people in the month of January. He said, " Fifteen long years we have prayed for this, and now our prayers are heard."

The disposition of those appointed to positions of authority, to act with the missionary element, tends to make the government unstable; and because they found I could not easily be led by them, they do not like me.

(2) The interference of the American minister, J. L. Stevens, in our local affairs, and conspiring with a few foreign people to overthrow me and annex these Islands to the United States, and by his actions, has placed me and my people in this unhappy position.

(3) My attempt to promulgate a new constitution. It was in answer to the prayers and petitions of my people. They had sent petitions to the late king, and to the legislature ever since 1887.

The legislature is the proper course by which a new constitution or any amendments to the constitution could be made ; that is the law. But when members are bribed and the legislature corrupted, how can one depend on any good measure being carried by the House? It is simply impossible. That method was tried and failed. There was only one recourse; and that was, that with the signature of one of the cabinet I could make a new constitution.

There is no clause in the constitution of 1887, to which I took my oath to maintain, stating " that there should be no other constitution but this ; " and article 78 reads that —

"Wheresoever by this constitution any act is to be done or performed by the king or sovereign it shall, unless otherwise expressed, mean that such act shall be done and performed by the sovereign by and with the advice and consent of the cabinet."

The last clause of the forty-first article of the constitution reads : —

"No acts of the king shall have any effect unless it be countersigned by a member of the cabinet, who by that signature makes himself responsible."

My cabinet encouraged me, then afterwards advised me to the contrary. In yielding to their protest I claim I have not committed any unconstitutional or revolutionary act; and having withdrawn, why should the reform party have gone on making preparations for war, as they did ?

(4) That on the afternoon of the 16th of January, at five P. M., the United States troops were landed to support the conspirators, by orders of the United States minister, J. L. Stevens.

That on Tuesday, the 17th of January, 1893, at about two thirty o'clock P. M., the Provisional Government was proclaimed, and Minister Stevens assured my cabinet that he recognized that Government; and that at six P.M. of the same day I yielded my authority to the superior force of the United States.

We have been waiting patiently, and will still wait, until such time as the Government of the United States, on the facts presented to it, shall undo the act of its representative.

I hope and pray that the United States and her President will see that justice is done to my people and to myself ; that they will not recognize the treaty of annexation, and that it may forever be laid aside ; that they will restore to me and my nation all the rights that have been taken away by the action of her minister ; that we may be permitted to continue to maintain our independent stand amongst the civilized nations of the world as in years gone by; that your great nation will continue those kind and friendly relations that have always existed for many years past between the two countries. I can assure you that Hawaii and her people have no other sentiment toward America and her President than one of the kindest regard.

The Provisional Government, instead of being under the guidance of the president and cabinet, as the responsible heads of the nation, are virtually led by irresponsible people, who compose the advisory councils and "provisional army," and who set the laws of the land at defiance. A continuation of this state of things I consider dangerous to life and to the community.

I pray, therefore, that this unsatisfactory state of things may not continue, and that we may not suffer further waste, that justice may be speedily granted, and that peace and quiet may once more reign over our land, Hawaii Nei.

LILIUOKALANI.

APPENDIX C.

FACTS AS TO SUBMISSION OF HAWAIIAN QUESTION TO
THE DECISION OF THE UNITED STATES.

By HER MAJESTY LILIUOKALANI, *with the approval of the
Provisional Government.*

Date of so-called
Revolution,
TUESDAY,
Jan. 17, 1893.
about 6 P.M.

J. O. C. being
"Queen's Councillor"
and still faithful.

Page 1330.

Page 1317.

Page 1674.
Also
"Alexander's
History," Oct. 1896.
Page 54.

S. B. Dole, S. M. Damon, and some
twenty or thirty others sent for J. O. Carter
to be of committee to be sent to palace to
assist her in making any protest she desired
to make against her deposition; he joined
the party, headed by Mr. Damon, and advised Her Majesty that any demonstration
on the part of her forces would precipitate
a conflict with the forces of the United
States; that it was desirable that such a
conflict be avoided; that her case would be
considered at Washington, and a peaceful
submission to force on her part would greatly
help her case. Mr. Damon had previously
informed Her Majesty of her deposition, and
that she might prepare a protest.   Mr. Damon in his sworn statement says, " I did
tell her that she would have a perfect right
to be heard at a later period by the United
States Government.   I was there as a member of the Provisional Government."   Mr.
Damon personally called on the queen at
nine o'clock that forenoon and told her that

he had decided to join the Provisional Government, and further that he was its first vice-president. He remains its minister of finance to the present date. The Provisional Government had been recognized at this time. The protest says, " I yield to the superior force of the United States of America — until such time as the Government of the United States shall, upon the facts being presented to it, undo the action of its representatives, and reinstate me in the authority which I claim as the constitutional sovereign of the Hawaiian Islands." Mr. Damon and the Cabinet returned to the Provisional Government and presented the protest; and President Dole indorsed on the same, " Received by the hands of the late Cabinet this seventeenth day of January, A.D. 1893." After this protest, the queen surrendered her arsenal. The letter sent by the same steamer on which (January 18) the annexation commissioners sailed (the queen having been refused the privilege of placing one representative on board), says to President Harrison, " This action on my part was prompted by three reasons : The futility of a conflict with the United States ; the desire to avoid violence, bloodshed, and the destruction of life and property ; and the certainty which I feel that you and your government will right whatever wrongs may have been inflicted on us in the premises."

Page 1318.

Page 1394.

Page 1399.

Page 1027.

received at
Executive office,
Feb. 3, 1893.

APPENDIX D.

THE TEXT OF THE TREATY.

How the Cession of the Islands is to be Accomplished.

THE full text of the treaty is as follows : —

The United States and the republic of Hawaii, in view of the natural dependence of the Hawaiian Islands upon the United States, of their geographical proximity thereto, of the preponderant share acquired by the United States and its citizens in the industries and trade of said islands, and of the expressed desire of the government of the republic of Hawaii that those islands should be incorporated into the United States as an integral part thereof and under its sovereignty, have determined to accomplish by treaty an object so important to their mutual and permanent welfare.

To this end, the high contracting parties have conferred full powers and authority upon the irrespectively appointed plenipotentiaries, to wit : —

The President of the United States, John Sherman, Secretary of State of the United States; the President of the republic of Hawaii, Francis March Hatch, Lorrin A. Thurston, and William A. Kinney.

ARTICLE II.

The republic of Hawaii hereby cedes absolutely and without reserve to the United States of America all rights of sovereignty of whatsoever kind in and over the Hawaiian Islands and their dependencies; and it is agreed that all territory of and appertaining to the republic of Hawaii is hereby annexed to the United States of America under the name of the Territory of Hawaii.

ARTICLE II.

The republic of Hawaii also cedes and hereby transfers to the United States the absolute fee and ownership of all public government, or crown lands, public buildings or edifices, ports, harbors, military equipments, and all other public property of every kind and description belonging to the government of the Hawaiian Islands, together with every right and appurtenance thereunto appertaining.

The existing laws of the United States relative to public lands shall not apply to such lands in the Hawaiian Islands; but the Congress of the United States shall enact special laws for their management and disposition; provided, that all revenue from or proceeds of the same, except as regards such parts thereof as may be used or occupied for the civil, military, or naval purposes of the United States, or may be assigned for the use of the local government, shall be used solely for the benefit of the inhabitants of the Hawaiian Islands for educational and other public purposes.

ARTICLE III.

Until Congress shall provide for the government of such islands, all the civil, judicial, and military powers exercised by the officers of the existing government in said islands shall be vested in such person or persons and shall be exercised in such manner as the President of the United States shall direct, and the President shall have power to remove said officers and fill the vacancies so occasioned.

The existing treaties of the Hawaiian Islands with foreign nations shall forthwith cease and determine, being replaced by such treaties as may exist, or as may be hereafter concluded between the United States and such foreign nations. The municipal legislation of the Hawaiian Islands, not enacted for the fulfilment of the treaties so extinguished, and not inconsistent with this treaty nor contrary to the Constitution of the United States, nor to any existing treaty of the United States, shall remain in force until the Congress of the United States shall otherwise determine.

Until legislation shall be enacted extending the United States customs, laws, and regulations to the Hawaiian Islands, the existing customs relations of the Hawaiian Islands with the United States and other countries shall remain unchanged.

ARTICLE IV.

The public debt of the republic of Hawaii, lawfully existing at the date of the exchange of the ratifications of the treaty, including the amounts due to depositors in the Hawaiian Postal Savings Bank, is hereby assumed by the government of the United States; but the liability of the United States in this regard shall in no case exceed $4,000,000. So long, however, as the existing government and the present commercial relations of the Hawaiian Islands are continued, as hereinbefore provided, said government shall continue to pay the interest on said debt.

ARTICLE V.

There shall be no further immigration of Chinese into the Hawaiian Islands, except upon such conditions as are now or may hereafter be allowed by the laws of the United States, and no Chinese, by reason of anything herein contained, shall be allowed to enter the United States from the Hawaiian Islands.

ARTICLE VI

The President shall appoint five commissioners, at least *two of whom shall be residents of the Hawaiian Islands*, who shall, as soon as reasonably practicable, *recommend* to Congress such legislation for the Territory of Hawaii as they shall deem necessary or proper.

ARTICLE VII.

This treaty shall be ratified by the President of the United States, by and with the advice and consent of the Senate, on the one part; and by the President of the republic of Hawaii, by and with the advice and consent of the Senate, in accordance with the Constitution of said republic, on the other; and the ratifications hereof shall be exchanged at Washington as soon as possible.

In witness whereof, the respective Plenipotentiaries have signed the above articles and have hereunto affixed their seals.

Done in duplicate at the city of Washington, this 16th day of June, 1897.

JOHN SHERMAN,	(Seal)
FRANCIS MARCH HATCH,	(Seal)
LORRIN A. THURSTON,	(Seal)
WILLIAM A. KINNEY.	(Seal)

APPENDIX E.

ARRANGED BY LILIUOKALANI.

No. 1.

GENEALOGY OF LILIUOKALANI.

ON HER MOTHER'S (KEOHOKALOLE) SIDE.

Three sisters . . . {
1. IKUAANA.
2. UMIULAIKAAHUMANU.
3. UMIAENAKU.

Father.	Mother.	Child.
Ahu a I.	Umiulaikaahumanu	{ Heulu
Ku a Nuuanu	"	{ Kamakaimoku
Heulu	Ikuaana	{ Keawe-a-Heulu
"	Moana	{ Hakau
Keawe-a-Heulu	Ululani	{ Keohohiwa
		{ Naihe
Kepookalani	Keohohiwa	Aikanaka
Aikanaka	Kamaeokalani	Keohokalole
Kapaakea	Keohokalole	{ Kaliokalani
		Kalakaua
		Liliuokalani
		Anna Kaiulani
		Kaiminaauao
		Miriam Likelike
		Leleiohoku W. P.
Cleghorn, A. S.	Likelike	Victoria Kaiulani

NOTE. — Keawe-a-Heulu was chief warrior and councillor of Kamehameha I. Ululani, his wife, was the most celebrated poetess in her day. Their daughter Keohohiwa married Kepookalani, my great-grandfather, first cousin of Kamehameha I. Her brother Naihe married Kapiolani, the celebrated queen who defied the goddess Pele. Naihe was one of the councillors to Kamehameha I., and chief orator of the council. Kamehameha's councillors were Keawe-a-Heulu, his son Naihe, and their cousins Kameeiamoku and Keeaumoku.

AUTHORITY. — C. Kanaina, A. Fornander, and others.

No. 2.

GENEALOGY OF LILIUOKALANI

ON HER FATHER'S (KAPAAKEA) SIDE.

KEAWEIKEKAHIALIIOKAMOKU. KING OF HAWAII.

Father.	Mother.	Child.
Keaweikekahialiiokamoku	(1st wife) Lonoma Ikanaka	Ka I–i mamao, *alias* Kalaninui Iamamao
Kalaninui Iamamao	Kaolanialii	Alapaiwahine
Kepookalani	Alapaiwahine	Kamanawa
Kamanawa	Kamokuiki	Kapaakea
Kapaakea	Keohokalole	Kaliokalani James. Kalakaua Liliuokalani Anna Kaiulani Kaiminaauao Miriam Likelike Leleiohoku, W. P.
Archibald Scott Cleghorn	Likelike	Victoria Kawekiu Lunalilo Kalaninuiahilapalapa Kaiulani

NOTE. — Liliuokalani's great grandmother, Alapaiwahine, is the same person given in the history of the "Tradition of Creation." Her husband, Kepookalani, was first cousin to Kamehameha I.

No. 1.

GENEALOGY OF KAMEHAMEHA I.

Three sisters . . . {
1. IKUAANA.
2. UMIULAIKAAHUMANU.
3. UMIAENAKU.

Father.	*Mother.*	*Child.*
Ahu a I.	Umiulaikaahumanu (brother)	Heulu.
Ku a Nuuanu	" (sister)	Kamakaimoku.
Keeaumokun Nui	Kamakaimoku	Keoua.
Keoua Kalanikupuapa	Kekuiapoiwa II.	Kamehameha I.

NOTE. — The relationship of the two families on my mother's side. Heulu, my ancestor, and Kamakaimoku were brother and sister. Keawe-a-Heulu, my ancestor, and Keoua, father of Kamehameha I., were first cousins. Keohohiwa, my great-grandmother, and Kamehameha I., were second cousins.

Kamehameha I. m. his aunt	Peleuli	Kahoanoku.
Kahoanoku	Wahinepio Kahakuakoi	Kekauonohi.

Kekauonohi was grand-daughter of Kamehameha I., and the same who adopted my sister Anna Kaiulani.

No. 2.

GENEALOGY OF KAMEHAMEHA I.

KEAWEIKEKAHIALIIOKAMOKU. KING OF HAWAII.

Father.	Mother.	Child.
Keaweikekahialiiokamoku	{ 2d wife Kalanikauleleiaiwi }	Kalanikeeaumoku
Kalanikeeaumoku	Kamakaimoku	Keoua Kalanikupua- paikalaninui
Keoua	Kekuiapoiwa II.	Kamehameha I.
Kamehameha I.	Keopuolani	{ Nahienaena Iolani Liholiho Kauikeaouli, K. III. }
"	Kaheiheimalie	{ Kamamalu I. Kinau }
Mataio Kekuanaoa	Kinau	{ Moses Kekuaina Lot Kamehameha Alexander Liholiho Victoria Kamamalu }

NOTE. — Comparing this genealogy and No. 2 of Liliuokalani's, you will find that Ka I-i Mamao and Kalanikeeaumoku were brothers, the latter marrying Kamakaimoku, sister of Heulu.

GENEALOGY OF KEPOOKALANI,

THE GREAT—GRANDFATHER OF LILIUOKALANI.

	Father.	Mother.	Child
Three brothers. { Twins. {	Haae a Mahi m. (1st wife)	Kalelemauliokalani	{ 1. Kamakaeheukuli { 2. Haalou
	Haae a Mahi m. (2d wife)	Kekelaokalani	3. Kekuiapoiwa II.
	Kamanawa (2d husband of)	"	4. Peleuli
	Kameeiamoku	Kamakaeheukuli	Kepookalani
	Kekaulike	Haalou	Namahaua
	Keoua Kalanikupua (1st wife)	Kamakaeheukuli	Kalaimamahu or Hoapilikane
	(2d wife)	Kekuiaoiwpa II.	Kamehameha I.
	Kamehameha I. (marries his aunt)	Peleuli	Kinau Kahoanoku
	Kinau Kahoanoku	Wahinepio	Kekauonohi.

(with brace on right labeled "Four sisters." grouping children 1–4)

NOTES. — Haae a Mahi and Kameeiamoku and Kamanawa were brothers, of one father and different mothers. The two latter brothers were twins, and called " The Royal Twins of Keeaumoku." They are also mentioned in history by the early missionaries or historians.

The above genealogy is most perplexing. Kepookalani (my great-grand-father), Namahana, and Kamehameha I., were first cousins. Kepookalani and Kalaimamahu were brothers by the same mother. Kalaiamamahu and Kamehameha I. were brothers by the same father. Kepookalani's mother was the oldest of the four sisters, and the third sister was mother of Kamehameha I.

Haae a Mahi, Kameeiamoku, and Kamanawa were half brothers by their mother to the grandfather of Kamehameha I.

Kepookalani being first cousin to Kamehameha I., my grandfather Kamanawa I., son of Kepookalani, becomes second cousin to Kamehameha I. The latter Kamanawa was named for the first.

The intermingling of the two families is not only from his mother's, but also by his father's side, and is both from my mother's as well as my father's side.

You will recognize Kekauonohi's name as the grand-daughter of Kamehameha I., and the same who adopted my younger sister, Anna Kaiulani.

Kalanikauleleiaiwi is the name of Haae's mother, also Kameeiamoku and Kamanawa. Kepookalani's mother was sister to Kamehameha I.'s mother.

Kepookalani's first wife was Keohohiwa, their child was Aikanaka; his second wife was Alapaiwahine, and Kamanawa was the child of that marriage. My father and mother were first cousins.

Keapo o Kepookalani was brother of Kamehameha I. and had no children. He was called Keliionaikai on account of his kindness to the people of Hana, Maui.

AUTHORITY. — Fornander and Kekuanaoa.

APPENDIX F.

SUBSTANTIATING PREVIOUS GENEALOGY, AND GIVING ADDITIONAL ANCESTRY.

COPIED BY PERMISSION FROM "A BRIEF HISTORY OF THE HAWAIIAN PEOPLE," BY W. D. ALEXANDER

SELECTED GENEALOGIES.

Chiefs of Hawaii about the end of the Eighteenth Century.

FAMILY OF KALANIOPUU, KING OF HAWAII.

Wives	Kalola, sister of Kahekili.	Kanekapolei.
Children . .	Kiwalao (k) married to Kekuiapoiwa Liliha (w)	Keona Kuahuula (k).
Grandchild .	Keopuolani (w) married to Kamehameha I.	

FAMILY OF KEOUA, HALF-BROTHER OF KALANIOPUU.

Wives	Kekuiapowa II.		Kamakaeheukuli
Children . .	Kamehameha I. married Keopuolani (w)	Keliimaikai (k) married * Kiilaweau (w)	Kalaimamahu (k) married Kalakua.
Grandchildren,	{ Liholiho (k) Kauikeaouli (k) Nahienaena (w) }	Kekuaokalani (k) and Kaoanaeha (w) married { John Young Fanny Kekela Emma Rooke }	Kekauluohi (w) married C. Kanaina (k)
Great-grandchildren			W. C. Lunalilo (k).

Additional names appearing on the right side of the family chart:
Kalola
Kekuiapoiwa
Liliha (w) married Kiwalao
Keopuolani (w) married Kamehameha I.

* This is an error. Keliimaikai (k) had no issue, and there was no chiefess by the name of Kiilaweau. Kiilaweau was a man, and uncle of Kekuanaoa.

FAMILY OF KAMEHAMEHA I.

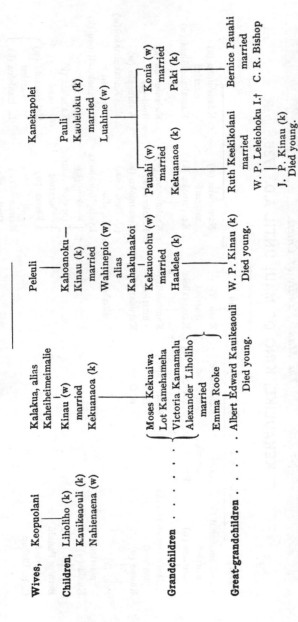

Wives,   Keopuolani

Children, Liholiho (k)
           Kauikeaouli (k)
           Nahienaena (w)

Kalakua, alias
Kaheiheimeimalie

Kinau (w)
married
Kekuanaoa (k)

Peleuli

Kahoanoku —
Kinau (k)
married
Wahinepio (w)
alias
Kahakuhaakoi —
Kekauonohu (w)
married
Haalelea (k)

Kanekapolei

Pauli
Kauleioku (k)
married
Luahine (w)

Konia (w)
married
Paki (k)

Pauahi (w)
married
Kekuanaoa (k)

Grandchildren . . . . .
Moses Kekuaiwa
Lot Kamehameha
Victoria Kamamalu
Alexander Liholiho
married
Emma Rooke

W. P. Kinau (k)
Died young.

Ruth Keekikolani
married
W. P. Leleiohoku I.†

Bernice Pauahi
married
C. R. Bishop

Great-grandchildren . . . . .
Albert Edward Kauikeaouli
Died young.

J. P. Kinau (k)
Died young.

* NOTE BY LILIUOKALANI.—This is an error. Kaoleioku married first Keona, who was the mother of Konia. His second wife was Luahine, the mother of Pauahi.

† Son of Kaianimoku (k) and Kuwahine (w).

The Maui Family of Chiefs.

KEKAULIKE, KING OF MAUI UNTIL A.D. 1736.

Wives,

Kekuiapoiwa I.

- Kamehamehanui (k) married Kukamano (w)
- Kalola (w) married Kalaniopuu (See No. I.)
- Kahekili (k) married Kauwahine (w)
  - Kalanikupule, Last king of Oahu
- Kalanihelemaiiluna (k) married Kawao (w)
  - Paki (k) married Konia (w)
    - Bernice Pauahi married C. R. Bishop

Hoolau

- Kaeo (k) married Kamakahelei
  - Kaumualii (k) married Kapuaamohu (w)
    - Kealiiahonui

Haalou

- Namahana (w) married Keeaumoku (k)
  - 1 Kaahumanu (w)
  - 2 Kalakua (w)
  - 3 Keeaumoku (k) (Or Gov. Cox.)
  - 4 Ria, alias Lydia Namahana
  - 5 { Kuakini (k) (or Gov. Adams) married Keoua (w)
    - Kamanele (w) Died in 1834.
- Kuamonoha (k) married Kamakahukilani (w)
  - 1 Kalanimoku (k)
  - 2 Boki (k)
  - 3 Wahinepio (w) alias Kahakuhaakoi (w) married
    - Kahoanoku–Kinau (k)
    - Kahalaia (k) and
    - Kekauonohi (w) married L. Haalelea (k)

PEDIGREE OF THE REIGNING FAMILY.

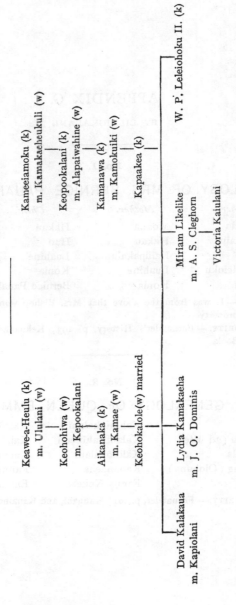

Keawe-a-Heulu (k)
m. Ululani (w)

Keohohiwa (w)
m. Kepookalani

Aikanaka (k)
m. Kamae (w)

Keohokalole (w) married

David Kalakaua
m. Kapiolani

Lydia Kamakaeha
m. J. O. Dominis

Kameeiamoku (k)
m. Kamakaeheukuli (w)

Keopookalani (k)
m. Alapaiwahine (w)

Kamanawa (k)
m. Kamokuiki (w)

Kapaakea (k)

Miriam Likelike
m. A. S. Cleghorn

Victoria Kaiulani

W. P. Leleiohoku II. (k)

APPENDIX G.

BY LILIUOKALANI.

No. 1.

GENEALOGY OF MRS. BERNICE PAUAHI BISHOP.

Father.	Mother.	Child.
Heulu	Moana	Hakau
Kanaina	Hakau	Hao
Hao	Kailipakalua	Luahine
Kaoleioku	Luahine	Konia
Paki	Konia	Bernice Pauahi Bishop

NOTE. — It was from the above that Mrs. Bishop won her position in Kanaina's property.

AUTHORITY. — Fornander's History, p. 193; Kekuanaoa's Book, p. 8; Kanaina's Book.

No. 2.

GENEALOGY OF QUEEN EMMA.

Heulu	Kahihiokalani	Kalaniwahineuli
Kalaniopuu (2d wife)	Kalaniwahineuli	Kalaipaihala
Kalaipaihala	Kalikokalani	Kaoanaeha
John Young (Olohana)	Kaoanaeha	Fanny Kekela
Naea	Fanny Kekela	Emma Kaleleonalani

AUTHORITY. — Fornander, p. 204; Kaunahi, and Kanaina's Book.

No. 3.

GENEALOGY OF PRINCESS RUTH KEELIKOLANI.

Heulu	Elepaio	Puhipuhiili
Kameeiamoku	Puhipuhieli	Loe or Uahine
Kauhiwawaeono	Loe	Keoua
Kaoleioku	Keoua	Pauahi
Kekuanaoa	Pauahi	Ruth Keelikolani

AUTHORITY. — Fornander, p. 150; Kaunahi; Kamokuiki, p. 15.

From Heulu, through his son Keawe-a-Heulu, and through his three daughters, Hakau, Kalaniwahineuli, Puhipuhieli, descended Mrs. Bernice Pauahi Bishop, Princess Ruth Keelikolani, Queen Emma, and Liliuokalani. The latter's ancestor was the son Keawe-a-Heulu. (See " Reigning Family," Appendix F.)

Liliuokalani is the only surviving representative of these four; and the Princess Kaiulani, heir apparent to the throne of Hawaii, is at present the last of her family line.

The authorities are given from which have been compiled these genealogies of Mrs. Bishop, Queen Emma, and Princess Ruth. A comparison with those given in Appendix F. will show that Mr. Alexander's able work is not entirely correct regarding the ancestry of Mrs. Bishop and Queen Emma.

The genealogies in Appendix E. begin with the names of three sisters, and give some of the descendants of Ikuaana and Umiulaikaahumanu. Following this note is a genealogy of the youngest sister Umiaenaku, who was an ancestress of both Princess Ruth and Mrs. Bishop.

GENEALOGY OF RUTH KEELIKOLANI.

AS A DESCENDANT OF UMIAEMOKU, YOUNGEST OF THE THREE SISTERS.

Father.	Mother.	Child.
Kauakahiahi	Umiaemoku	Kanekapolei
Kalaniopuu	Kanekapolei	Kaoleioku
Kaoleioku	Keoua	Pauahi
Kekuanaoa	Pauahi	Ruth Keelikolani

AUTHORITY. — Kanaina's Book, Kekuanaoa's Book.

EPILOGUE

Liliuokalani's story thus ends with her forced abdication and retirement to lovely Washington Place, where she lived quietly "among her flowers." Writing, music, and her many welfare projects occupied her time, and, before her death in 1917, she was revered and admired by a younger generation. Audiences always rose in her honor when "Aloha Oe" was played. In 1911 she was an interested observer and guest at the opening ceremonies of Pearl Harbor, which she witnessed from the *USS California,* seated with her old enemy and successor Sanford B. Dole. When the United States entered World War I, she presented a Red Cross flag to the first Hawaiian chapter of the American Red Cross, and, for the first time, the Stars and Stripes flying over Washington Place proclaimed her loyalty.

Hawaii's story, of course, does not end with Liliuokalani's. The long struggle for statehood, the growing pains of a multi-racial territory, the development of the enormous sugar and pineapple industries, and tourism in this crossroads of the Pacific are too well known for recounting here. World War II, with its influx of military and civilian personnel, and the mushrooming of air travel all served to bind Hawaii closer to the mainland. In 1959 all Americans were proud to claim this Pacific paradise as their fiftieth state.

BIBLIOGRAPHY

The following books are suggested reading for those who are interested in learning more about Hawaii. Titles marked with an asterisk are out of print but are generally available in public libraries.

Allen, Edward W.: *The Vanishing Frenchman: The Mysterious Disappearance of Lapérouse*. Tokyo and Rutland, Vermont: Tuttle, 1958.

Allen, Gwenfread: *Hawaii's War Years, 1941–1945*. Honolulu: University of Hawaii Press, 1955.

*Buck, Peter: *Vikings of the Sunrise*. New York: Stokes, 1938.

*Chickering, William: *Within the Sound of These Waves*. New York: Harcourt, 1941.

Day, A. Grove: *Hawaii and Its People: Paradise and Paradox of the Pacific*. New York: Duell, Sloane and Pearce, 1955.

——: *Hawaii: Fiftieth State*. New York: Duell, Sloane and Pearce, 1960.

*Fergusson, Erna: *Our Hawaii*. New York: Knopf, 1942.

Field, Isobel: *This Life I've Loved*. New York: Longmans, 1940.

*Gessler, Clifford: *Tropic Landfall: The Port of Honolulu*. New York: Doubleday, 1942.

Gray, J. A. C.: *Amerika Samoa*. Annapolis: U.S. Naval Institute, 1960.

Hawaii State Society of Washington, D.C.: *Hawaiian Cuisine*. Tokyo and Rutland, Vermont: Tuttle, 1963.

Kelly, John M., Jr.: *Folk Songs Hawaii Sings*. Tokyo and Rutland, Vermont: Tuttle, 1963.

Kuykendall, Ralph S., and Day, A. Grove: *Hawaii: A History*. New York: Prentice-Hall, 1948.

*McKee, Ruth Eleanor: *The Lord's Anointed*. New York: Doubleday, 1942.

Mellen, Kathleen: *Lonely Warrior*. New York: Hastings House, 1949.

——: *The Magnificent Matriarch*. New York: Hastings House, 1952.

Michener, James A.: *Hawaii*. New York: Random House, 1959.

Pratt, Helen Gay: *The Hawaiians: An Island People*. Tokyo and Rutland, Vermont: Tuttle, 1963.

von Tempski, Armine: *Born in Paradise*. New York: Duell, Sloane and Pearce, 1940.

Twain, Mark: *Roughing It*. New York: Harper, 1871.

Webb, Nancy and Jean Francis: *The Hawaiian Islands: From Monarchy to Democracy*. New York: Viking Press, 1958.

Westervelt, William D.: *Hawaiian Legends of Ghosts and Ghost-Gods*. Tokyo and Rutland, Vermont: Tuttle, 1963.

——: *Hawaiian Legends of Old Honolulu*. Tokyo and Rutland, Vermont: Tuttle, 1963.

——: *Hawaiian Legends of Volcanoes*. Tokyo and Rutland, Vermont: Tuttle, 1963.

Other TUT BOOKS available:

BACHELOR'S HAWAII *by Boye de Mente*

BACHELOR'S JAPAN *by Boye de Mente*

BACHELOR'S MEXICO *by Boye de Mente*

A BOOK OF NEW ENGLAND LEGENDS AND FOLK LORE *by Samuel Adams Drake*

THE BUDDHA TREE *by Fumio Niwa; translated by Kenneth Strong*

CALABASHES AND KINGS: An Introduction to Hawaii *by Stanley D. Porteus*

CHINA COLLECTING IN AMERICA *by Alice Morse Earle*

CHINESE COOKING MADE EASY *by Rosy Tseng*

CHOI OI!: The Lighter Side of Vietnam *by Tony Zidek*

THE COUNTERFEITER and Other Stories *by Yasushi Inoue; translated by Leon Picon*

CURIOUS PUNISHMENTS OF BYGONE DAYS *by Alice Morse Earle*

TYPHOON! TYPHOON! An Illustrated Haiku Sequence *by Lucile M. Bogue*

UNBEATEN TRACKS IN JAPAN: An Account of Travels in the Interior Including Visits to the Aborigines of Yezo and the Shrine of Nikko *by Isabella L. Bird*

ZILCH! The Marine Corps' Most Guarded Secret *by Roy Delgado*